IMAGES
of America

BROWNSBURG

On the Cover: This c. 1908 photograph shows children in front of William F. Evans Furniture and Undertaking. Based on the heavy-handed marketing, this is likely a demonstration for Majestic Ranges. A similar demonstration was held in Indianapolis in 1909. For every range sold, "free useful" utensils were given away. See entire image and additional information about Evans on pages 114 and 115. (Courtesy of Brownsburg Public Library, Brownsburg Then and Now digital collection.)

IMAGES
of America

BROWNSBURG

Linda Lichte Cook

ARCADIA
PUBLISHING

ISBN 978-1-4671-1426-4

Published by Arcadia Publishing
Charleston, South Carolina

Printed in the United States of America

Library of Congress Control Number: 2015931260

For all general information, please contact Arcadia Publishing:
Telephone 843-853-2070
Fax 843-853-0044
E-mail sales@arcadiapublishing.com
For customer service and orders:
Toll-Free 1-888-313-2665

Visit us on the Internet at www.arcadiapublishing.com

To Shannon Careen Lichte, who passed on her love of the library—you are missed and loved.

Contents

Acknowledgments

My sincere thanks goes to my family, my husband for traipsing through woods and water with me to confirm my hunches, and my sons Zach and Jake, who took my role and became the encouragers; I am exceedingly proud of you both. I would like to thank my sister Lori for her ever-present love and support and Sharon for modeling perseverance. I could not thank the Brownsburg Public Library enough, from Wanda Pearson, mentor and friend, who fostered my love of the local history department; to Denise Robinson, Amie Thomas, and Emily Fleischer for initially thinking of me, allowing me to submerge in history, and letting me take home history books and photographs to study; and to past and present staff for working to preserve the town's history. Roger Zimmerman and Laura Thomas, I am sure there are many people out there with collections about Brownsburg that I would love to see, but I am thankful that you came across my radar and for your desire to share what you have. I would like to thank my writing friend Stacy Post for always checking in. I thank Reann Poray for being willing to do whatever she could to show the way. I also wish to thank Mickie Myers for always helping me figure out what I was looking at in photographs and in life. Tracy Burgoyne, your excitement for this project and for me was uplifting. I thank all of my friends who allowed me to drop off the face of the earth and waited patiently for me to surface again. To all the people and businesses who contributed to the library photograph collection over the years, we, at the library, owe you a big thank-you. There would be no collection without you. Julia Simpson, my editor, thank you for knowing how to manage people and trusting me to do my work and answering my questions when needed. And, last but never ever least to me, dad, there simply is no better example than you.

Unless otherwise indicated, all images appear courtesy of the Brownsburg Public Library, Brownsburg Then and Now digital collection.

INTRODUCTION

This is not a history book. It is a photo album full of history, and I have come to realize, hoping the reader does as well, the magnitude of what our predecessors accomplished.

It must have initially seemed like a lonely and intimidating location to plan a life. When James B. Brown arrived in the area now known as Lincoln Township, in Hendricks County, Indiana, around 1824 there were few if any known settlers to the west and north of him. Most of the area was covered in water at least part of the year. Yet, he stayed, and the township at the time was named Brown after him, and rightly so, considering he had the foresight to see past what was, to what would be. Eventually, there would be no area remaining that would remind anyone of how the land used to be. The swamps were drained and the forests cut down, making way for fields of grass and grain.

In 1828, the Crawfordsville Road, US 136, was not much more than a path or rudimentary road cut through the wilderness. In 1832, a stagecoach line was established along this road to connect the travel from Indianapolis to Crawfordsville. When William Harris arrived, that was likely a deciding factor in his selection of a place to plan his town. It would be the perfect location to offer respite on the long stagecoach journey between the two locations and a profitable one as well. So he proceeded and platted out the land in 1835 and named it after himself, Harrisburg. It was later changed to Brownsburg when the post office was established, avoiding confusion with another Harrisburg, and paying homage to early settler James B. Brown. Benjamin M. Logan was the first postmaster and store merchant, and amazingly enough, he is still here buried in Lingeman Cemetery. The area to become Brownsburg would draw the attention of many pioneer families seeking a place to call home.

Brown Township was the original township. It engulfed all of the land now known as Brown and Lincoln Townships, but in 1863, Brown Township was separated into two parts. When the Civil War draft came in 1863 it was discovered that the southern half of the township was more Republican and the northern more Democratic. A division was favored and granted by the Commissioners, and Lincoln Township was formed

The railroad came later in 1869 and would continue to change the shape of the town as factories, mills, population, and prosperity grew. It brought with it shipments of stock, lumber, flour, and other necessities.

Around this time, churches and schools were founded. Men and women of faith gathered initially in homes until log structures and then more modern buildings could be built. The community would not be what it is today if not for the churches and people of faith; those strong citizens of the early years whose determination for establishing values and building a town upon them made the town grow because they wanted a better place for families. The schools started in much the same way, from the gathering of these families who wanted more for their children. They went from one-room schoolhouses scattered about the townships to organized schools built in town. In

1899, the first two-story schoolhouse opened on the corner of School Street and College Avenue, and the schools of today carry on the legacy.

The hope is that this book will pique people's interest in Brownsburg's history. Someone discovers a tidbit here, someone finds a photograph there, and soon, a clearer picture of the past has been assembled. History and information are not items to be possessive of; they are something to share. The key is getting the information assembled in a central location, like a library, for future generations to access.

I have tried to be as historically accurate as possible, and I have gathered numerous documents to support what I can. I have searched and have endeavored to use original source documentation.

This is a collection of photographs that I hope you have not seen in a while or have never seen. It is a small representation of the over 1,000 photographs that are currently housed in the Brownsburg Then and Now digital collection. The photographs have been donated over the years by organizations, businesses, and patrons who all have the same desire to preserve our past. There was no guideline or criteria. It was not my intent to exclude or omit any person, place, or thing. The truth is that it was very difficult to pick out photographs and leave some behind. Some photographs were left behind simply because there was no information to corroborate them. That is where the public comes in and can help identify and preserve the history. In the end, the criteria became what brings smiles, laughs, and remembrance.

My hope is that the public will want to view the rest of the photographs in the library collection, online at Brownsburg Then and Now, part of the Indiana Memory Collection. It is an honor for the town to be a part of this collection. The hope is also, that others will donate photographs or scans of photographs for the future generations. Brownsburg deserves to have its history preserved, and there is history out there that we can add. The following quote from an 1889 article in the *Brownsburg Record* sums the book's goal up well: "It is altogether too pretty a town to be permitted to go into decay. It is the unavoidable duty of its men [and women] of intelligence, property, and business, to take hold of it and push it along in the high road of prosperity."

So as you look through this book, may it bring memories, may it bring new information, and may it make us willing to preserve it and push it along.

One

Main and Green Streets

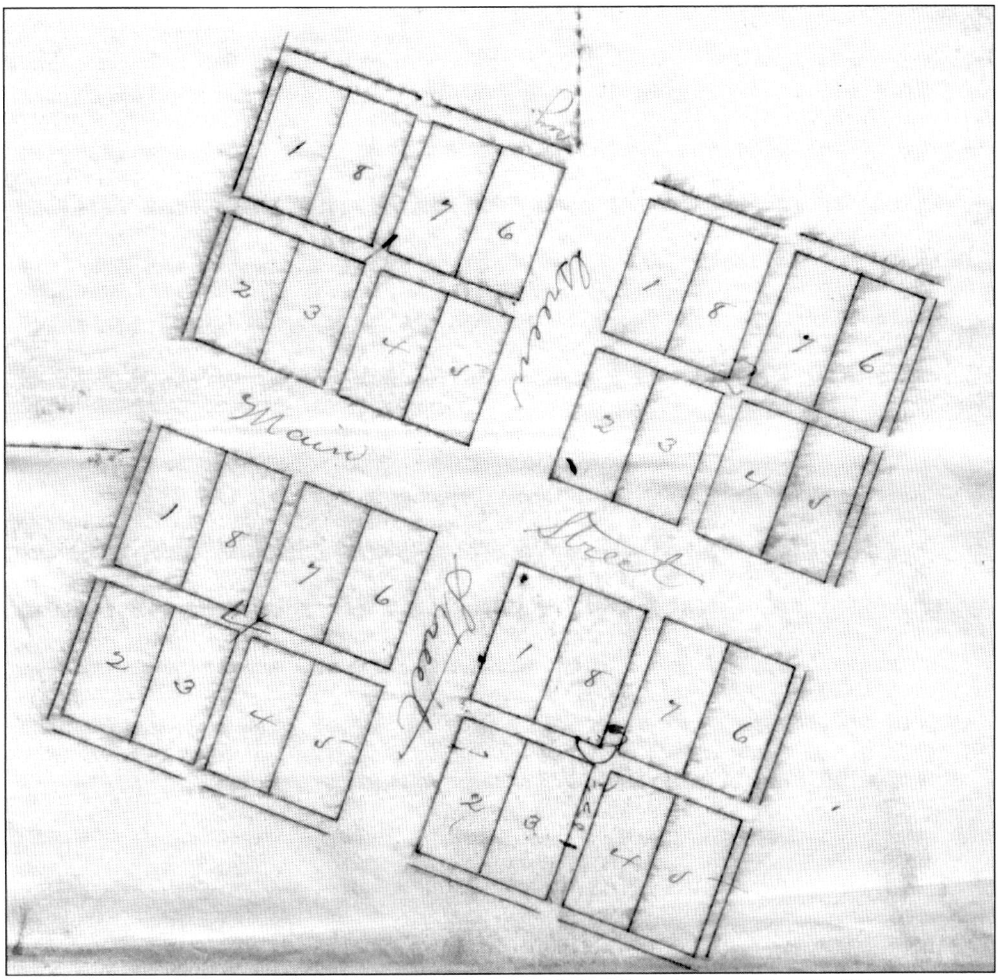

William Harris acquired plats of land along White Lick Creek in Section No. 11 of Township No. 16 North, Range No. 1 East, the area now known as Main and Green Streets. Harris recorded a deed, on August 25, 1835, for the purpose of forming a town. This plat map shows how Brownsburg, originally named Harrisburg, was arranged into four principal blocks.

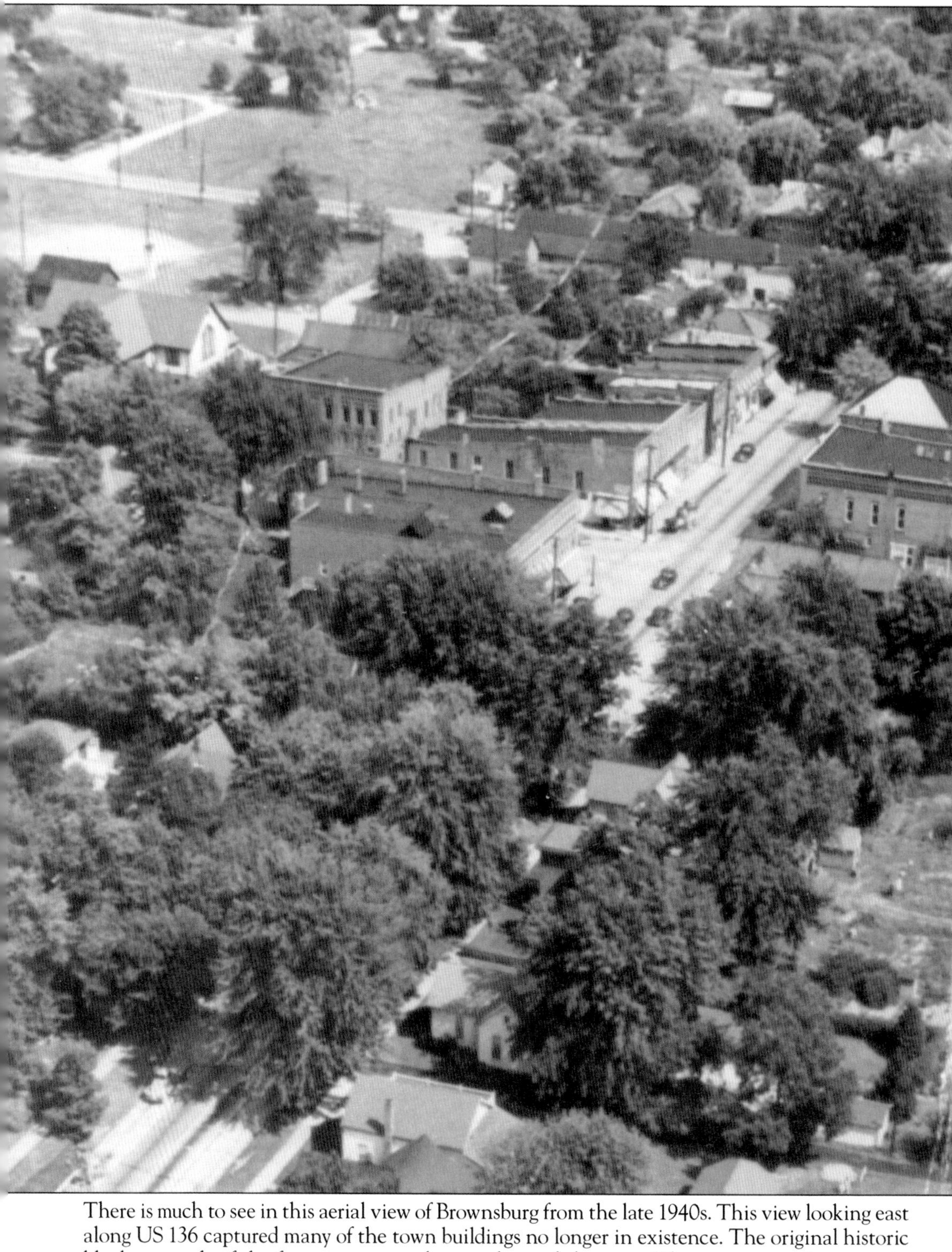

There is much to see in this aerial view of Brownsburg from the late 1940s. This view looking east along US 136 captured many of the town buildings no longer in existence. The original historic blocks on each of the four corners can be seen beyond the trees. The water tower in town sits to the right of the photograph. The former Brownsburg Christian Church can be seen directly

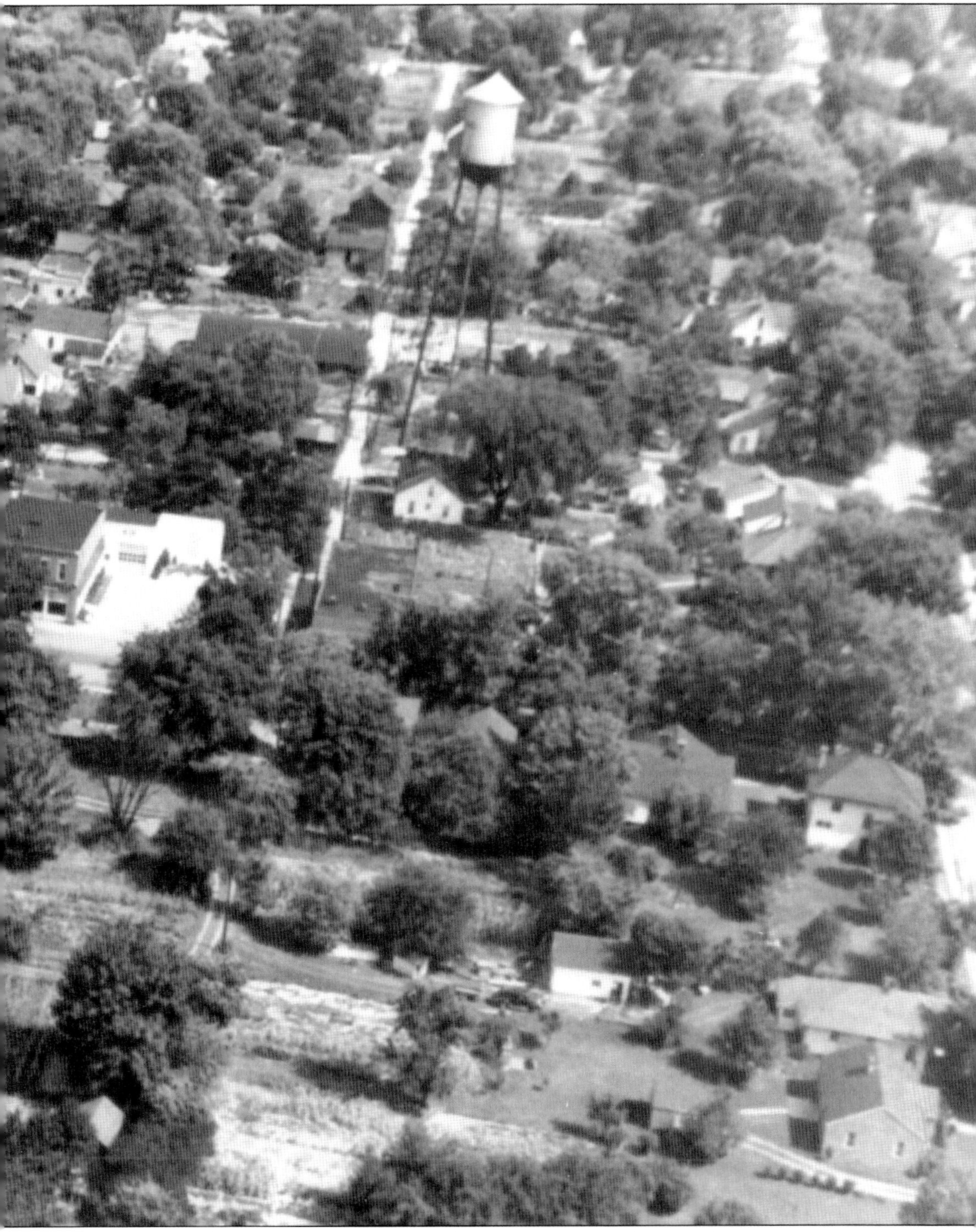

to the left or north of the existing Knights of Pythias building. Sitting behind the Brownsburg Christian Church are the ball diamond and green spaces of then Eaton Park, which is now home to the Brownsburg Municipal Buildings. A keen observer will recognize many other buildings, including the old Methodist church in the far top of the photograph.

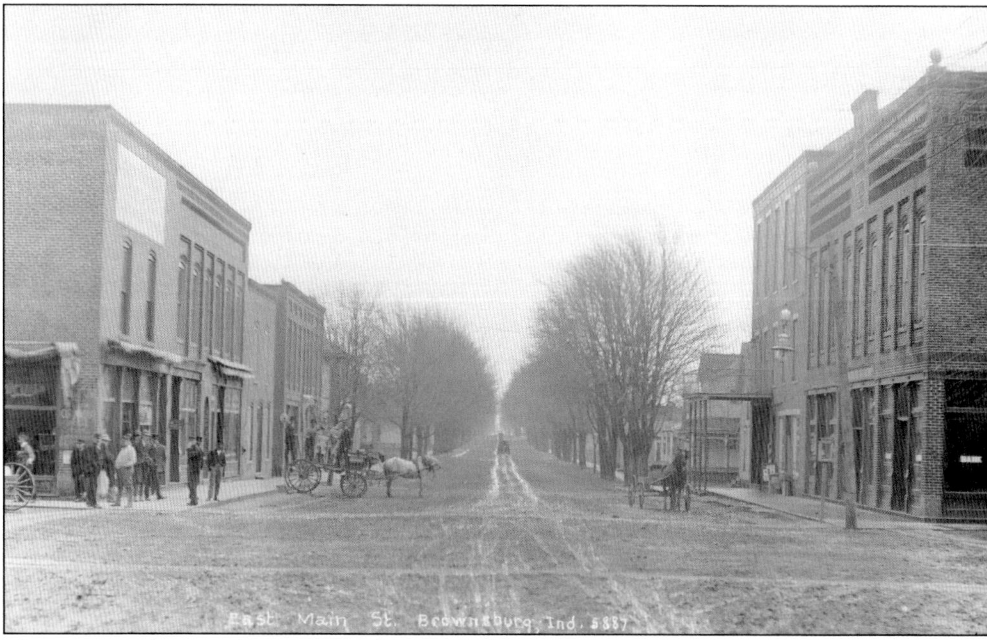

These postcard views of Main Street facing east from Green Street in the early 1900s give a glimpse of the town in two different seasons. The photograph above captured the business of the day from horses and wagons traveling on the dirt road to the men gathered on the northeast corner in front of the E.M. Henderson Drugstore. Earl Henderson, the druggist, also sold paints and dry goods. Today, this corner building still exists at 2 East Main Street. The "ghost sign" of Henderson's Drugstore can still be seen today on the front of the building. Sadly, it is the only historic block existing in town. Maple trees that once lined the streets can be seen in each photograph. The Independent Order of Odd Fellows (IOOF) building is on the right in each photograph, housing the Brownsburg State Bank at one time.

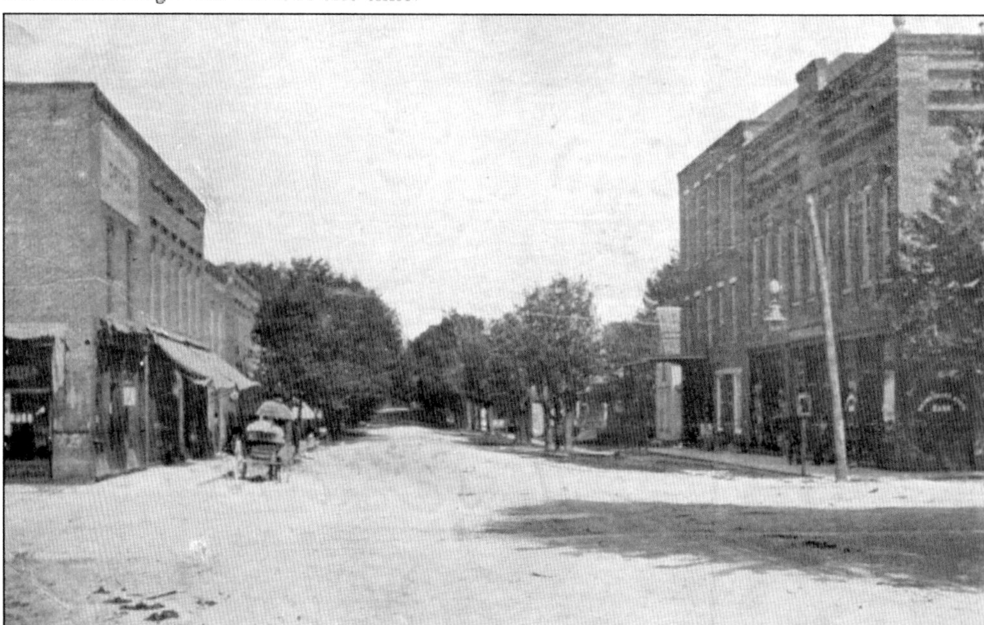

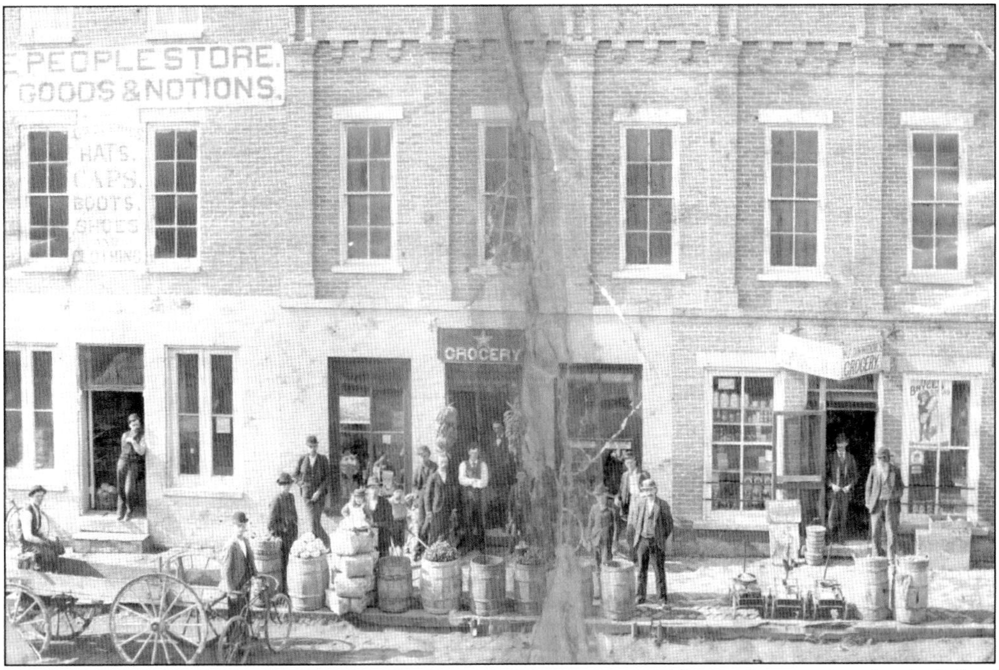

This shot captures the storefronts in the 1890s on the southeast block of town. On the far left of the photograph is the People's Store. The center building, known as the Eaton building, housed two grocery stores, Roberts and W.F. Dinwiddie's on the far right. The Nash building, unseen in this photograph, sat to the right of Dinwiddie's on the corner. On March 6, 1900, a fire starting in Robert's grocery, destroyed most of this block. Two hose companies were sent to assist by way of the Big Four Railroad. The IOOF building shown in the photograph below was erected later in 1900 as a replacement. Here, it is being torn down to make way for the Hendricks County Bank and Trust building at 1 East Main Street.

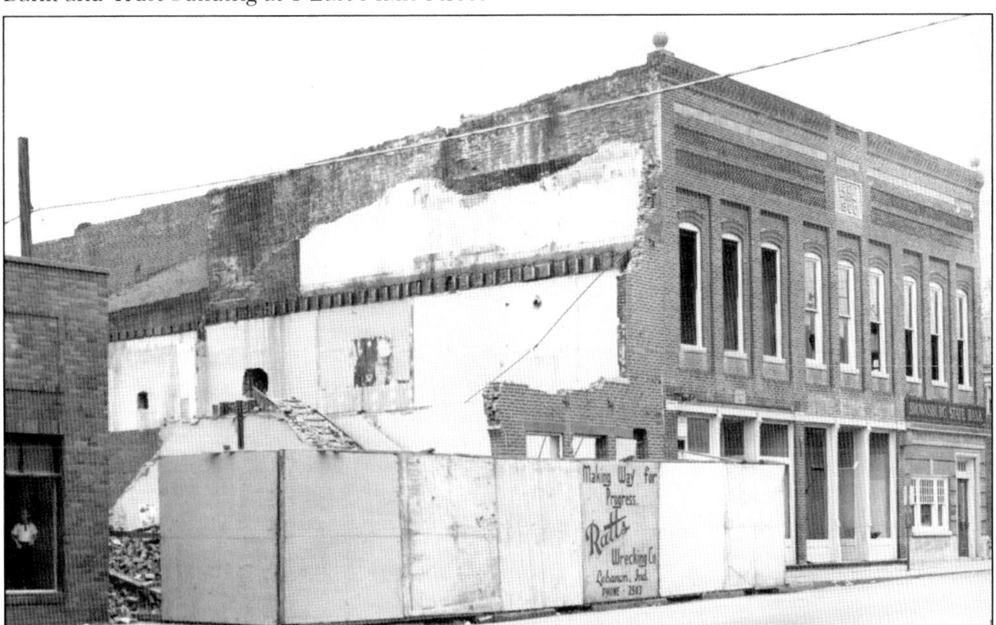

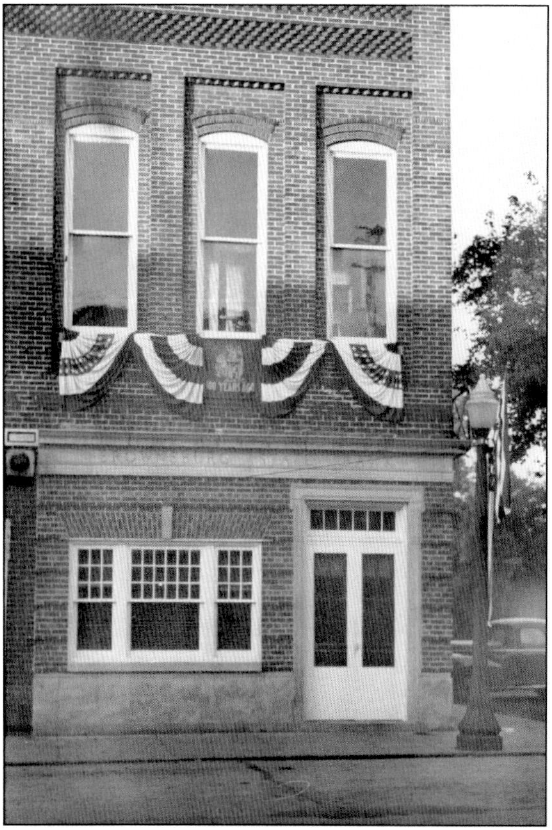

The Brownsburg State Bank, with its name etched in the building above the front door with pride, was a well-known landmark in town beginning in 1908. Here, it is shown in the IOOF building on the southeast corner of Main and Green Streets in 1948. The photograph looks ever so slightly down south Green Street to the right. The bank merged with Hendricks County Bank and Trust in 1974.

The IOOF building on the southeast corner of Main and Green Streets, shown here in 1948, was dedicated in December 1900 on the site of the previously burned building. Completed with two stories of iron, brick, and stone, the $10,000 structure housed many shops throughout the years including the Family Store, Brownsburg Bakery and Confectionery, and Brownsburg Hardware.

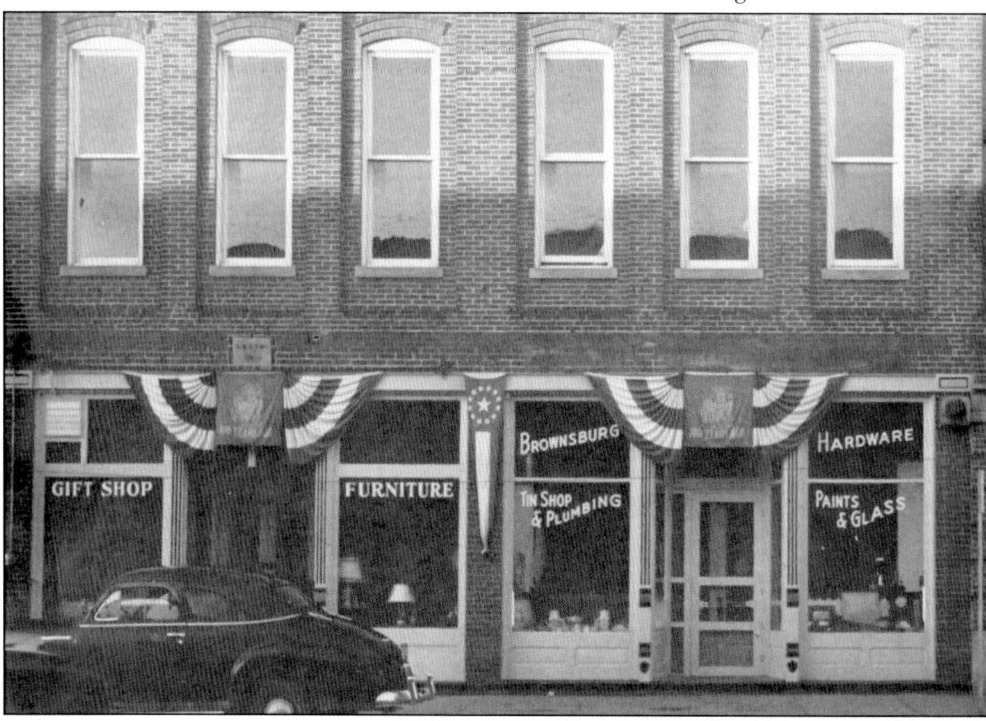

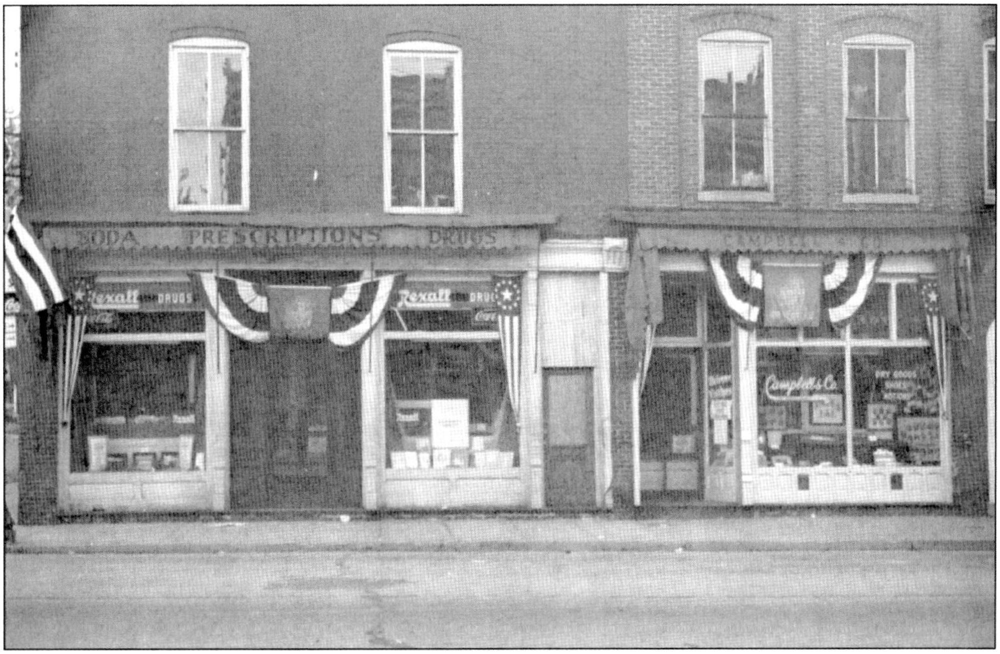

These two photographs, taken at different times, capture the building located on the northeast corner of Main and Green Streets. In the above 1948 photograph, Hollett and Harmon Rexall Pharmacy occupies the space at 2 East Main Street. Campbell's Dry Goods store occupies the location at 8 East Main Street. The facade of the location was updated to attempt to provide a more beautiful suburban look. The outdoor facade and care of the old brick was completed around 1956. At some point during the makeover, the stone added to the building fronts covered up doorways in the original building. An aluminum marquee was also added over the sidewalk.

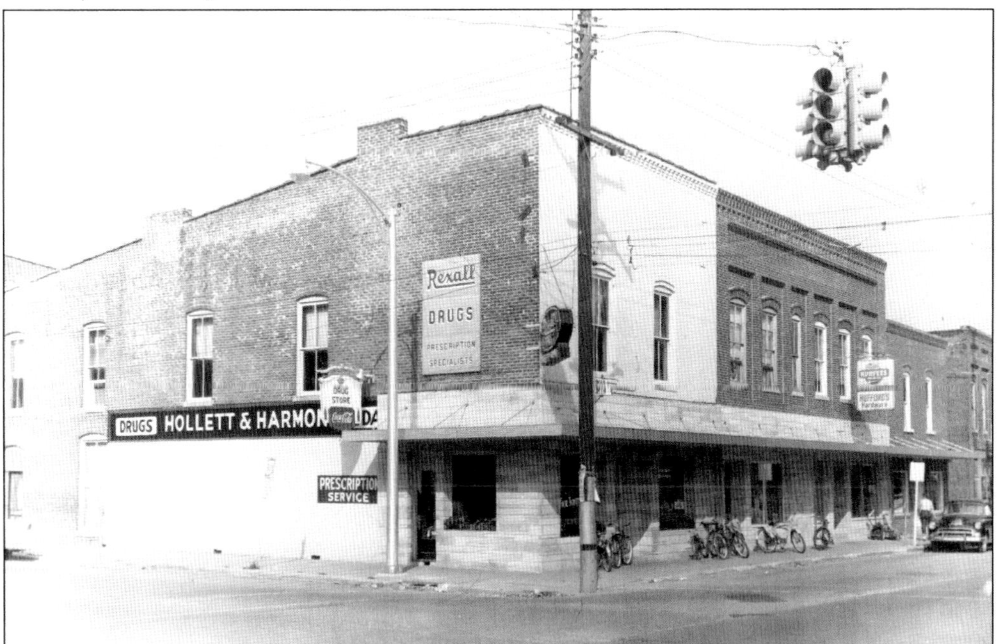

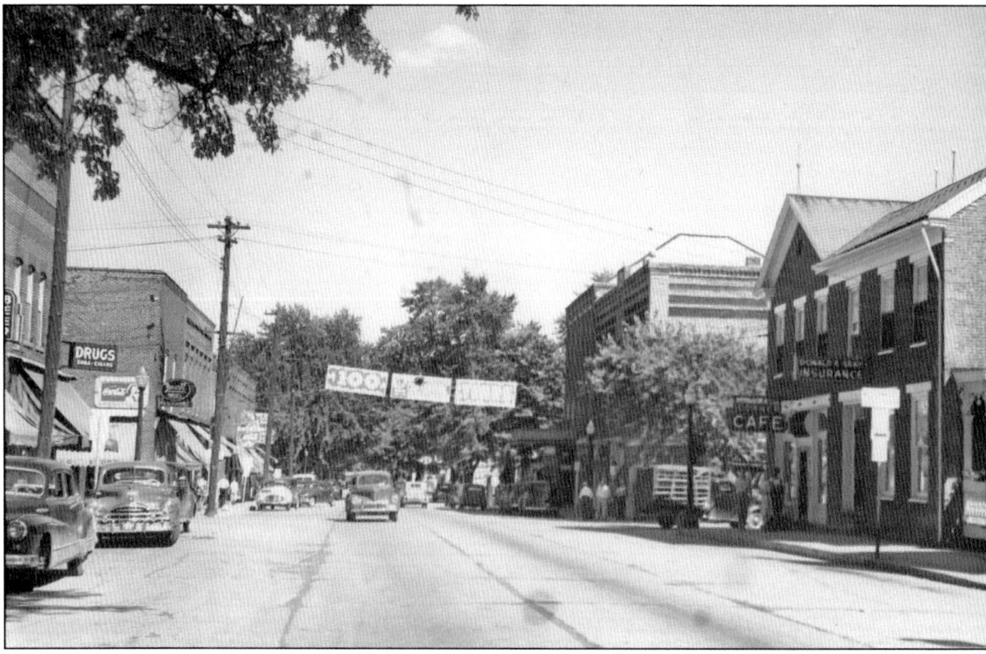

Slightly west of Green Street, this busy street view looks to the east along Main Street and beautifully shows the four historic corners as they were in 1948 with the residential section among the trees in the distance. The town is celebrating its centennial anniversary as indicated by the sign hanging above the street.

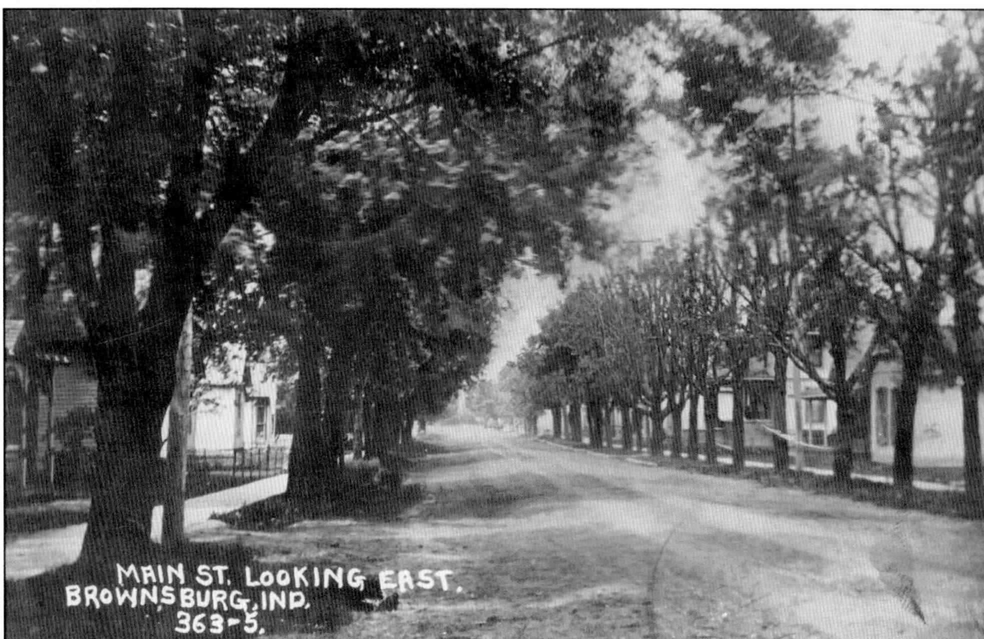

Taken from a postcard dated 1911, this scene of Main Street looking east shows the beautiful tree lined residential section of the town. Clean and neat sidewalks and some curbing show the improvements made to the streets. The dirt roads would have caused quite a mess for the residents until they were treated or paved in the 1920s.

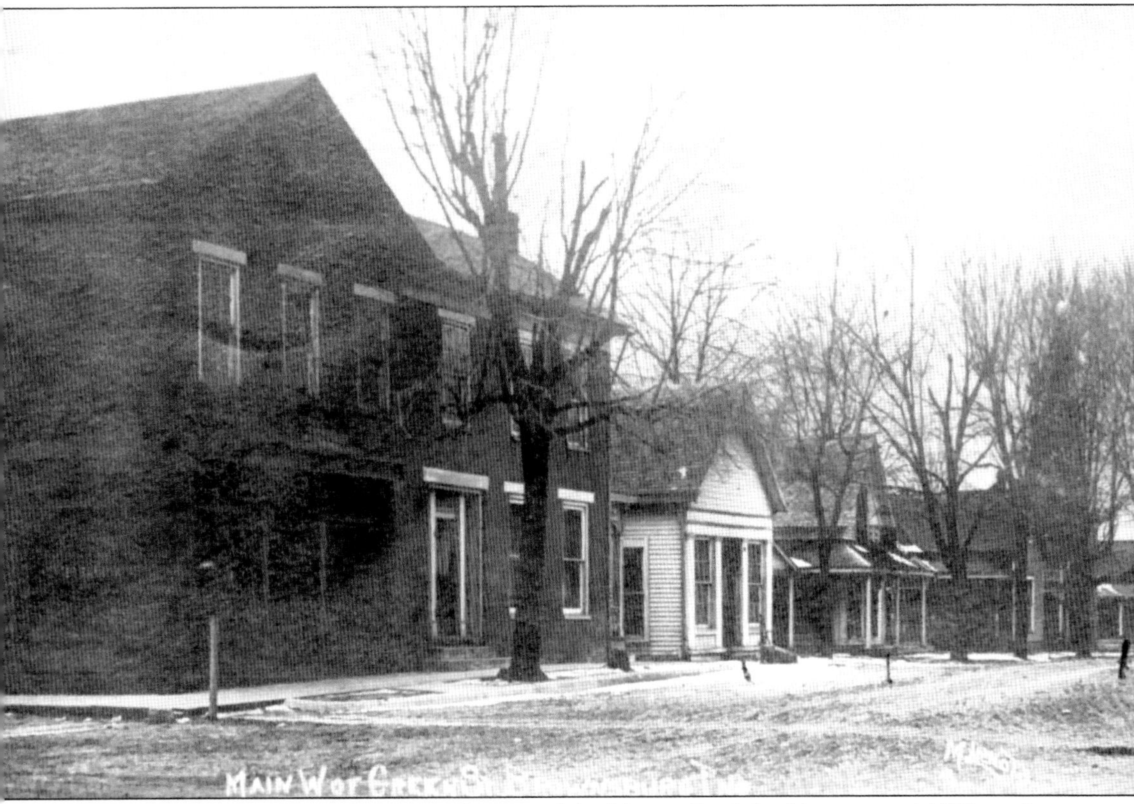

This is a cold winter day and a rare early view of the Hunter Bank building around 1910 on the southwest corner of Main and Green Streets looking slightly west. Erected in the 1870s, the structure housed the general merchandise store of Jesse R. Cope and Cyrus N. Hunt. It was at this time that they established a banking service as a convenience to their customers. After their deaths, M.T. Hunter, a well-known banker from Danville, Indiana, stepped in to manage the bank from 1907 to 1932. During this time it became known as the Hunter Bank building or Hunter building; the name can be seen in the corner window. It housed many businesses throughout the years, including the Corner Café, Dale's TV, and Rocking Horse Saloon. Today, the building is gone, and in its place in the corner location is CVS Pharmacy at 21 West Main Street.

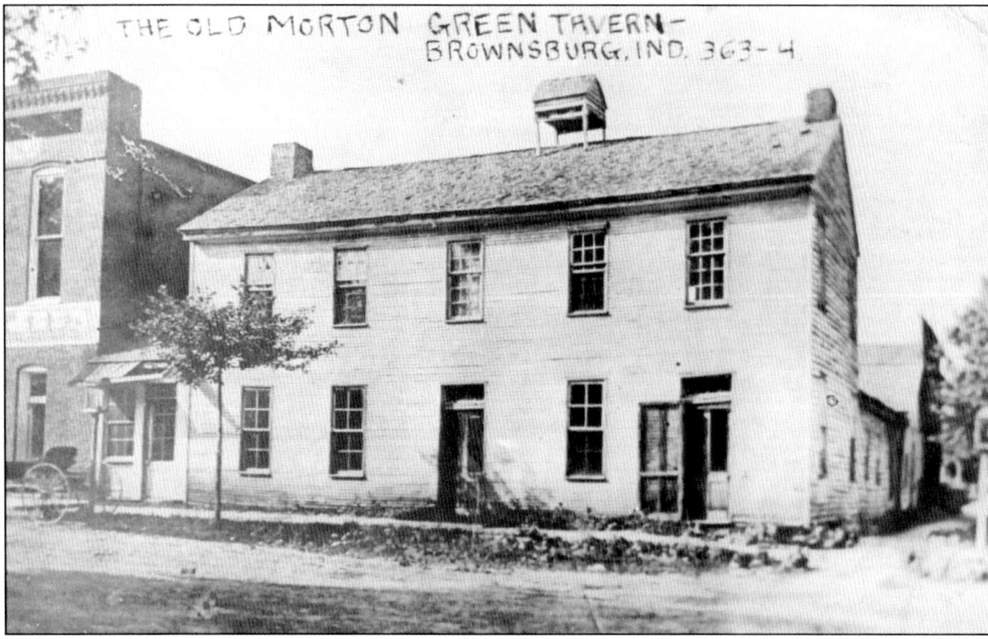

Originally erected in 1837, the building seen here as the Morton Green Tavern housed many other taverns and hotels throughout the years. Its location along the Crawfordsville Road on the northwest corner of Main and Green Streets made it the perfect stop on the stage route from Indianapolis westward. In May 1900, while functioning as the Union Hotel, it was destroyed by fire. In 1903, the Stevenson [*sic*] building was constructed in its place, as seen in the photograph below. It was home to yet another hotel, the *Brownsburg Record* newspaper, and a grocery. Opening by Christmas 1903, the hotel was managed by Martha Smith. Today, this corner is occupied by Walgreens at 20 West Main Street. (Above, courtesy of Roger A. Zimmerman.)

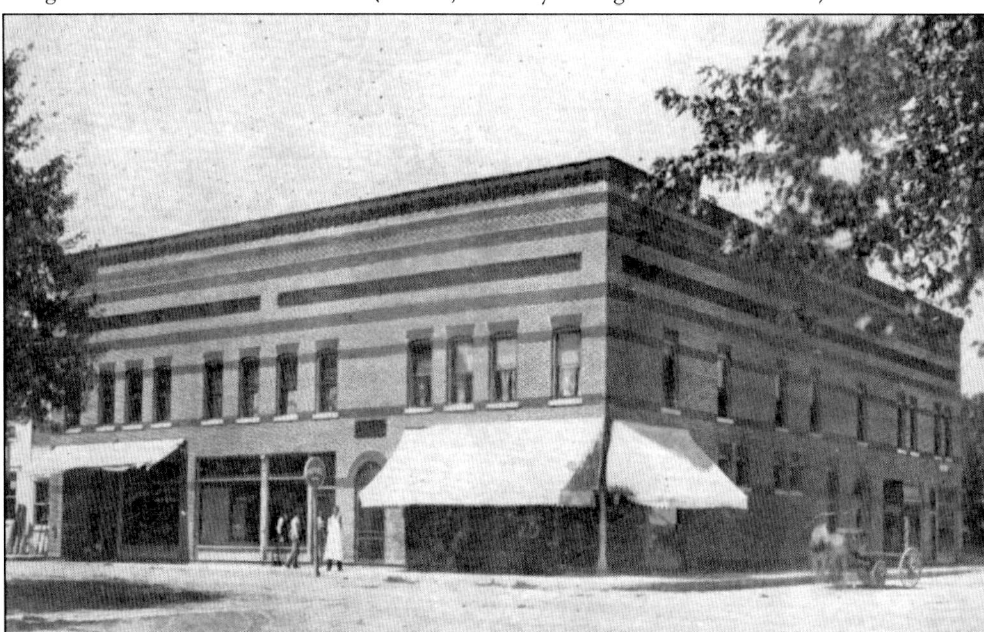

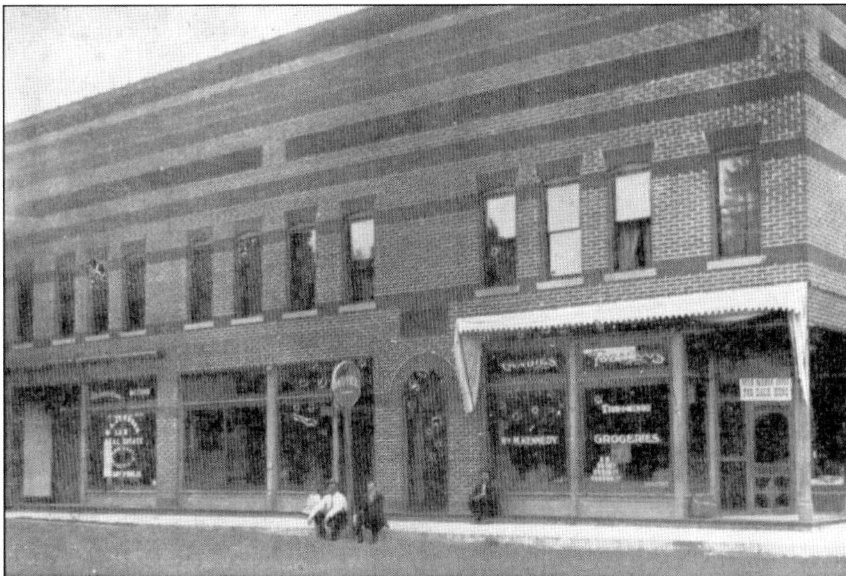

HUNTER BLOCK, BROWNSBURG, IND.

The stately Stevenson [*sic*] building, seen in the above photograph, on the northwest corner of Main and Green Streets became a prime location for thriving businesses. Among those shown here with the hotel are George Andrew Johnson's law, real estate, and notary business, as well as the Kennedy Grocery Store (also known as the Kennedy Hughes Grocery Store) where one could buy "Good Groceries Always." The man in the photograph below is unidentified but if presumed to be Kennedy would date the photograph around 1910–1914. Fruits and vegetables line the windows and Tish-I-Mingo cigars, Indianapolis, are advertised prominently. William Kennedy was the proprietor for a time, along with his wife, Ruth Hughes Kennedy, who is buried in Greenlawn Cemetery. (Both photographs courtesy of Roger A. Zimmerman.)

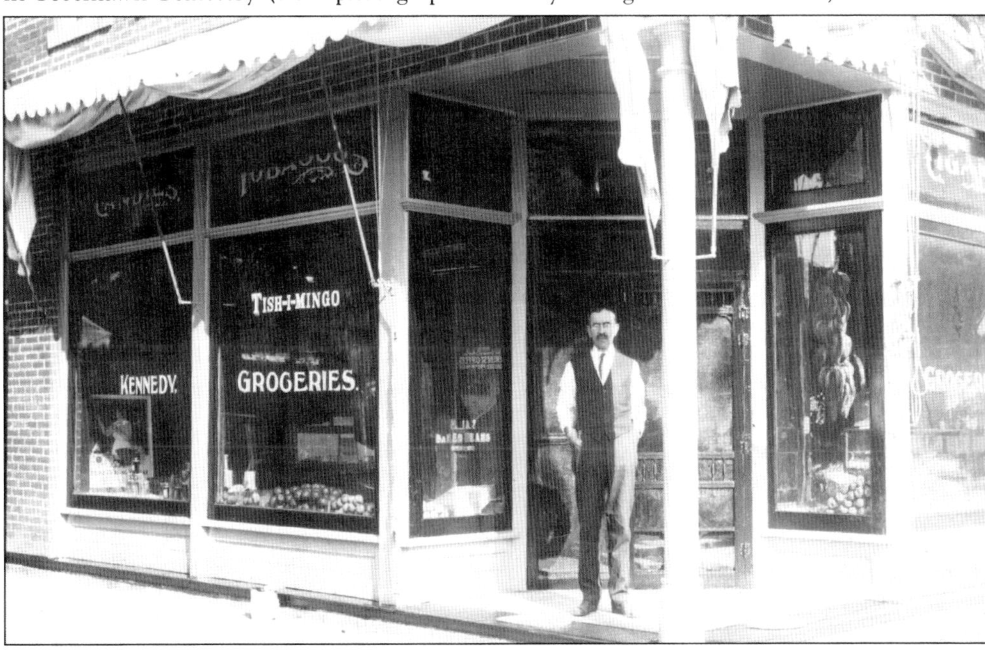

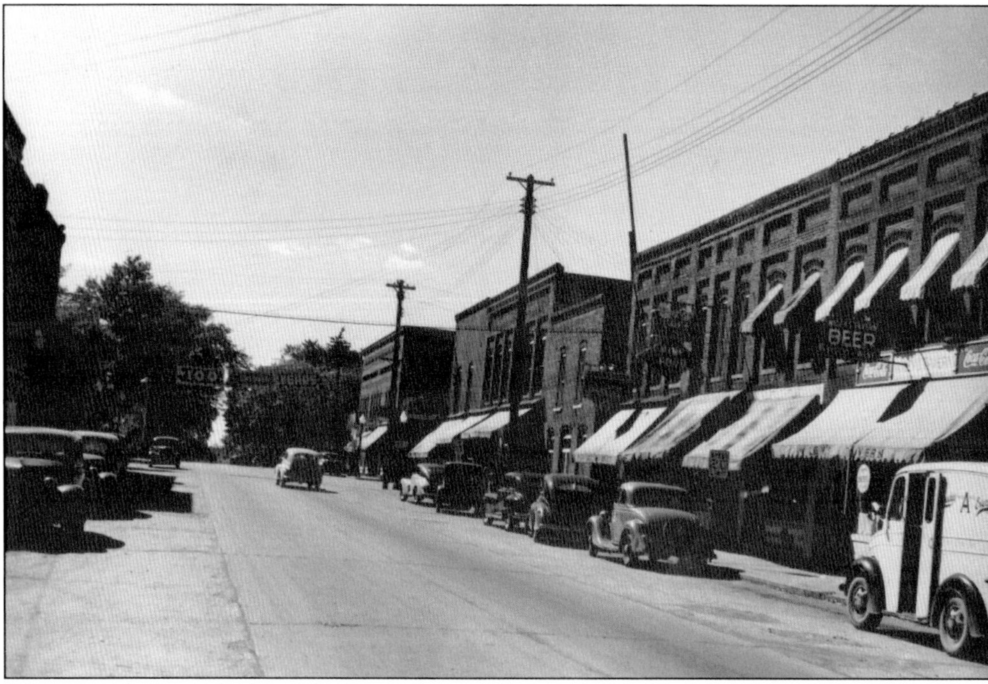

This 1948 photograph shows the businesses on the north side of Main Street heading west. The signs for North Side Café and Wiley's Tavern can be seen. Wiley's Tavern occupied the location at 36 East Main Street. The slight dip in the road as it travels out of town toward Pittsboro can be seen in the distance.

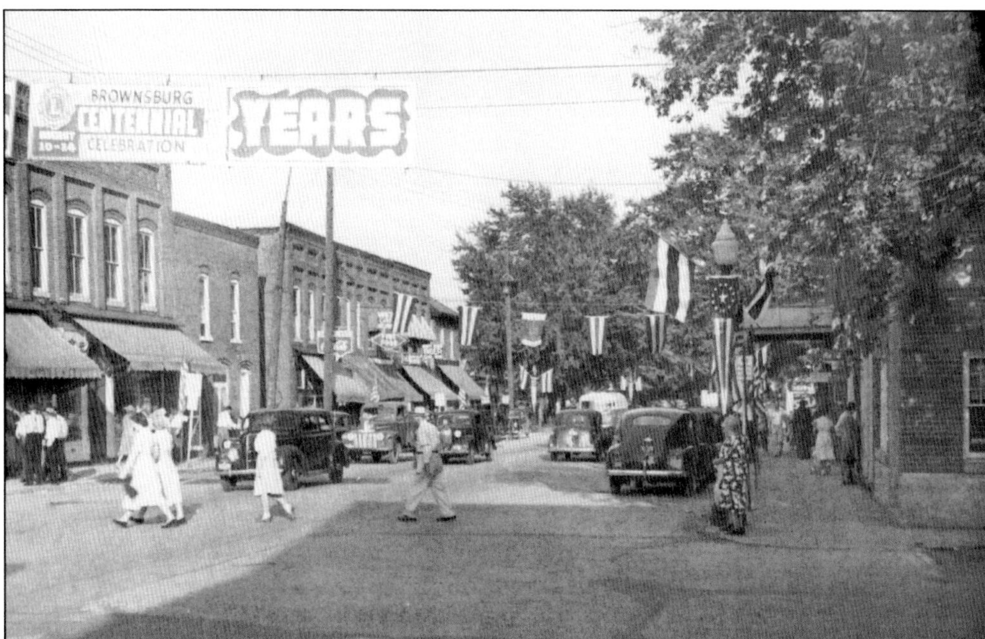

Looking east on Main Street at the same block of businesses offers an additional view of the busy town in 1948. The town is decorated for its centennial celebration August 10 through 14. The Brownsburg State Bank can be seen on the corner in the far right of the photograph.

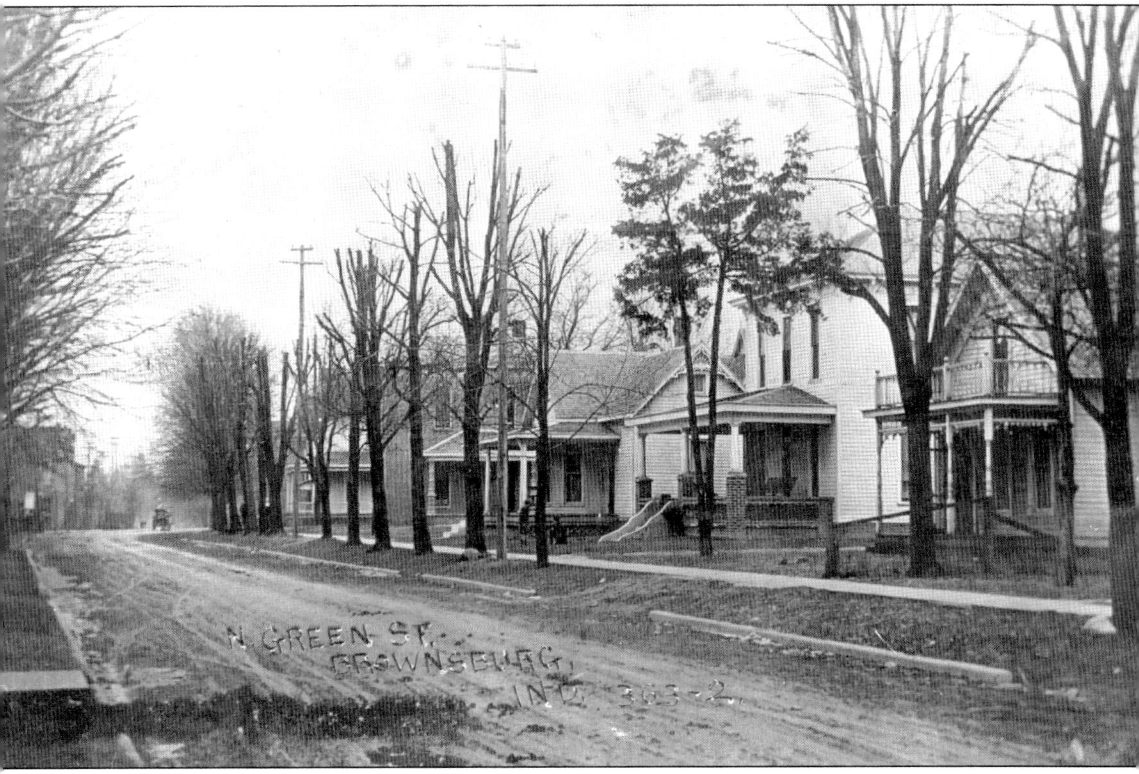

The wagon in the distance is likely heading south into town along Green Street. At the time, trees lining the street framed many residential homes. In this undated winter photograph taken from a 1911 postcard, the careful observer will notice the beautiful brick home on the right in the middle of the photograph that is still standing on the corner at 44 North Green Street and Vermont Street. Originally, the street that residents know now as Vermont did not run east and west alongside the brick home. Eventually, additional land in the area would become part of Tharp and Thompson's Addition, and an east-west road was added. Not many of the original homes remain in this area. The beginning of the town buildings of the northeast block can be seen in the distance on the left. Green Street still curves gently on the approach to town. (Courtesy of Roger A. Zimmerman.)

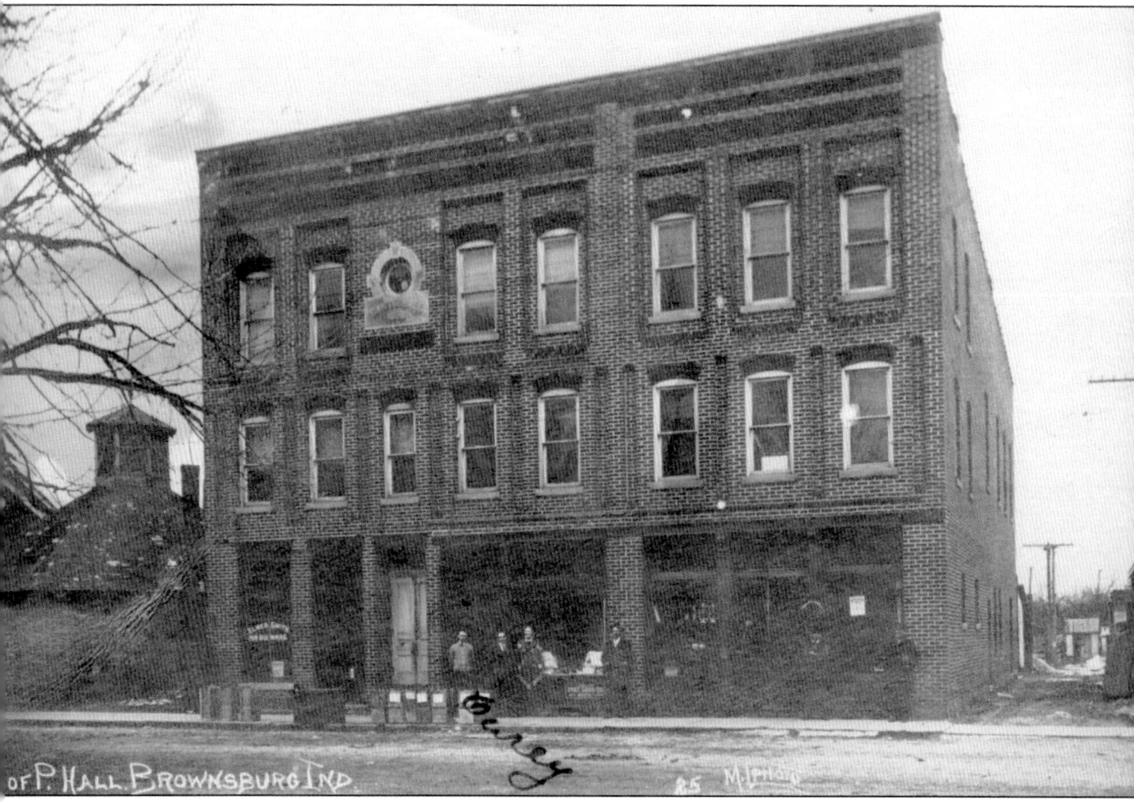

This recognizable building is a landmark in town. The Knights of Pythias Castle Hall building was constructed in 1898 on the east side of north Green Street. The second floor of the building accommodated minstrel shows, music, and other large gatherings featuring local performers. One gathering in 1912 included singing, plays, and readings, presided over by the master of ceremonies C.L Hunt. In this particular view, the Elmer Smith Hardware store can be seen on the left of the building and a harness shop on the right. The round building to the far left of the photograph served for many years as a blacksmith shop and, as of latest record in 1922, a battery repair station. Peeking out slightly behind the blacksmith shop was the top of the Brownsburg Christian Church.

Two

AROUND TOWN

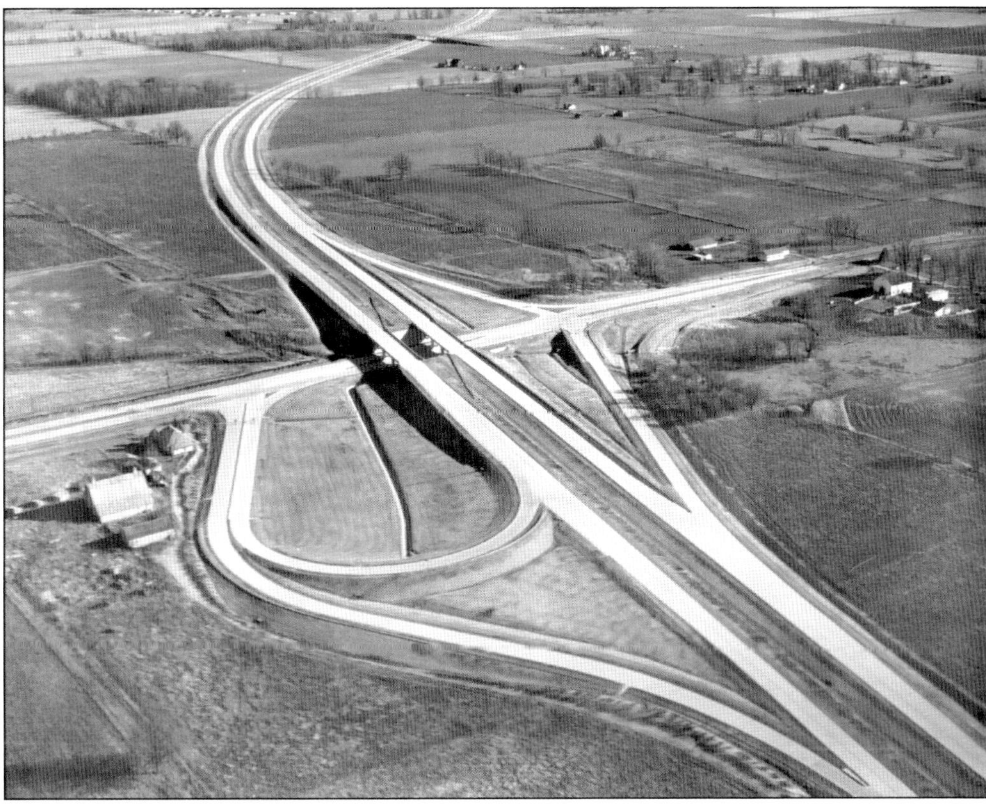

This aerial shot of the Brownsburg interchange with Interstate 74, opening in 1961, faces east toward Indianapolis. Green Street or SR 267 is running from the left and right. A long way removed from the plank road days, the road system has been updated numerous times since this photograph. Local residents will likely remember the days of exiting the interstate and rounding the ramp past the old barn.

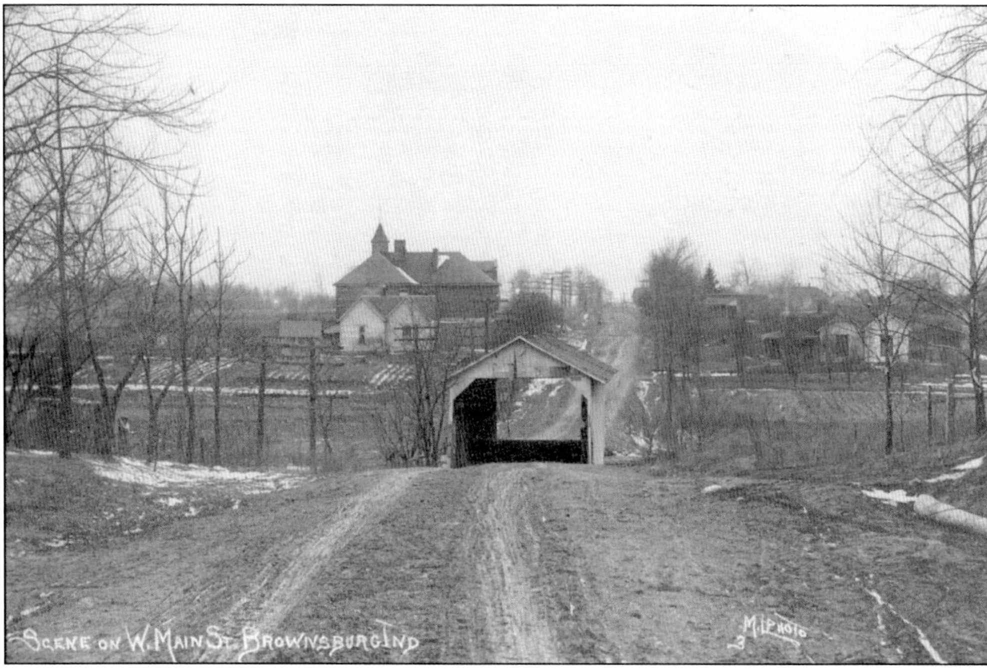

At one time, a very recognizable feature of the town was the covered bridge along the Crawfordsville Road, US 136, heading west. Originally built in 1861 by Oliver Peters to replace a wooden trestle, it was part of the Brownsburg to Indianapolis plank road and one of the first toll roads in the state. The purportedly oak structure was torn down in 1927 to make way for a modern bridge of cement and steel. The road bed for the new bridge was raised so as not to be as steep as before. The house to the right in the photograph still stands at 250 West Main Street. The house on the left still stands as well, and beyond it the old West Point school can be seen.

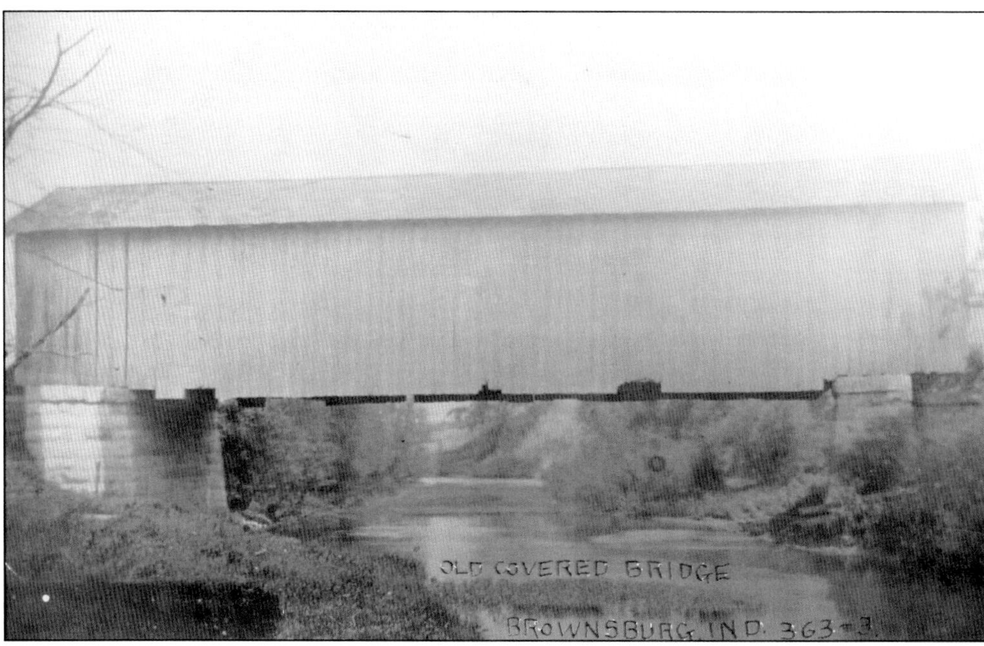

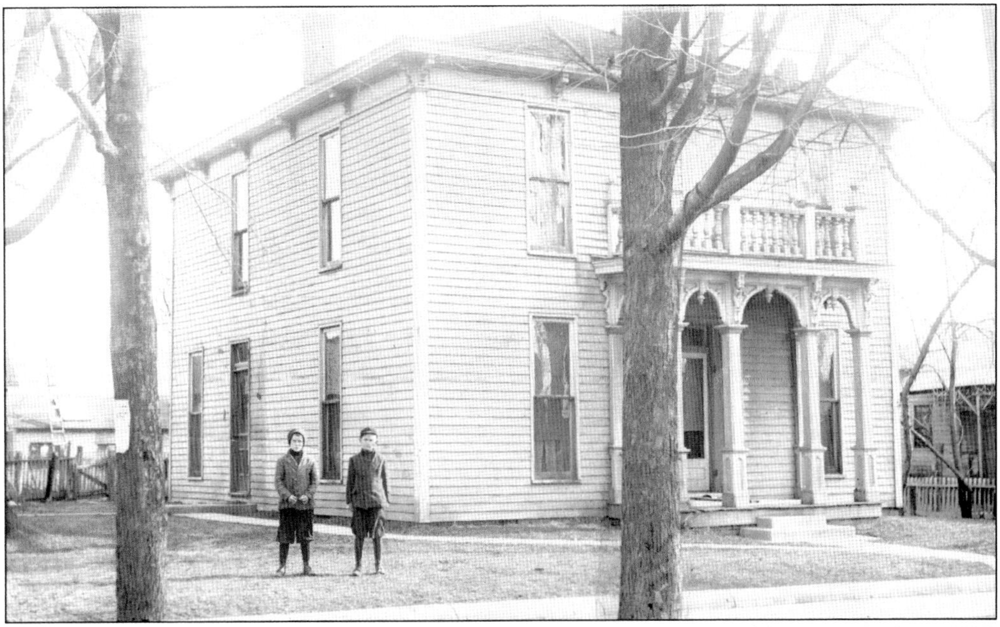

In 1916, Brownsburg citizens moved to form a library and secure a good location. In June 1917, Laura and Sherman Talbert sold their lot on the corner of Main and Mill Streets (now Adams) to the newly formed Board of the Carnegie Library Association. The Lingeman brothers offered to pay $375 for the buildings on the lot. Talbert boys Merrill (left) and Herschell pose here in front of their home.

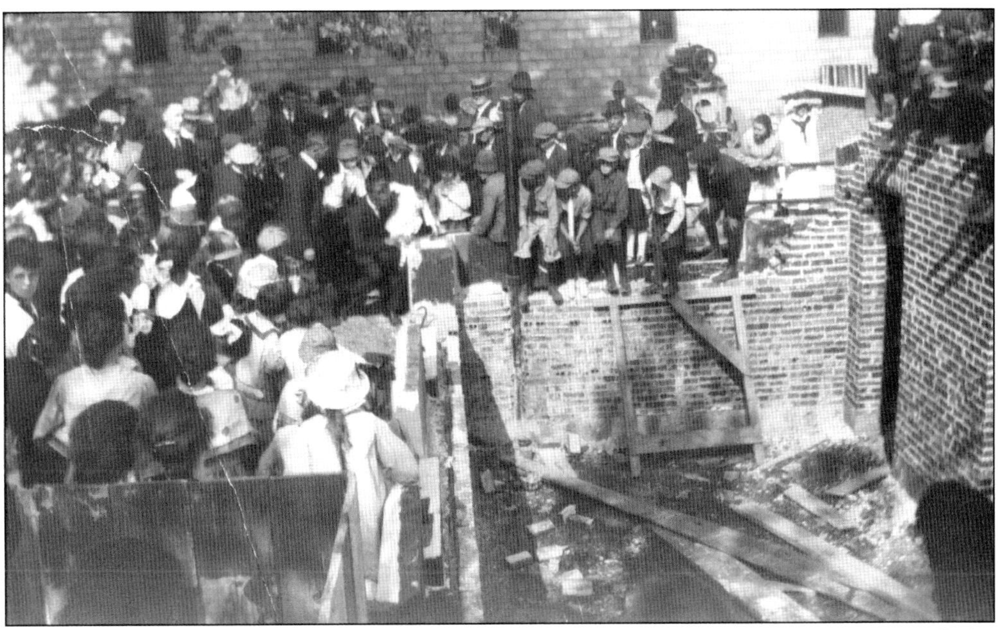

The cornerstone of the Brownsburg Library was laid on September 18, 1917. Lois Reitzel, the little girl dressed in white and held by her father, George, in the middle of the photograph, was chosen to place several items in the cornerstone; included were the names of the board members, a flag wrapped around the names of 40 local boys enlisted in World War I, and a list of Civil War veterans, among other items.

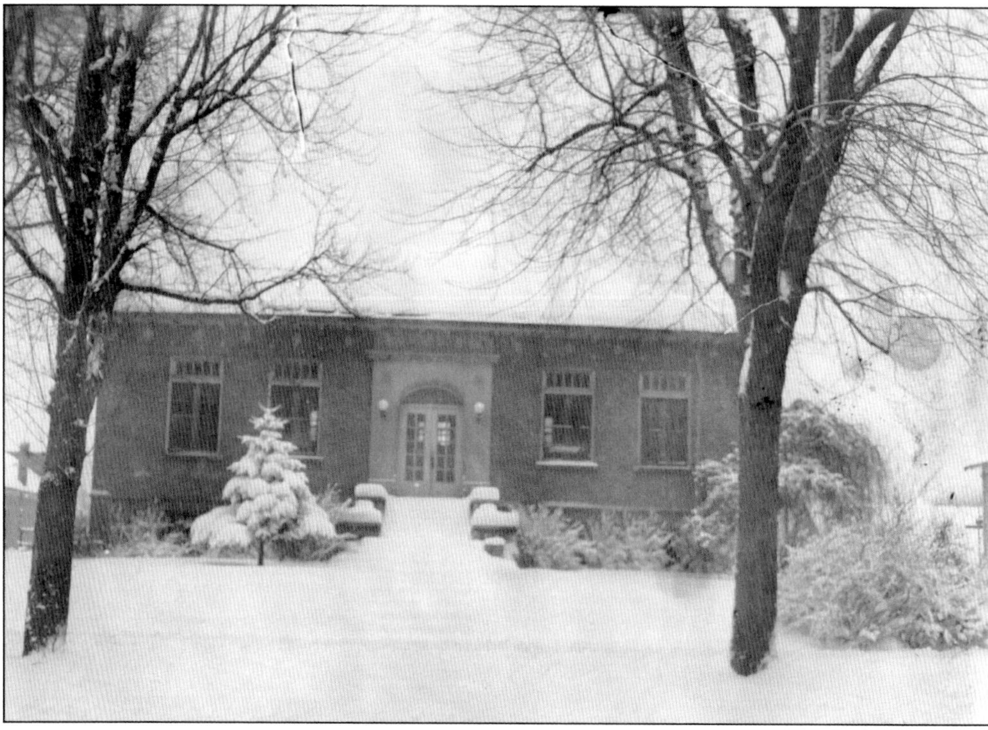

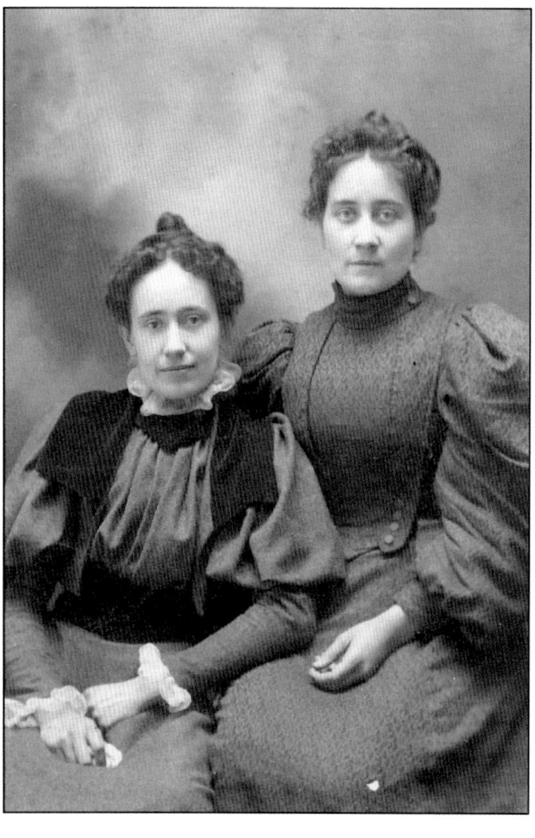

On January 3, 1917, Elza Henson, president of the Brownsburg Town Board, wrote to James Bertram, secretary of the Carnegie Corporation in New York. In the letter, he explained that citizens had raised the amount required to contribute to a library. After collecting books and opening a reading room, they requested the Carnegie Corporation to consider donating funds for a building. In the latter part of 1918, the building was complete.

Ottie Roberts, the first librarian for the town, can be seen here with her sister Minnie Roberts Smith. The back of the photograph indicates that Ottie is on the left. Roberts also taught for Brownsburg Public Schools. She lived with her sister and brother-in-law Dr. T.G. Smith in their home across from the library. The glorious brick house is still located at 111 East Main Street.

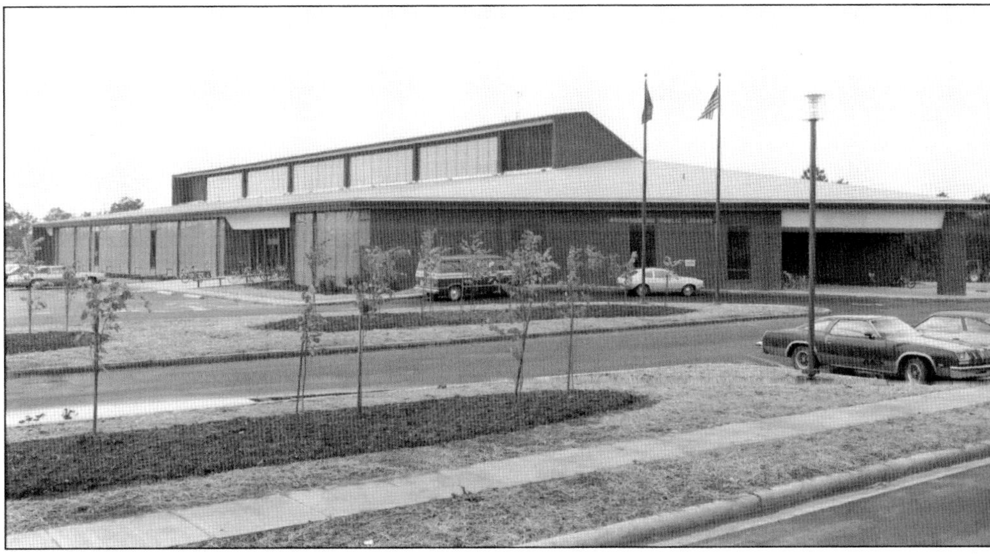

When it became evident that the Carnegie Library building was no longer efficiently serving the growing community or collection, a new library building was completed in 1981 at 450 South Jefferson Street. Books were placed into boxes color coded by stickers, and the collection was moved to the new building with help from volunteers and staff. Growing yet again, a renovation was necessary and began in 1998. The library has grown alongside the community, offering programs and services throughout the years. Summer reading programs have been a popular part of keeping children active in reading. The 1962 photograph below shows the summer reading club in front of the Carnegie building. 254 participants in the first through eighth grades completed the program. By the summer of 2014, the summer reading enrollment for children and teens had reached 1,617 participants.

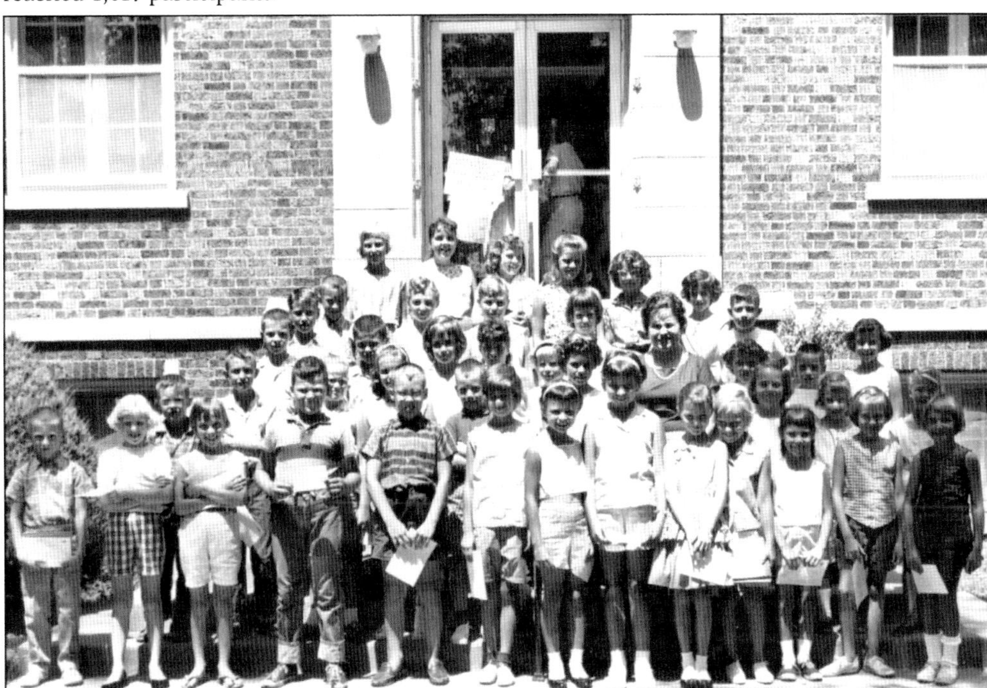

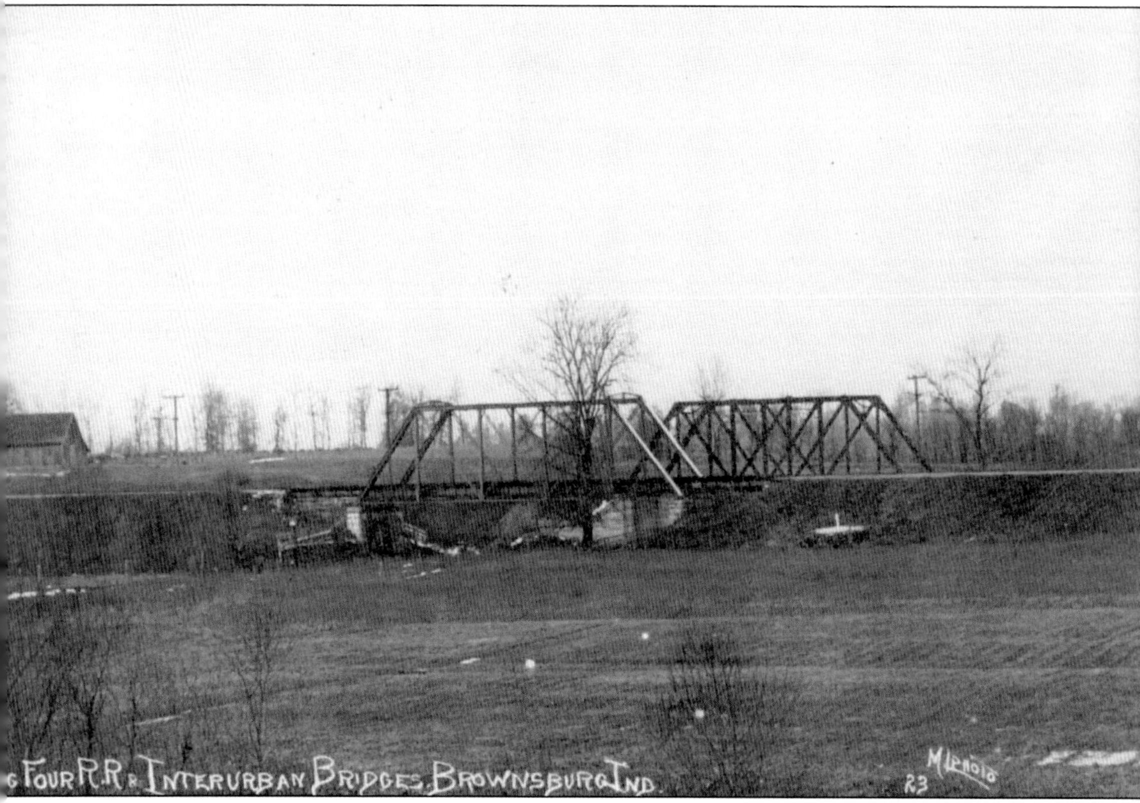

Rising majestically from the land surrounding them, the twin railroad bridges in Brownsburg were captured in this rare photograph for a postcard printed in 1911. The Big Four Railroad and interurban rail tracks ran side by side through Brownsburg crossing north Green Street at what is now the entrance to Arbuckle Acres Park. The interurban track is no longer there. The track used by the Big Four is still crossed today by traffic heading north and south through town. These two trestles met together over the White Lick Creek on the land now part of Arbuckle Acres. Tragically, in July 1911, a 22-year-old engineer named Fred Garlick met his demise at the bridges when he fell from a westbound train on the Big Four track. W.F. Evans was the undertaker to see to his arrangements. Although the trestles are no longer there, a bridge still exists on the CSX track. The piers for the interurban track are the only remnants that speak of its existence.

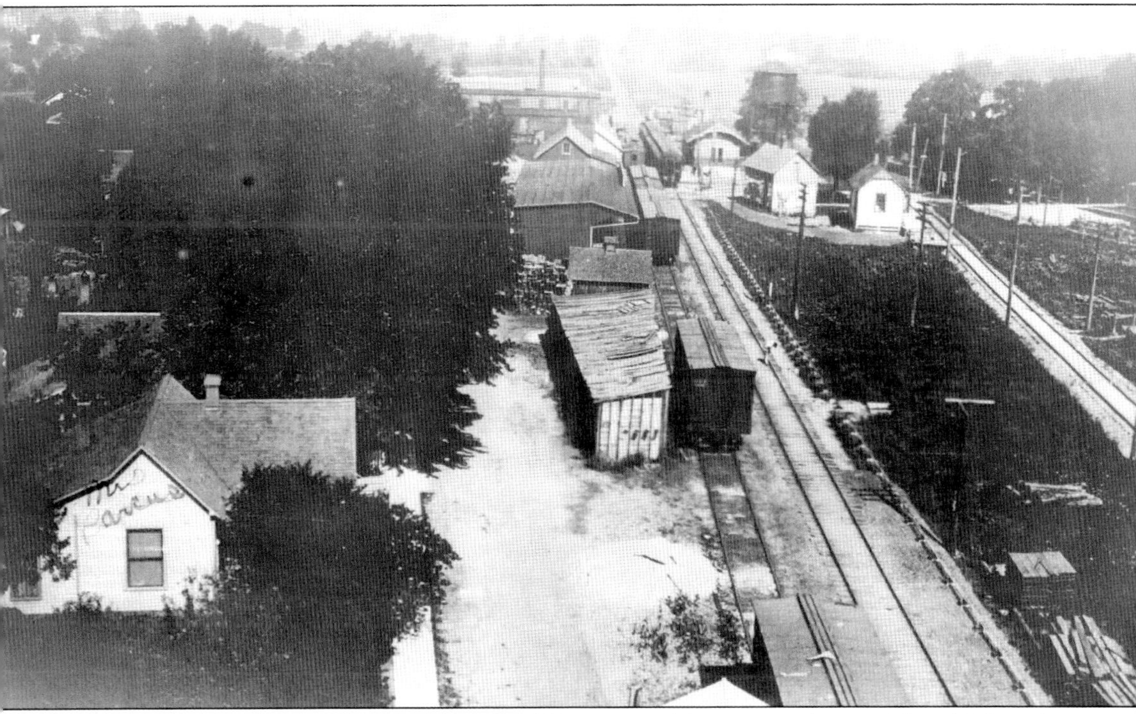

This 1912 postcard view is facing west from the old Lingeman-Adams grain elevator. The odd-shaped building in the center functioned as a coal shed around this time. The buildings heading along the track to the west operated as lumber sheds for the Greer-Wilkinson Lumber Company at one time. The farthest building to the right of the photograph next to the interurban electric track is the interurban or I&E Traction Company passenger and freight depot. Locals will recognize this building still in existence at 205 North Green Street. A second depot sits next to the water tower on the west side of Green Street. Follow the tracks to the top of the photograph, and a keen eye will see the twin trestle bridges faintly in the background. (Courtesy of Roger A. Zimmerman.)

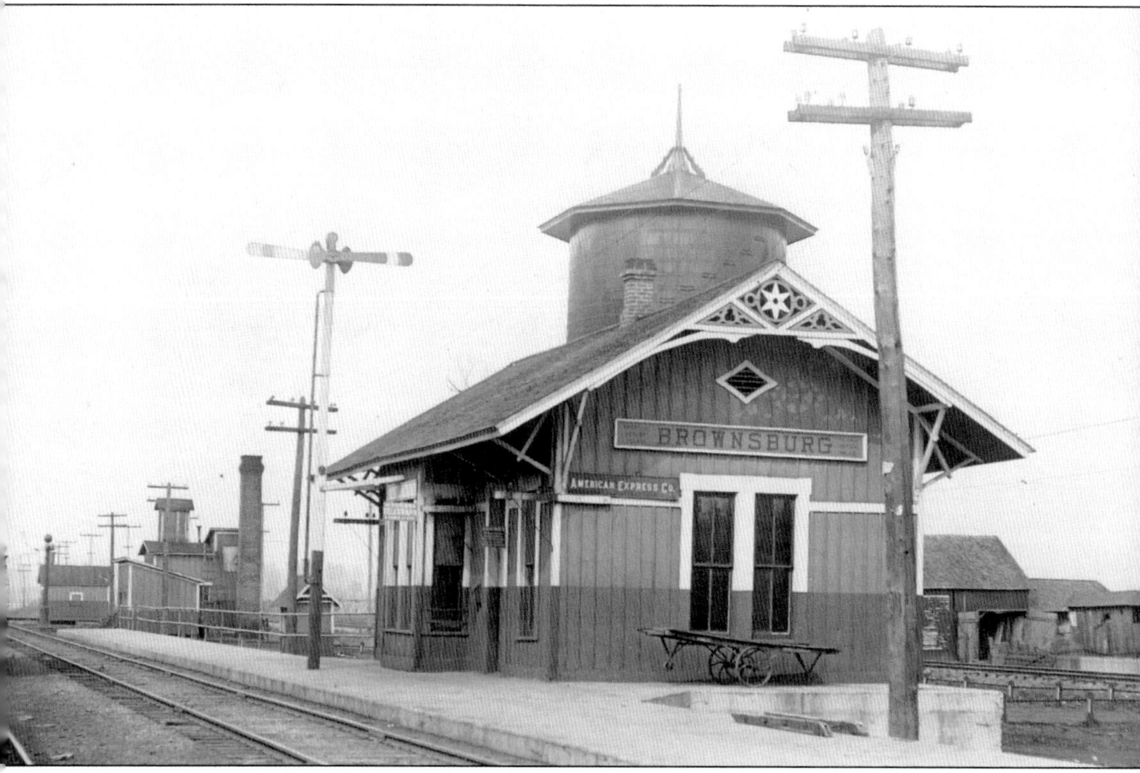

The beautiful Big Four depot on the west side of north Green Street, north of the railroad track, at one time served the Peoria & Eastern Railroad. The depot advertised its American Express and Western Union Telegraph capabilities. A Brownsburg sign announced the distance to Springfield and Peoria, Illinois. A wooden water tank with steel base, behind the depot 40 feet in elevation, served the thirst of the steam engines. Both sat approximately in the location of the entrance to Arbuckle Acres Park. There were two tracks at this location, a main track and a switch, which can be seen to the left of the photograph. In 1914, a tragedy occurred at this crossing when a man driving a horse and buggy across the tracks was struck. The boxcars, sheds, and even canning factory were cited as reasons that the gentleman's view was blocked. The train, traveling 55 to 65 miles per hour, was violating a Brownsburg town ordinance at the time that limited the speed of trains over town crossings to 6 miles per hour. (Courtesy of Roger A. Zimmerman.)

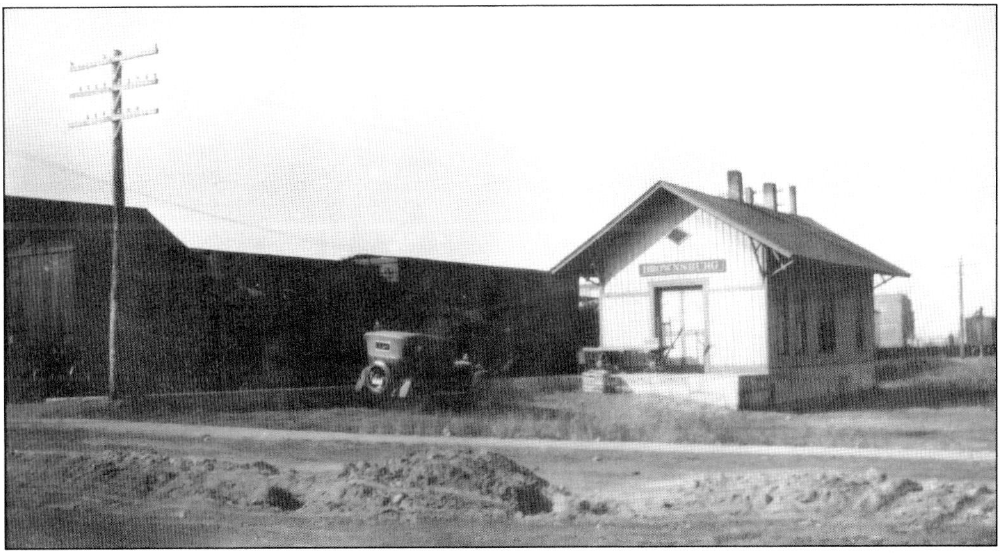

Later, becoming part of New York Central Railroad, the old depot in this undated photograph went through another change. In 1964, a group of citizens headed by Mary Wilson worked to salvage the depot to use as the Brownsburg Historical Museum. The public library, with the help of citizens, began collecting objects. Plans were drawn, and repairs were underway, but the cost of insuring the building prohibited the project.

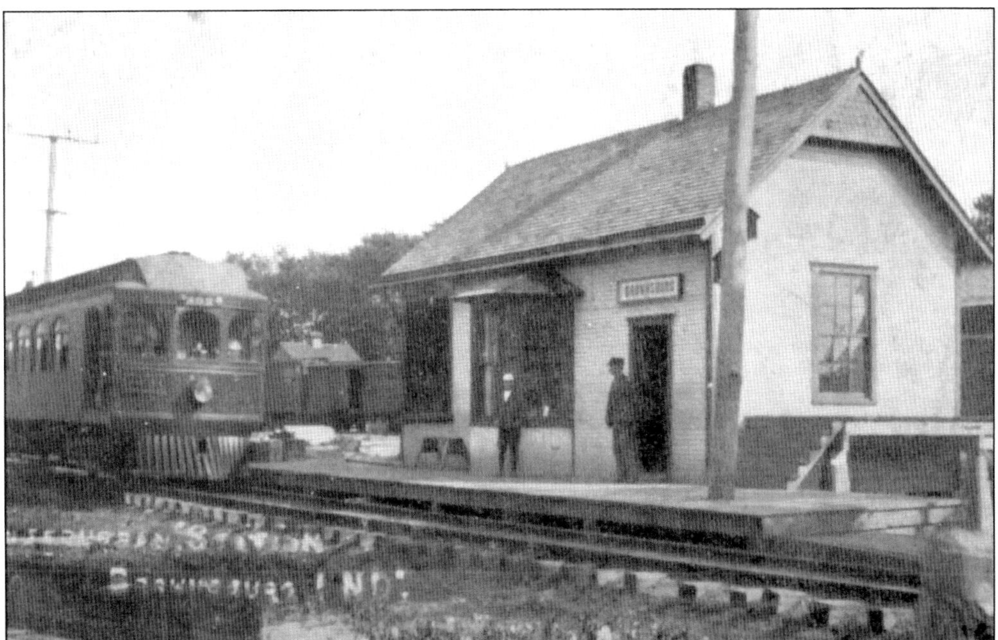

The interurban depot, pictured here and still located today at 205 North Green Street, provided cheap and dependable transportation. The line, opening around 1907, allowed residents to expand their horizons and work jobs in Speedway and Indianapolis. The line ran from Indianapolis to Brownsburg and on west to Crawfordsville. (Courtesy of Roger A. Zimmerman.)

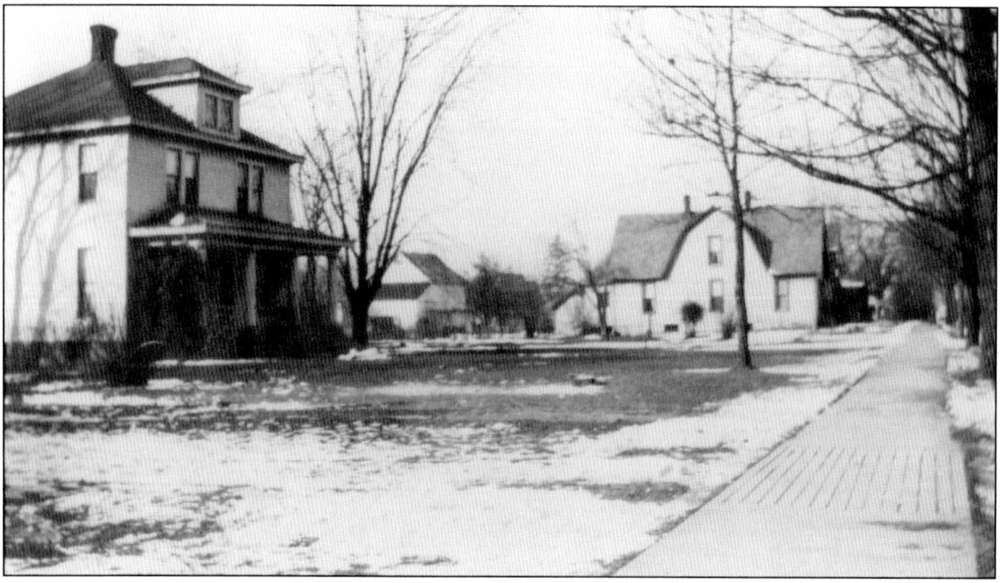

On the left, the Foursquare home, built around 1910, is located at 111 East College Avenue. The home on the right, with its gambrel roof, is located at 103 East College and was likely built prior to 1900. This undated photograph was taken before the rest of the property had been developed. These two homes have been beautifully preserved and still stand today.

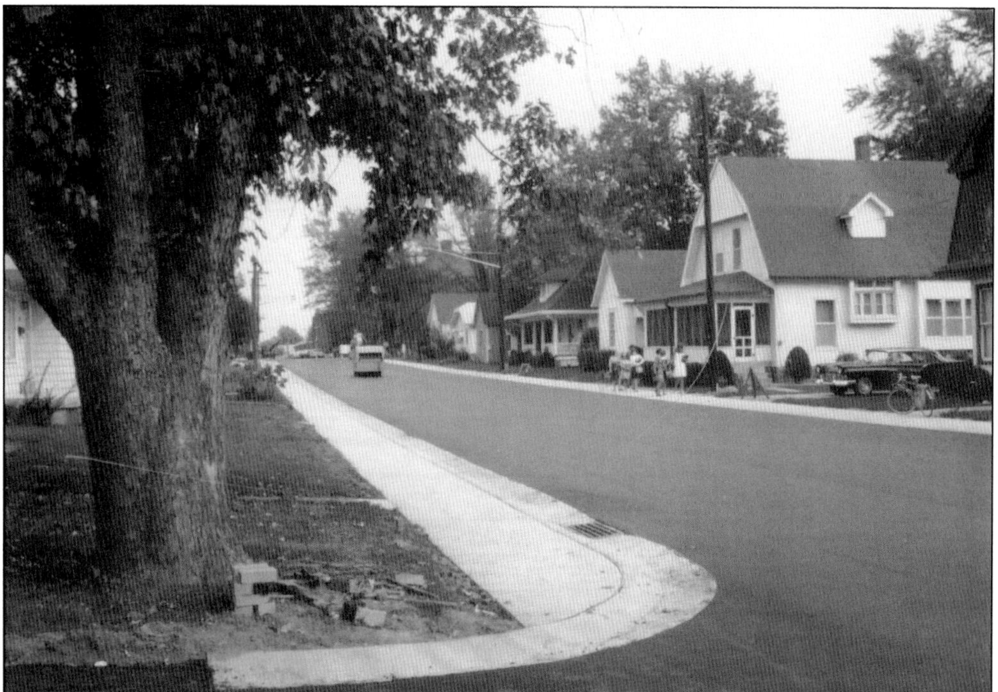

Looking east on College Avenue at the south side of the street sits another lovely row of well-preserved homes. College Avenue was resurfaced in 1965 and curbs and sidewalks were added. Many trees were removed at that time. The Brownsburg school buildings can be seen down the street through the trees.

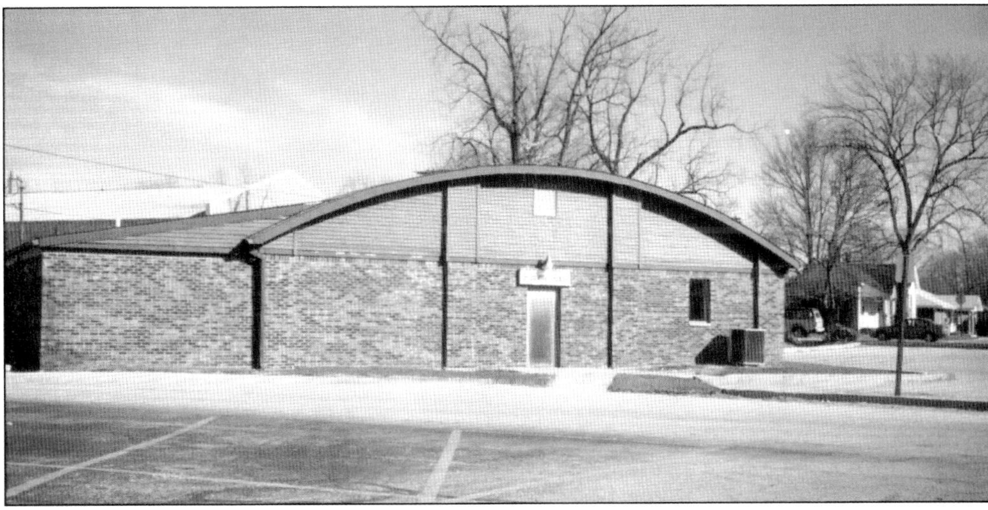

Prior to his death in October 1922, Grandison Eaton, a veteran of the Civil War and one of Brownsburg's most substantial citizens, had expressed his desire to donate land he and his wife owned to the town of Brownsburg for a park. His wife presented the deed for the land to the town board in November 1922, after his passing. The land was located just east of the then Brownsburg Christian Church and directly west of Lingeman-Adams mill on what is now Adams Street. The land was only to be used for park purposes and was to be known as Eaton Park, preserving their memory. The park went through stages of change from picnic land to a park with shelter house, shown in these two photographs. Eaton Hall was an open shelter that was enclosed and remodeled for use in the late 1960s. The land is still owned by the town and is home to the Brownsburg Municipal Buildings at 61 North Green Street. Residents will still see Eaton's name on Eaton Hall.

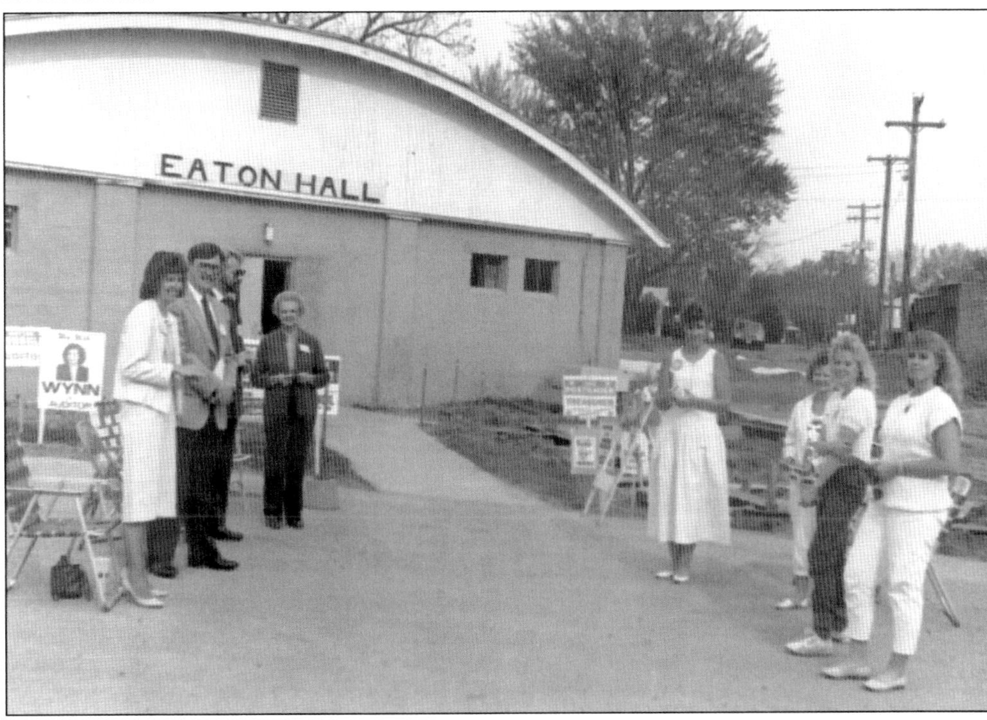

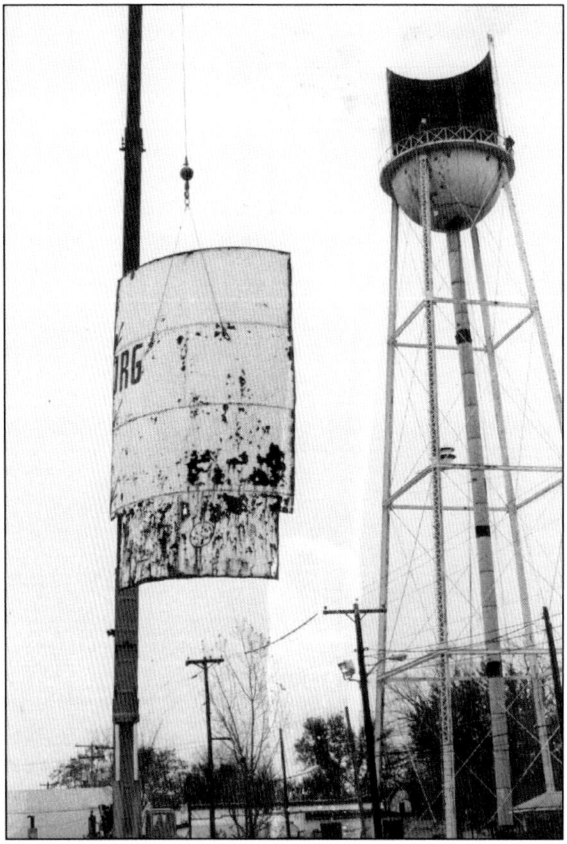

The old water tower was a landmark that residents may remember stood south of Main Street and east of Green Street just off of a small alley. When the use of water towers for town supply became obsolete, the tower deteriorated and was dismantled piece by piece in November 1984.

The former Brownsburg Town Hall and the gazebo sit in close proximity in this photograph. The town board approved the plans to build the town hall in 1987. Initially, there was opposition to the building due to the architectural style, timing, and location in Eaton Park. This town hall sat facing Main Street in the approximate location of the Brownsburg Municipal Buildings today.

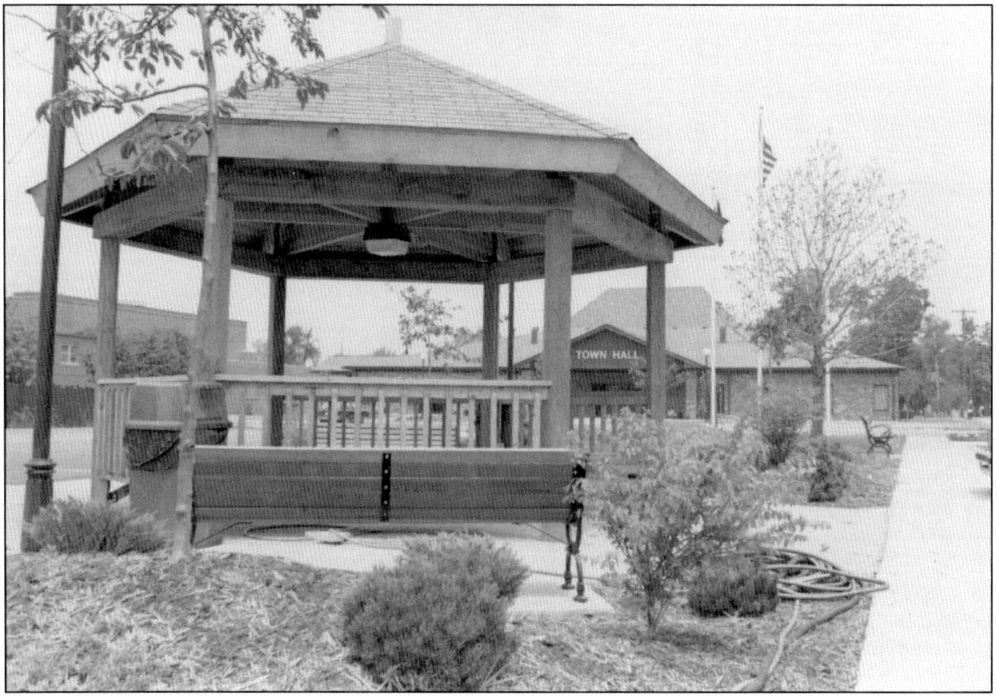

Three

Businesses

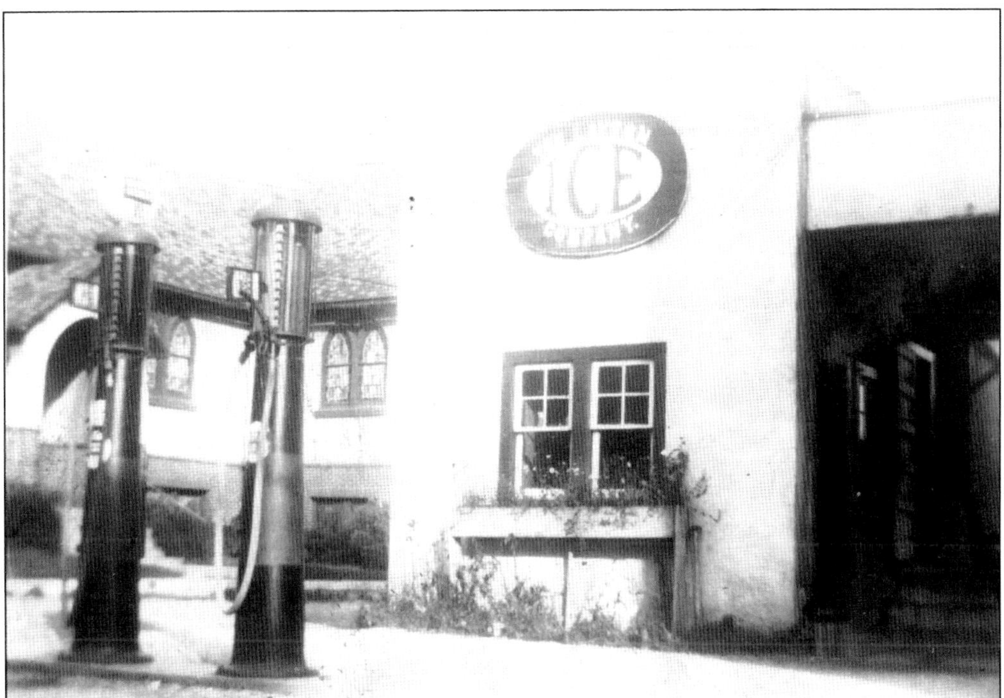

Sometime after 1922, the old roundhouse that sat between the Christian Church and Knights of Pythias building was torn down. In the late 1920s to early 1930s, the icehouse filled this location. R.M. "Bundy" Garner delivered ice from the icehouse in his truck to the people in town. (Courtesy of Roger A. Zimmerman.)

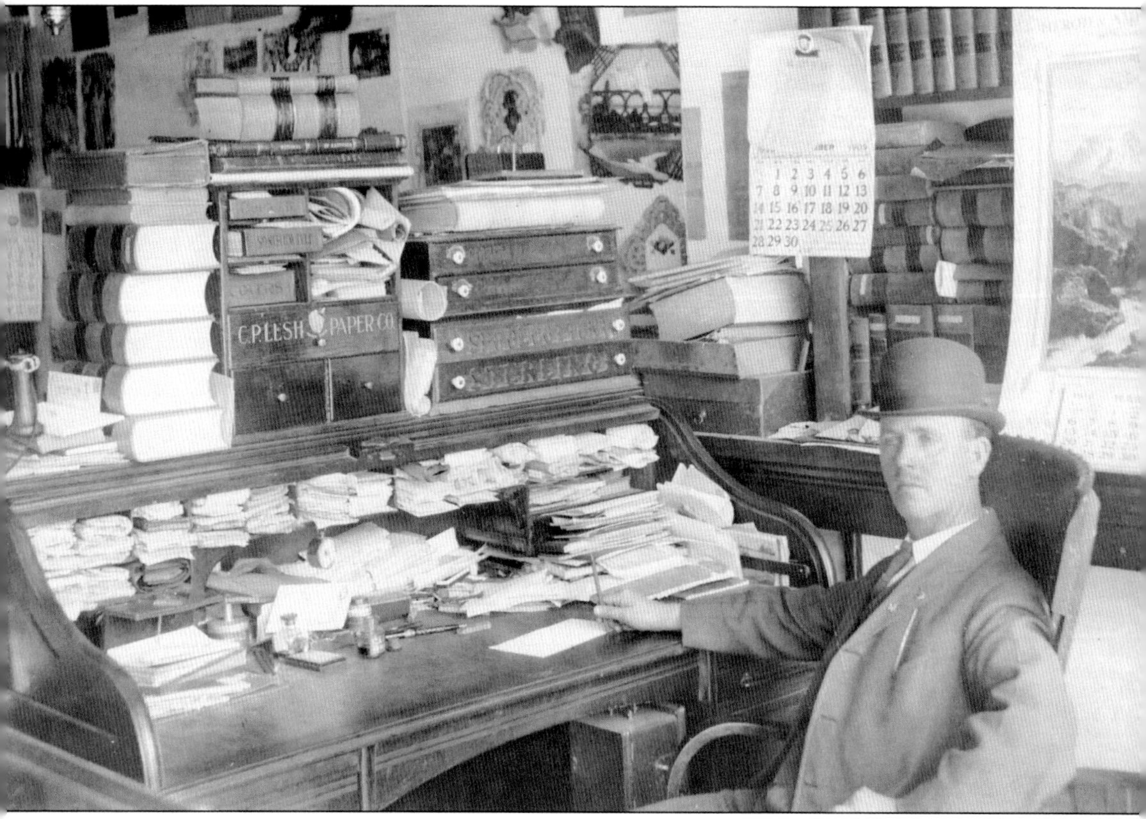

George Andrew "Andy" Johnson sits at his desk around 1909–1910. As indicated by the stacks of paperwork, various calendars, and writing books, Johnson was a man of many talents. He wore several business hats in the community serving as lawyer, insurance agent for Aetna farm policies, real estate agent, notary, and publisher of the *Brownsburg Record*. Johnson's office, shown in this photograph, was located in the Hunter Block on the northwest corner of Main and Green Streets and was most likely taken during his newspaper days based on the C.P. Lesh paper box on top of the desk. Lesh was a paper dealer in Indianapolis in the late 1800s to 1900s. While serving as the notary in 1897, Johnson witnessed and notarized the incorporation of citizens responsible for creating the Greenlawn Cemetery Association. Johnson and his wife, Nora Belle Hopkins Johnson, are buried in Greenlawn Cemetery.

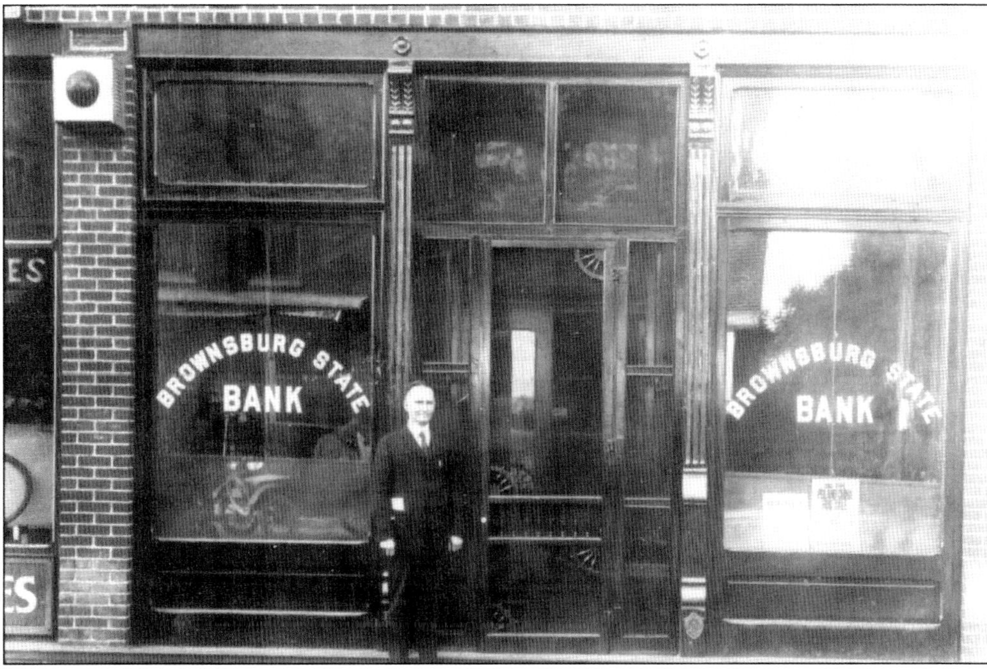

An unidentified man stands in front of the Brownsburg State Bank located then at the southeast corner of Main and Green Streets in the Odd Fellow Block, possibly around 1910. The bank was organized in 1908 and operated under the assistance of many well-known names, including Grandison Eaton, Dr. John L. Marsh, and William F. Evans.

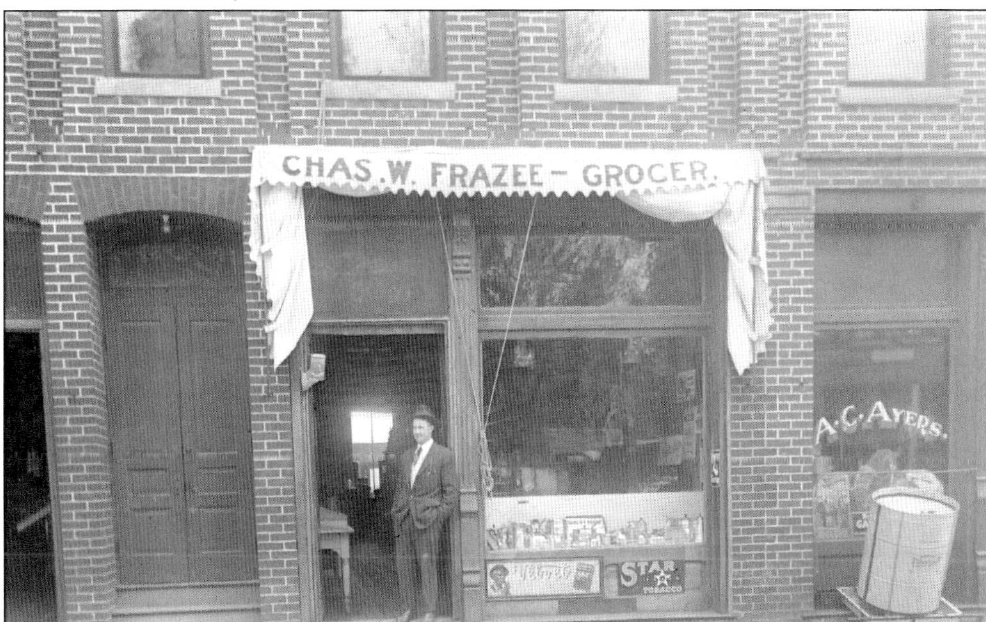

In the center of the Knights of Pythias building, at 21 North Green Street, the Charles W. Frazee grocery store operated. Frazee managed his grocery store next door to Albert C. Ayers, who ran a harness shop out of the corner location. The back of this postcard view is dated 1917 and is addressed to Mrs. Otis Frazee.

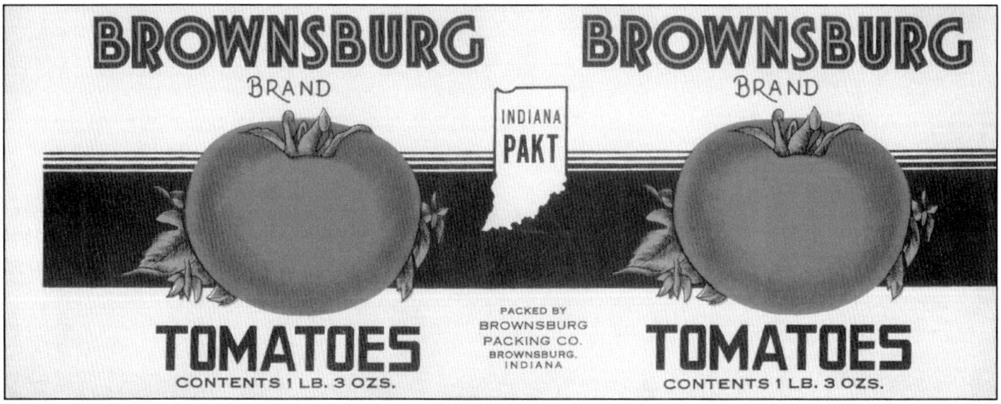

The label above proudly displays Brownsburg Brand tomatoes. The canning factory in Brownsburg was located on the west side of north Green Street just south of the railroad track. Around 1909, it was operating, in summers, as the Ladoga Canning Company. In 1916, the start of Brownsburg Schools was delayed a week due to the number of children employed at the factory whose assistance with the tomato crop was vital. Operating as the Princeton Canning Company in 1918, a peeler's shed was added to the southwest corner around that time. The peeler's checks below were purportedly either used as a system of payment for wages for peeling tomatoes or to track use of equipment. The factory continued for many years until it was destroyed in 1956 as part of a fire department exercise. (All photographs courtesy of Roger A. Zimmerman.)

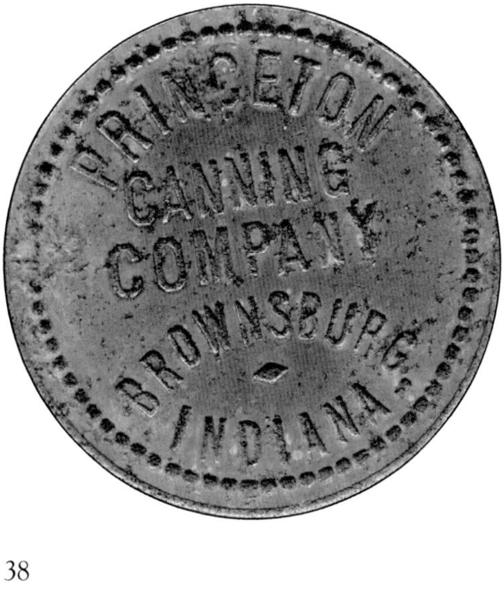

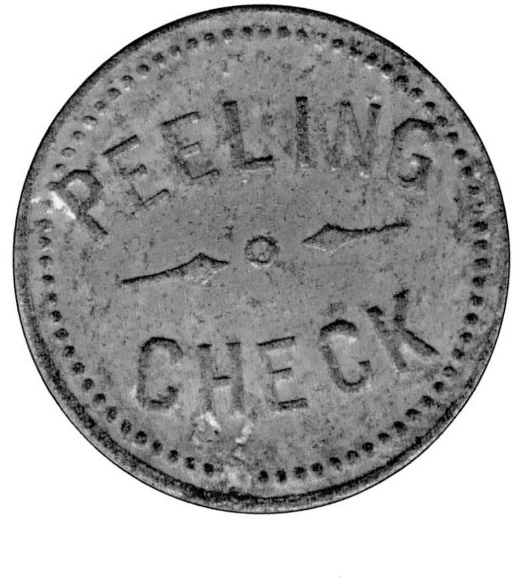

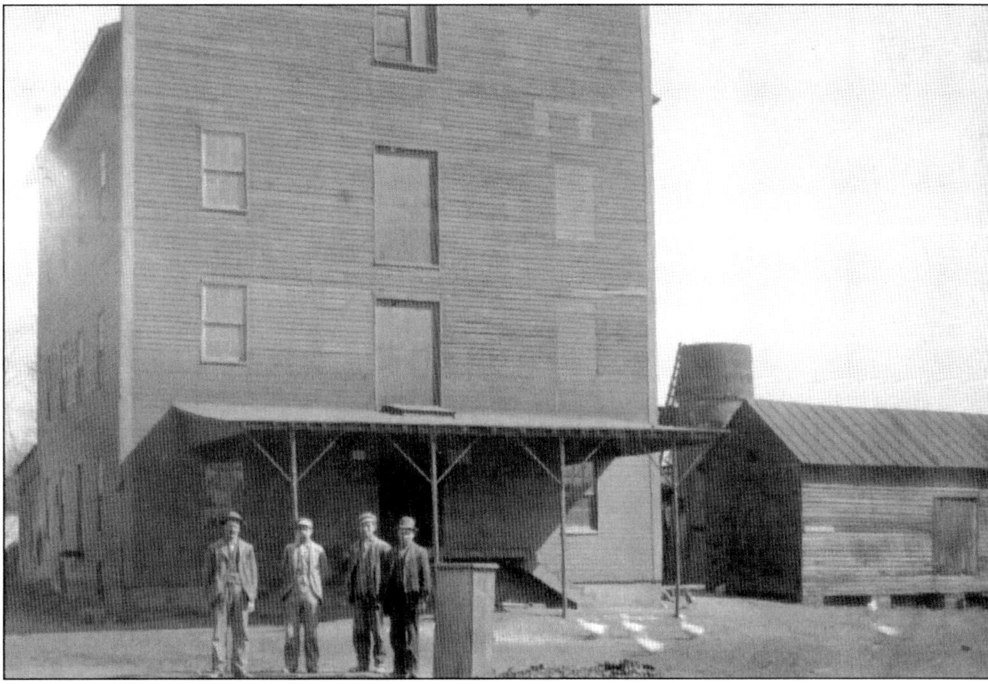

The year 1899 was a tragic one for the Lingeman-Adams companies. The gristmill, shown here, sat on the east side of Mill (Adams) Street north of Main Street. In July 1899, a boiler exploded and wrecked the mill without injuries. In October 1899, the boiler at the sawmill, leased by Willis Tyler, exploded causing death to three men and injuring five others. The boiler landed in the rear of the Methodist church about 200 yards away.

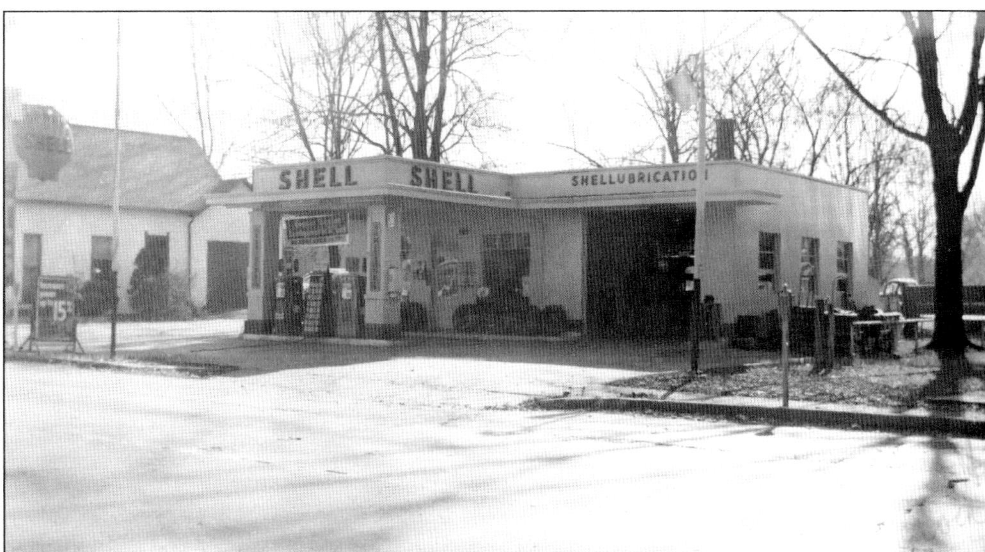

The Shell gas station, photographed around 1945, was located just east of the large brick Italianate home at 27 West Main Street. It was owned and operated at one time by R.D. "Mike" Wilson along with other employees. The station was located on the south side of Main Street.

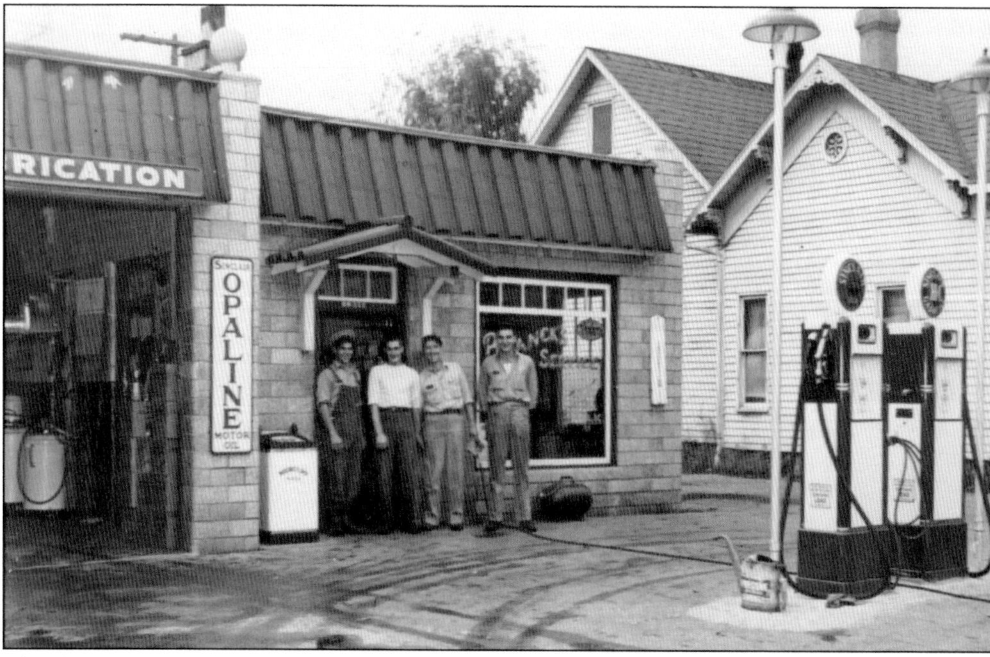

Blanck's Service and the Sinclair gas pumps are pictured at the west end of the Blanck Chevrolet Company and in front of the old water tower on the south side of Main Street. In no particular order, Carl Kelsheimer, Carl "Jerry" Blanck, Tommy Ballard, and Mickey Poole handled car maintenance and station management.

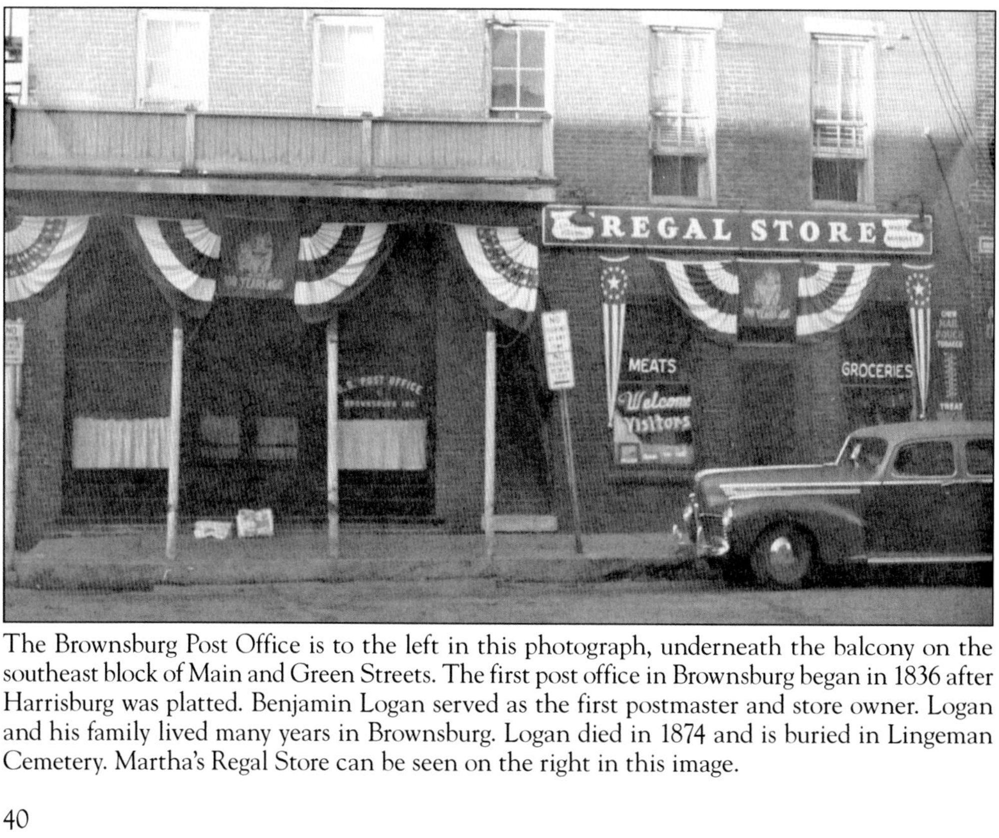

The Brownsburg Post Office is to the left in this photograph, underneath the balcony on the southeast block of Main and Green Streets. The first post office in Brownsburg began in 1836 after Harrisburg was platted. Benjamin Logan served as the first postmaster and store owner. Logan and his family lived many years in Brownsburg. Logan died in 1874 and is buried in Lingeman Cemetery. Martha's Regal Store can be seen on the right in this image.

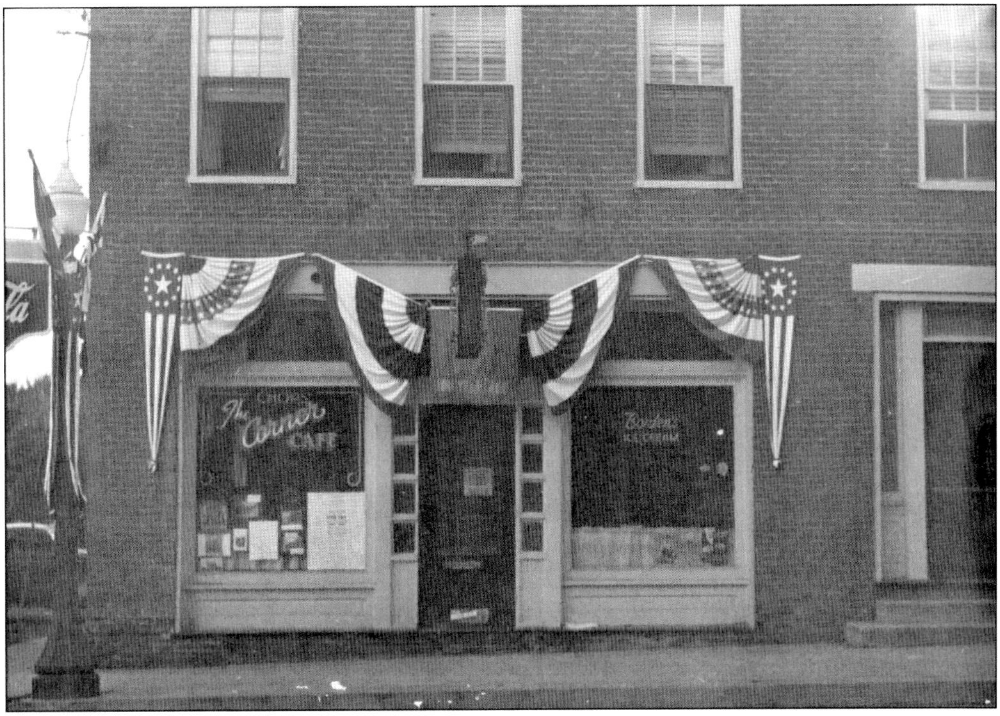

The Corner Café, shown in the photograph, was housed in the Hunter Bank building on the southwest block of Main and Green Streets. The building stood unused for a time in the 1930s, until it was sold. Around 1936, a tavern called Wonder Bar opened in the corner store. Randall Roberts bought the location in 1938 and changed the name to the Corner Café. Eventually, the café would be sold and resold many times. The café served the community for 30 years. It was remodeled to accommodate Dale's TV store around 1968–1969. (Below, courtesy of Roger A. Zimmerman.)

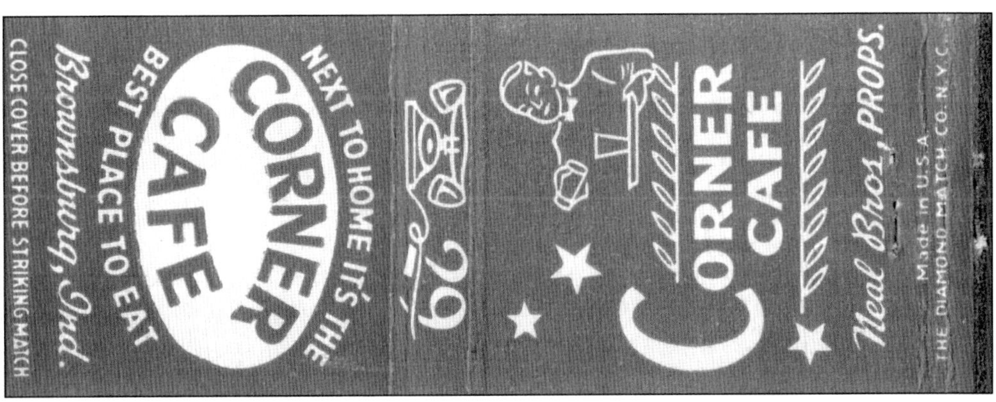

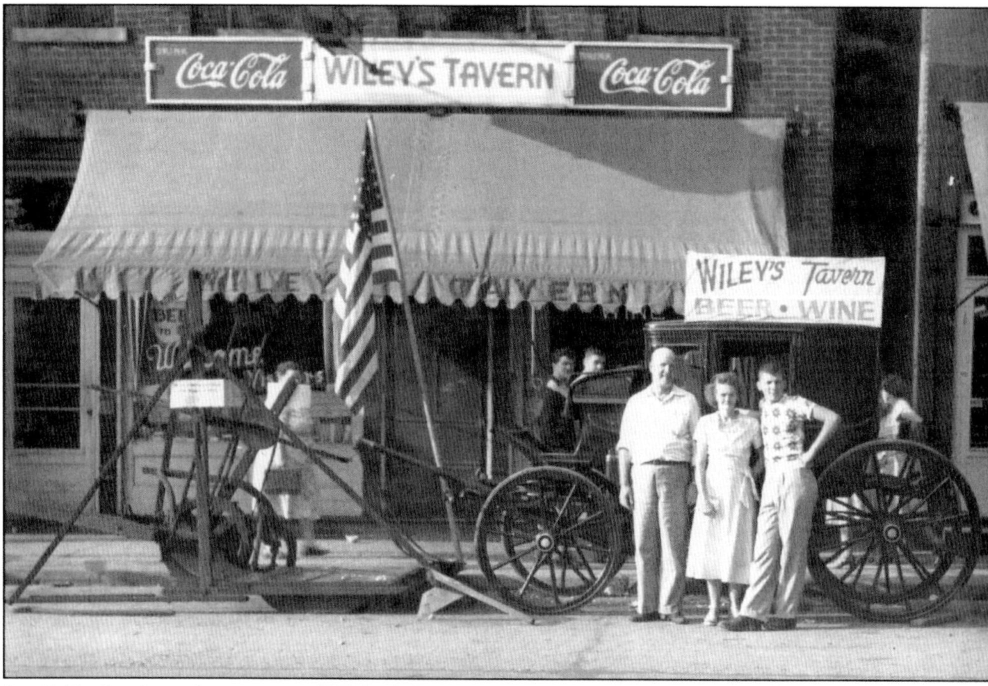

In 1942, the formal opening of Wiley's Tavern was announced three doors east of the previous location on the north side of Main Street. In this photograph, Mr. and Mrs. Russell Wiley pose with their son in front of an 1831 reaper and old cab.

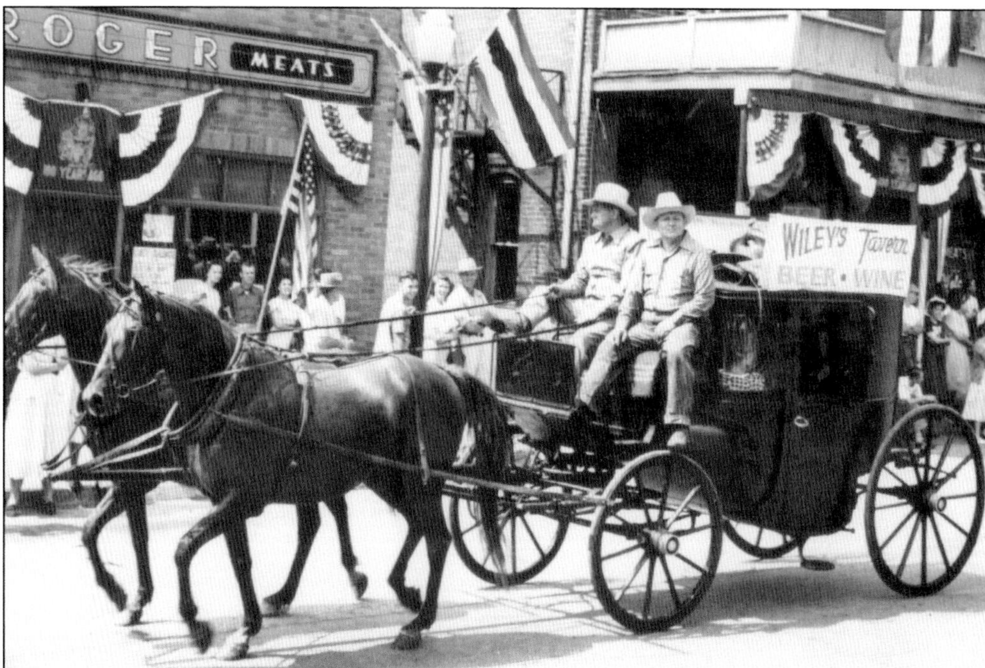

Wiley's Tavern used the 1948 centennial parade as a prime opportunity to advertise. At the time, they advertised a new electrically cooled bottle and smart decorations. To every lady attending the grand opening, a rose was presented, and the men received a cigar.

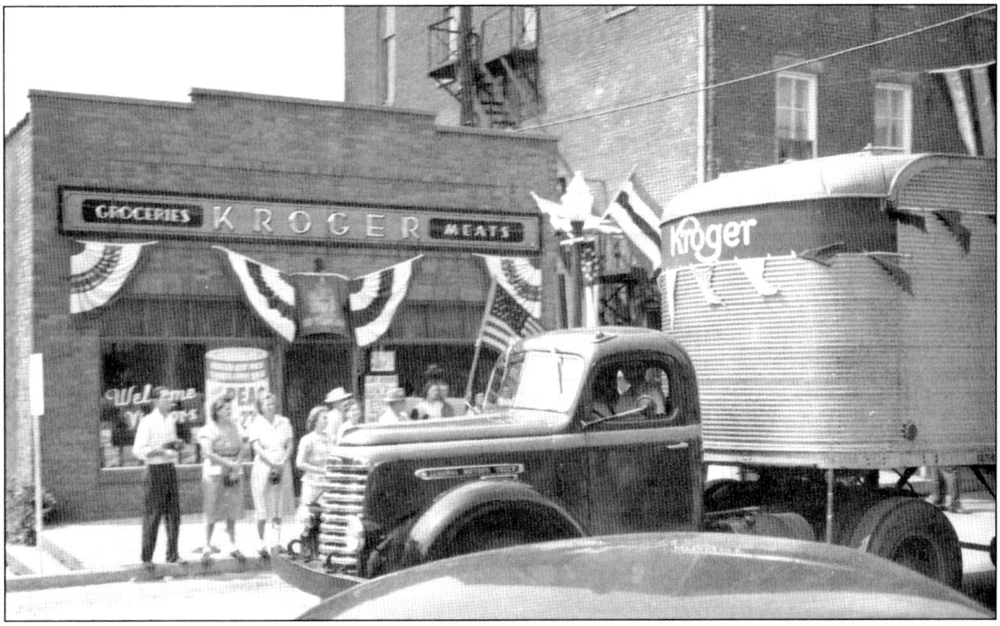

Brownsburg's Kroger Grocery was the hometown market for many years. Situated on the south side of east Main Street, the market was overshadowed by the Masonic Hall and balcony. In this photograph, a Kroger delivery truck makes its way east on Main Street during the centennial celebration parade.

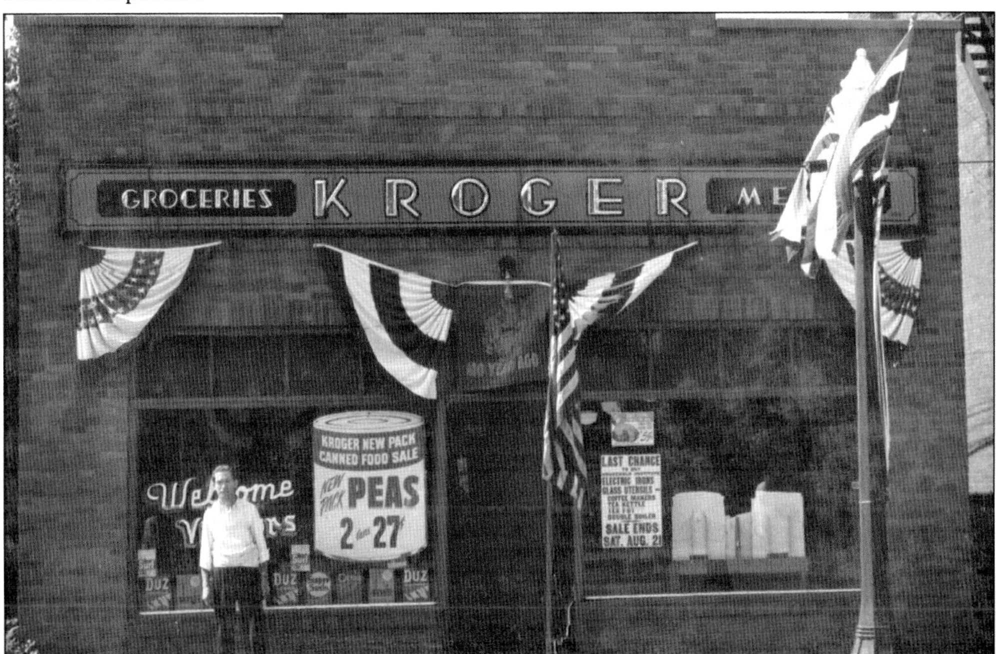

Frank Glass, manager of the Kroger Grocery, stands in front of the store. The Kroger Grocery and Baking Company opened its first store in Indianapolis in 1924–1925 when Bernard Henry Kroger decided to expand from Cincinnati to other locations. Kroger entered the market business, establishing the "neighborhood grocery store."

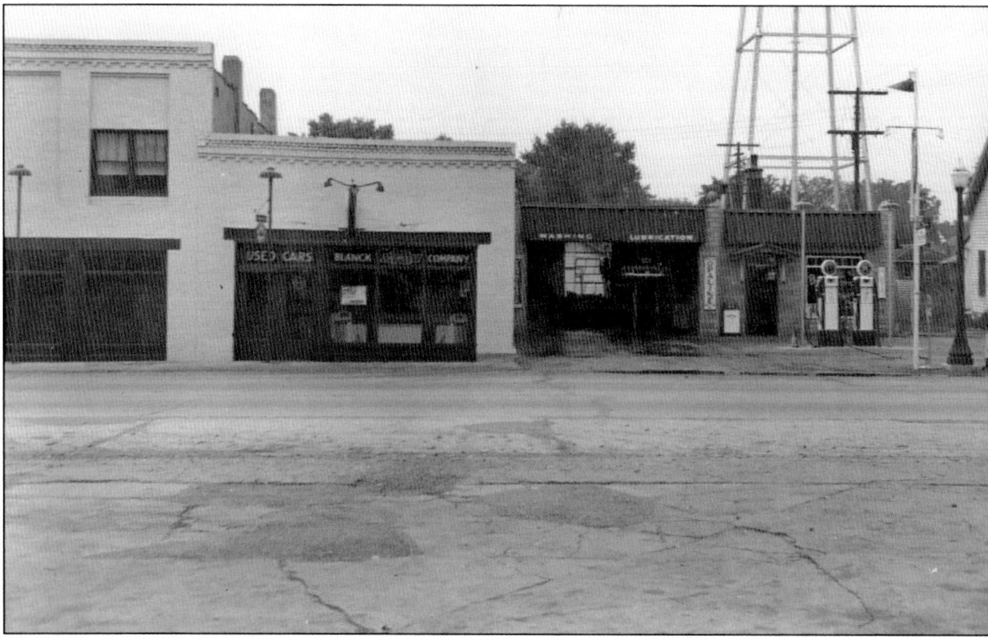

Moving farther east past the water tower and next to the Sinclair gas pumps sat Blanck Chevrolet on the south side of Main Street. The old town water tower can be seen in the background. Although this was the second home for Blanck Chevrolet, the firm remained there until it moved to the east edge of Brownsburg around 1955.

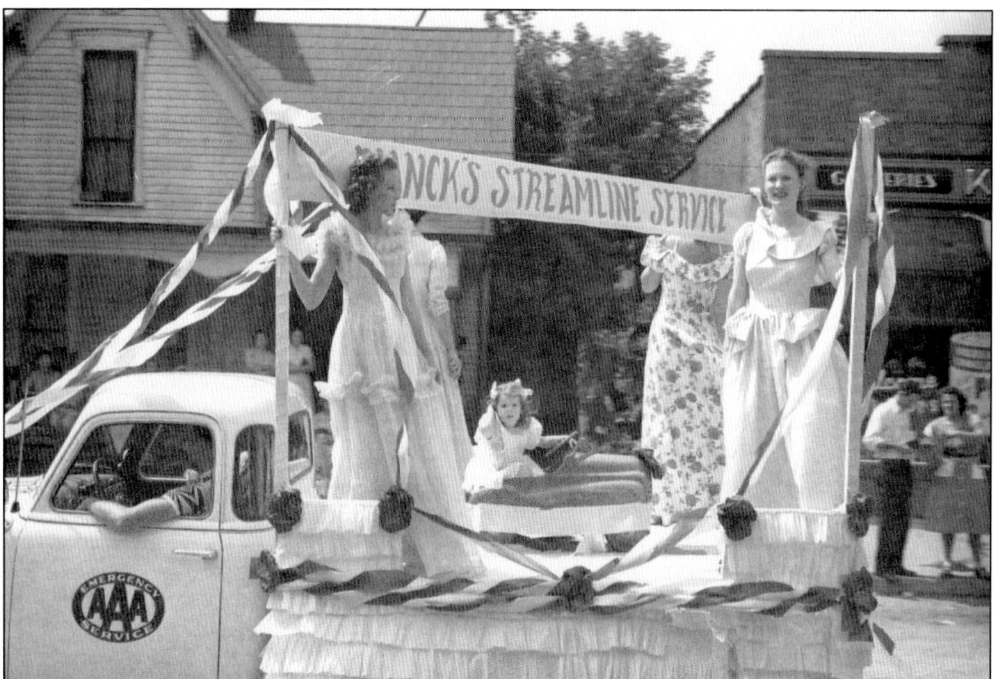

The Blanck Streamline Service float moves east on Main Street in the centennial parade. Ed Blanck Sr. officially opened the Chevrolet business in a garage in Brownsburg in 1928. The float was a fine representation of a company with many ties to the community.

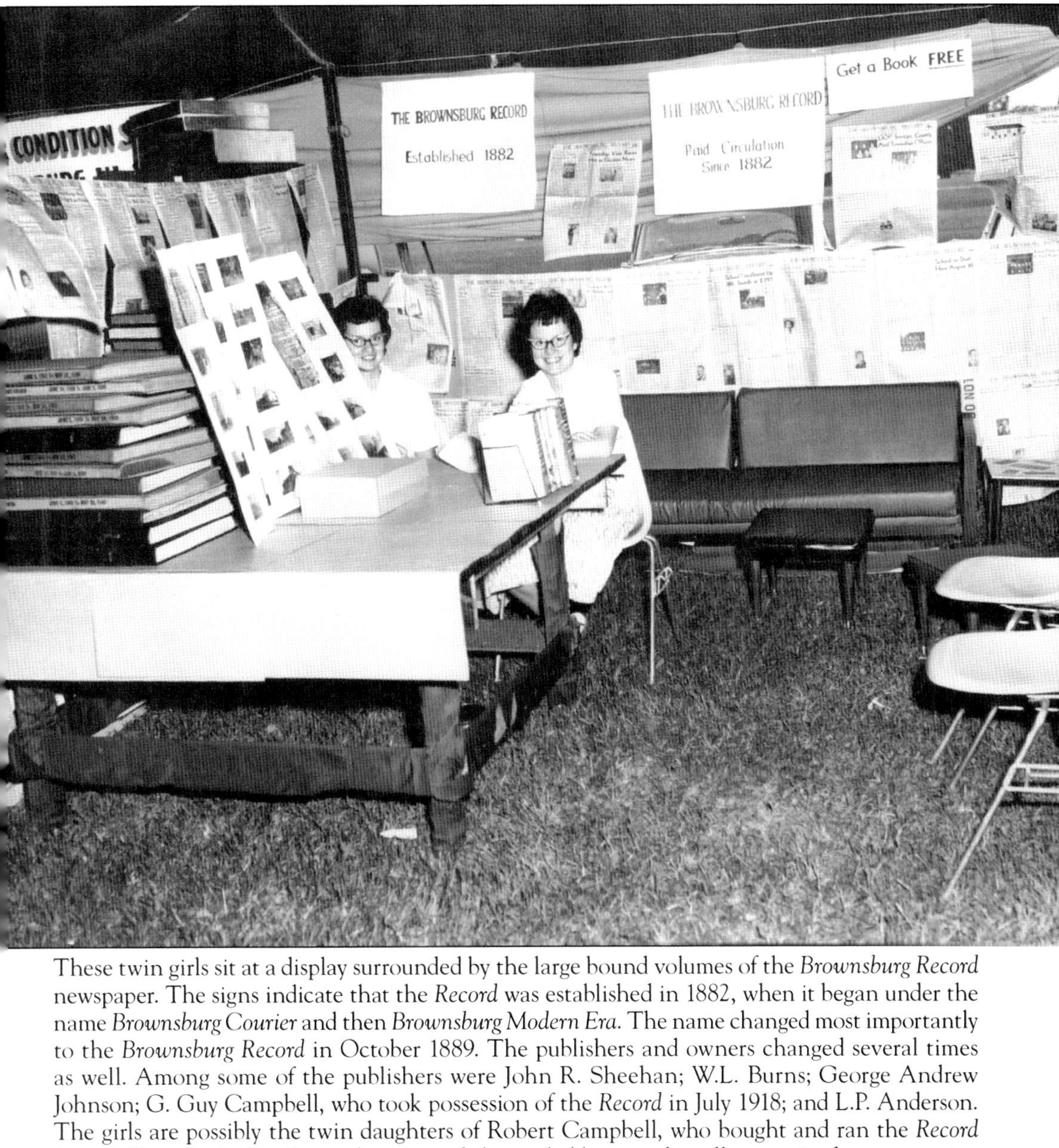

These twin girls sit at a display surrounded by the large bound volumes of the *Brownsburg Record* newspaper. The signs indicate that the *Record* was established in 1882, when it began under the name *Brownsburg Courier* and then *Brownsburg Modern Era*. The name changed most importantly to the *Brownsburg Record* in October 1889. The publishers and owners changed several times as well. Among some of the publishers were John R. Sheehan; W.L. Burns; George Andrew Johnson; G. Guy Campbell, who took possession of the *Record* in July 1918; and L.P. Anderson. The girls are possibly the twin daughters of Robert Campbell, who bought and ran the *Record* from 1953 to 1966. The *Brownsburg Record* chronicled large and small events in the community. Local advertisers throughout the years also help tell the tale of the changing business face of the community within its pages.

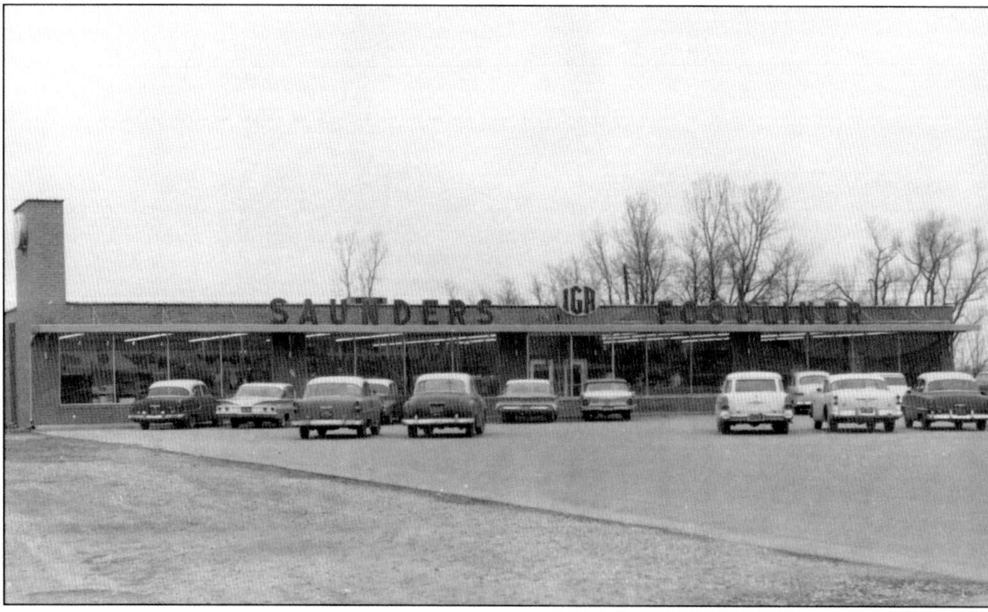

Saunders IGA Foodliner, shown here in the Brownsburg shopping center east of town on the north side of US 136, was built in 1955. Marion Saunders from Danville was the owner. The modern building had new checkout counters and automatic cash registers.

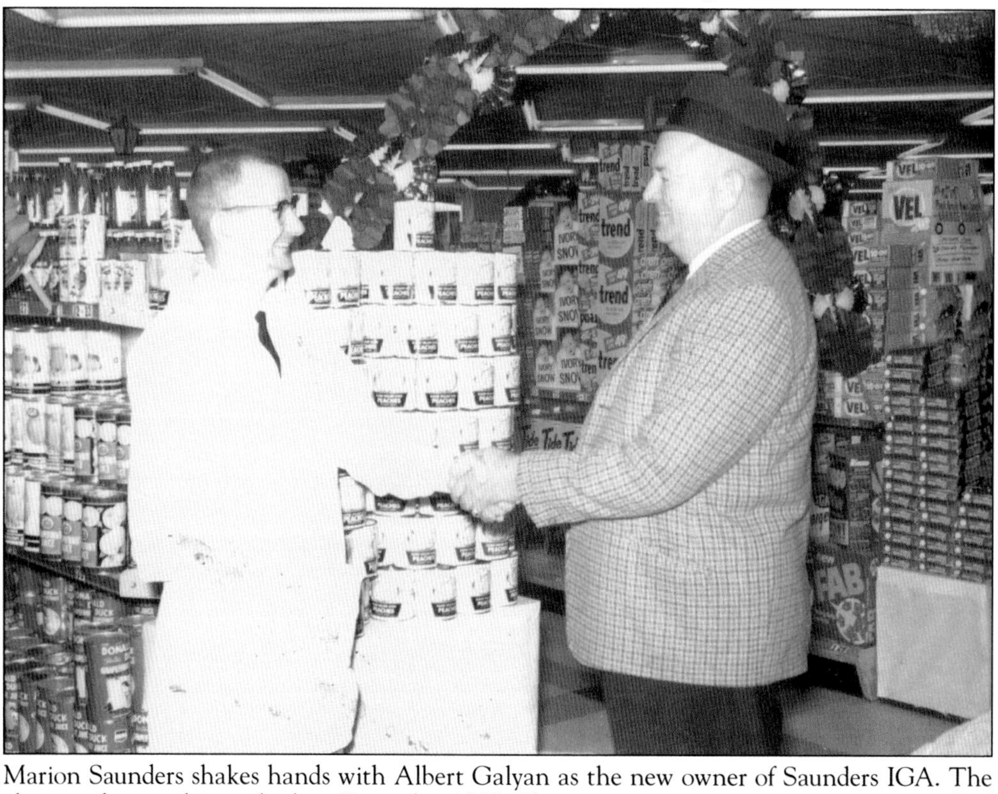

Marion Saunders shakes hands with Albert Galyan as the new owner of Saunders IGA. The change of ownership took place December 1963. The store was to continue operating as it had with no closing planned at that time. Many residents will remember Galyan's Grocery store.

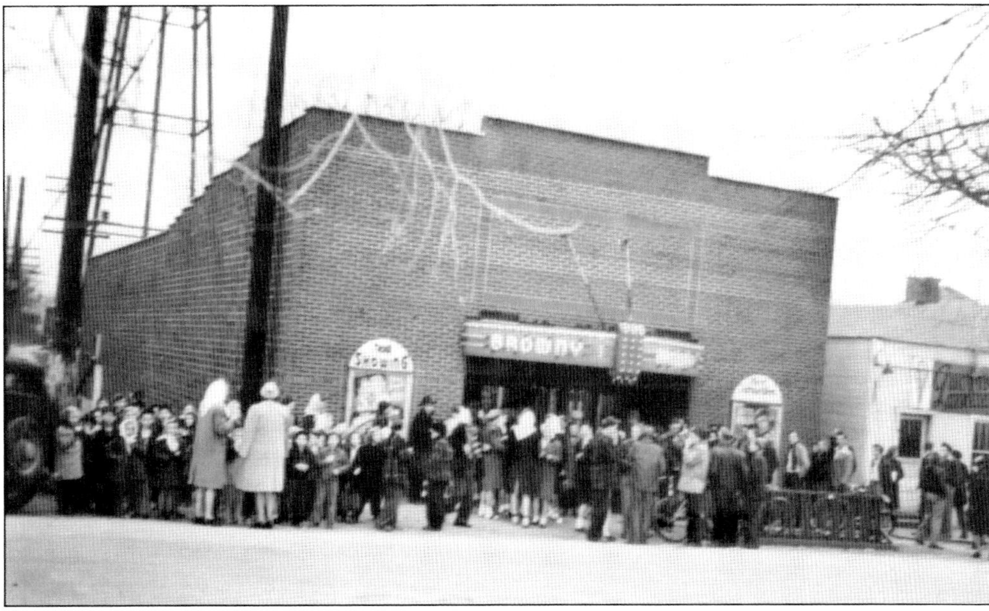

The Browny Theatre [Theater] was located at 25 South Green Street. Around the 1950s, the Browny was the only movie house in the county with a wide screen to show films like *Ma and Pa Kettle*. It closed for a while in July 1953, reopened, and closed again in May 1955; this would not be the end of its revival attempts throughout the years.

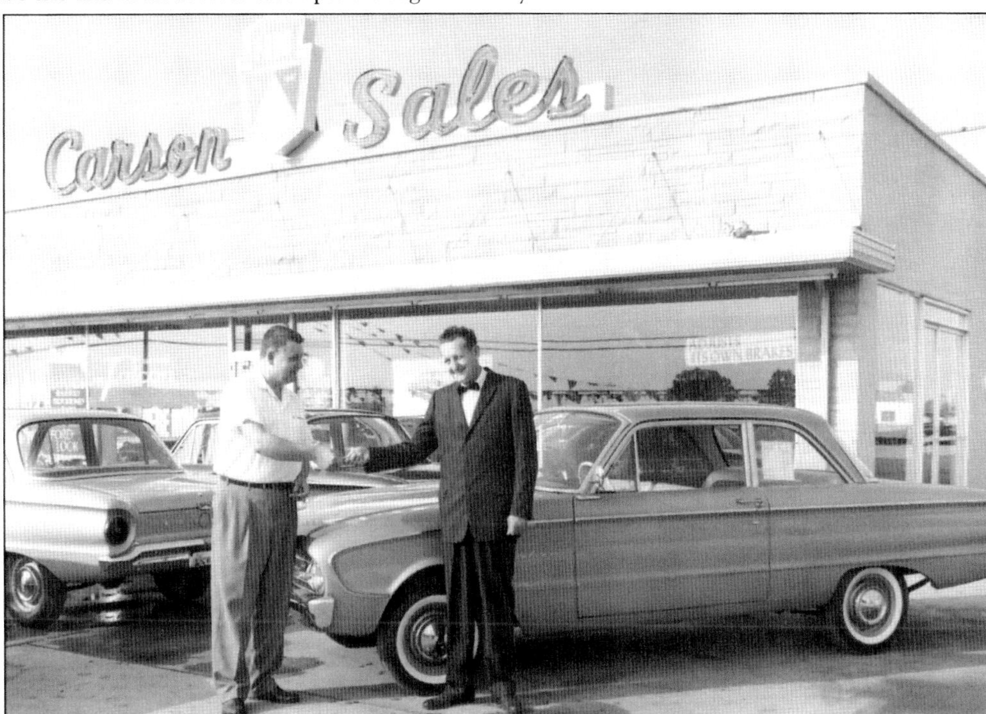

Carson Ford Sales at one time was located in the Brownsburg Shopett shopping center area. In 1959, Carson packed up and moved to the Shopett location on the far east end of town. The move gave the company a larger space to accommodate a showroom and service department.

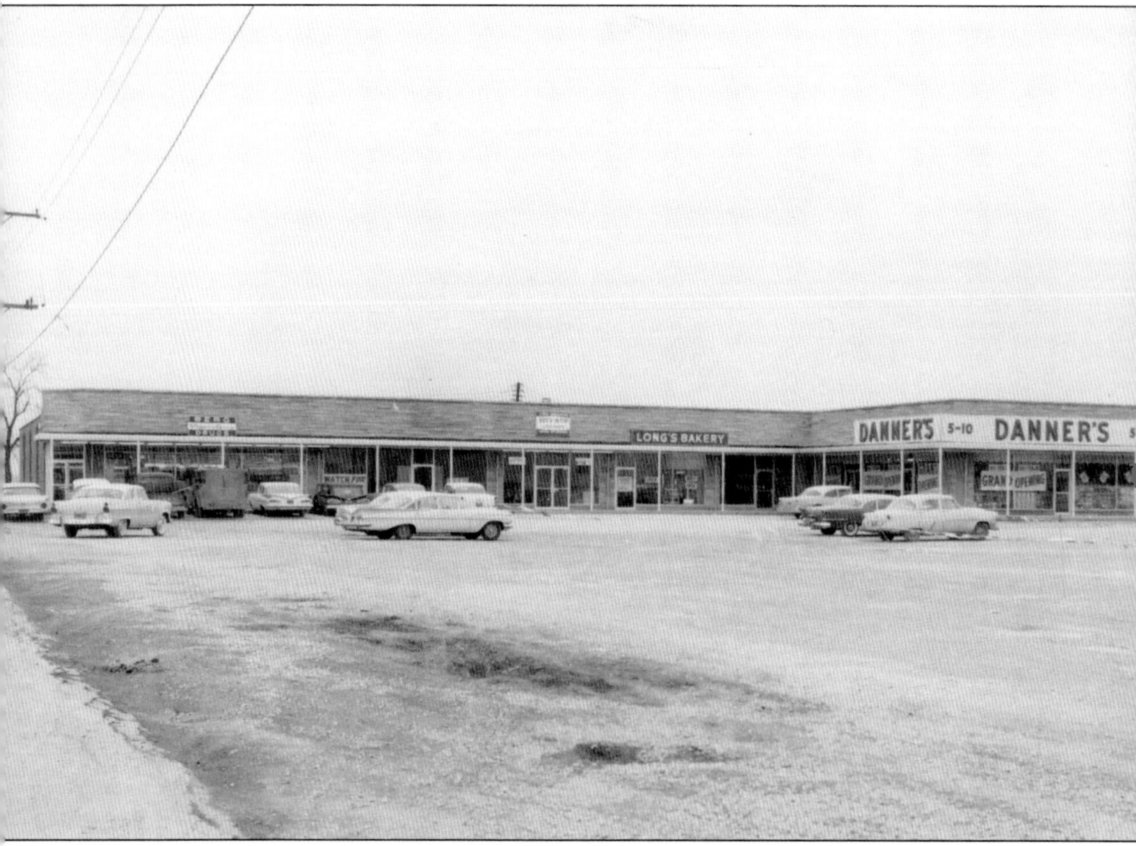

This photograph of the east side Shopett was taken in 1960. Some of the stores included were Berg's Drugstore, Brouhard's Quick Wash Laundry, Long's Bakery, and Danner's 5 and 10. Danner's offered a well-lighted and modern display room where shoppers could purchase many different items. The store carried clothes, personal items, gift items, and even lawn and garden items. On December 18, 1981, a fire started in the back of Danner's, and it was destroyed. Many other stores suffered damage from the blaze. The Shopett was Bert "Bud" Carson's brainchild. When looking for a property to expand his Ford Dealership, Carson thought big and planned for a shopping center that would accommodate several businesses for the community for years to come. The Shopett, shown here, is on the east end of town on the north side of Main Street, or US 136.

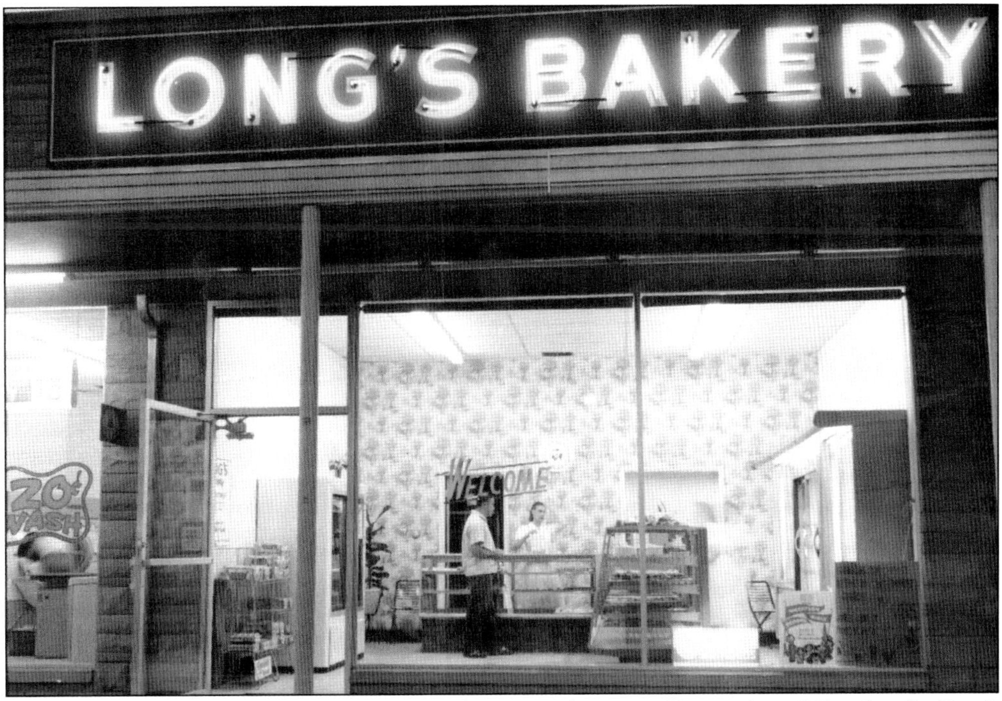

Long's Bakery was at one time nestled in the corner between Danner's and Brouhard's Quick Wash Laundry in the east side Shopett. The bakery was owned and operated by Carl W. Long. The bakery, shown here in 1960, offered a complete line of pastries.

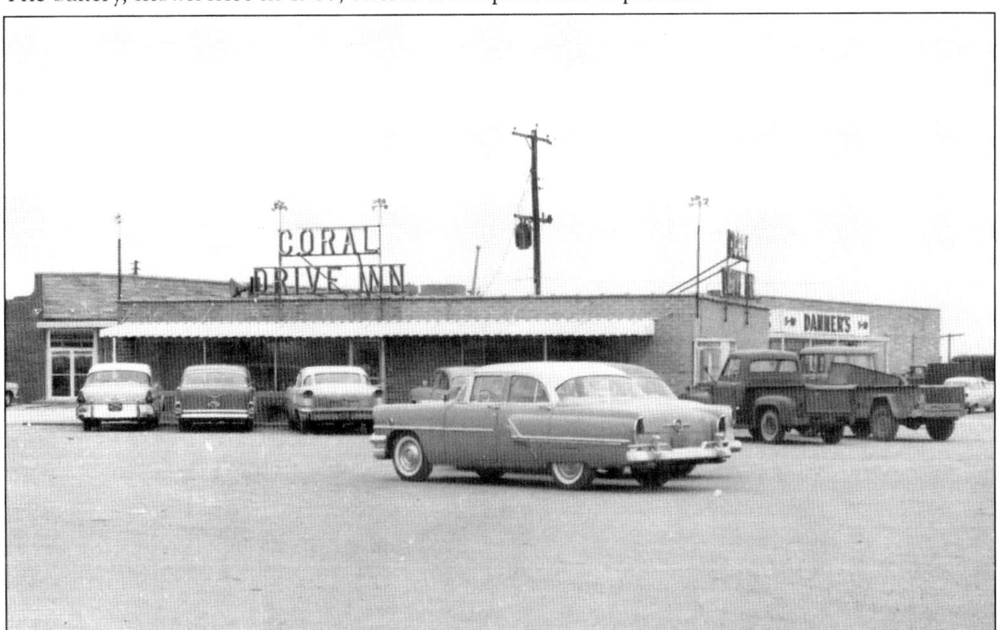

A photograph labeled August 1960 shows cars and trucks gathered around the Coral Drive Inn at the east side Shopett. Danner's can be seen in the background. The Coral Drive Inn expanded in the late 1950s and added a new 24-by-32-foot dining room. They used the space to offer regular meals seven days a week and to cater for special parties.

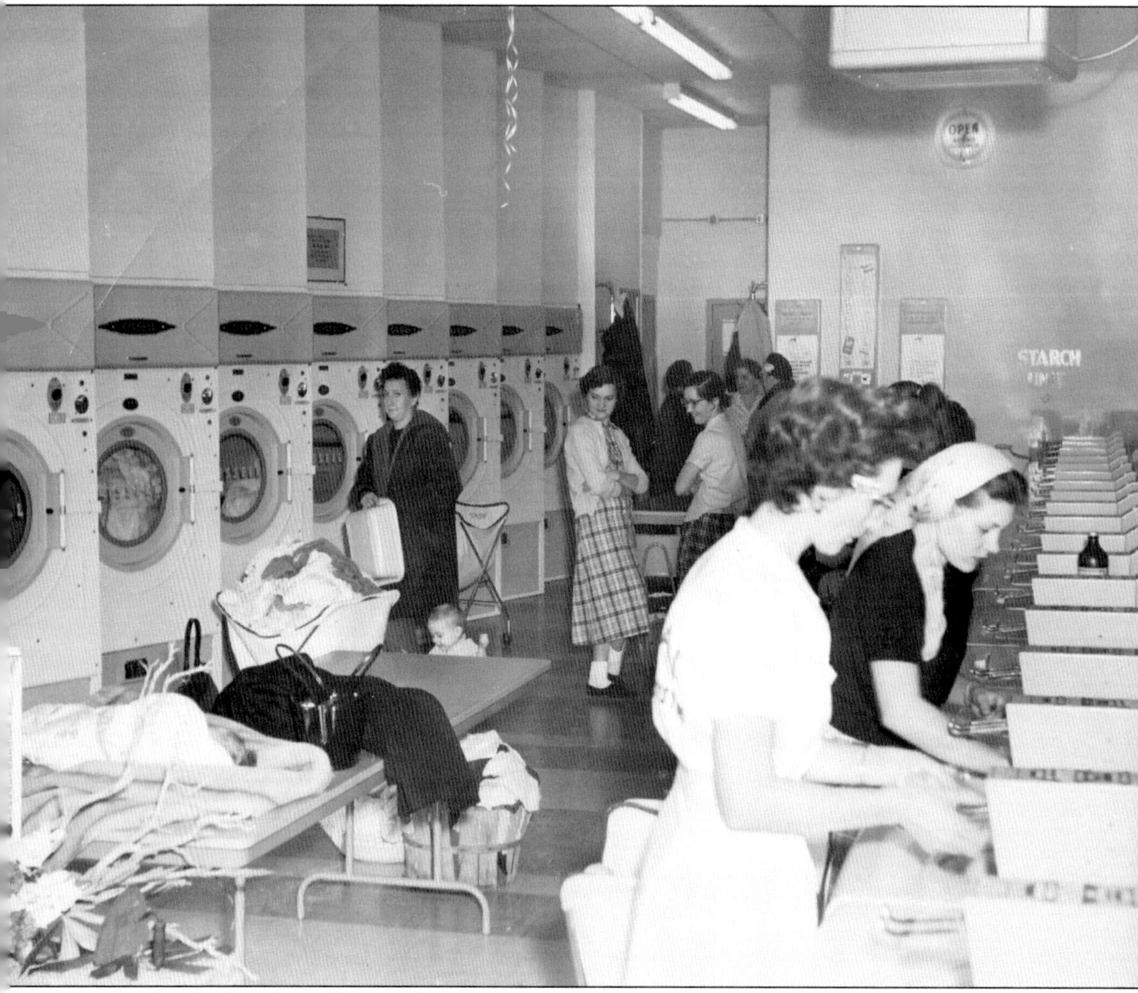

Brouhard's Quick Wash Laundry was one of the first units to open in the Brownsburg Shopett. These hardworking women are pictured going about the task of finishing the wash. The laundry was completely coin operated and open for business 24 hours a day. There were 21 washers in all, 20 for clothes washing and 1 machine was reserved for dyeing clothes. Eight dryers were placed diagonally on the west wall of the shop to offer greater privacy for the operators. Brouhard's also installed vending machines to provide candy and drinks for the patrons or their children. Owned by Harry Brouhard, the laundry was well located to offer the patrons a choice by day of staying and chatting with friends or shopping at the additional Shopett stores. By night, the laundry provided a bright spot shining through the night for townspeople.

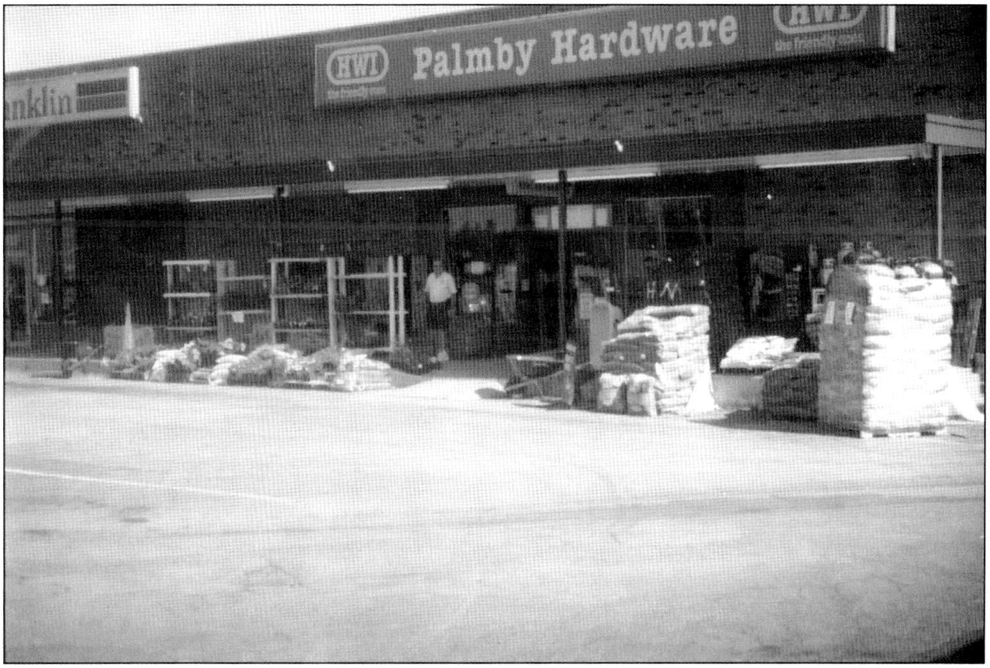

Although gone, thoughts of Palmby Hardware still bring a smile. Palmby occupied a corner shop at the far east end of town on the north side of Main Street or US 136. The hardware store began as part of a franchise chain but made the decision to switch to an independent store, focused on meeting the needs of the community that it served. Locals will indeed remember it for its hometown feel.

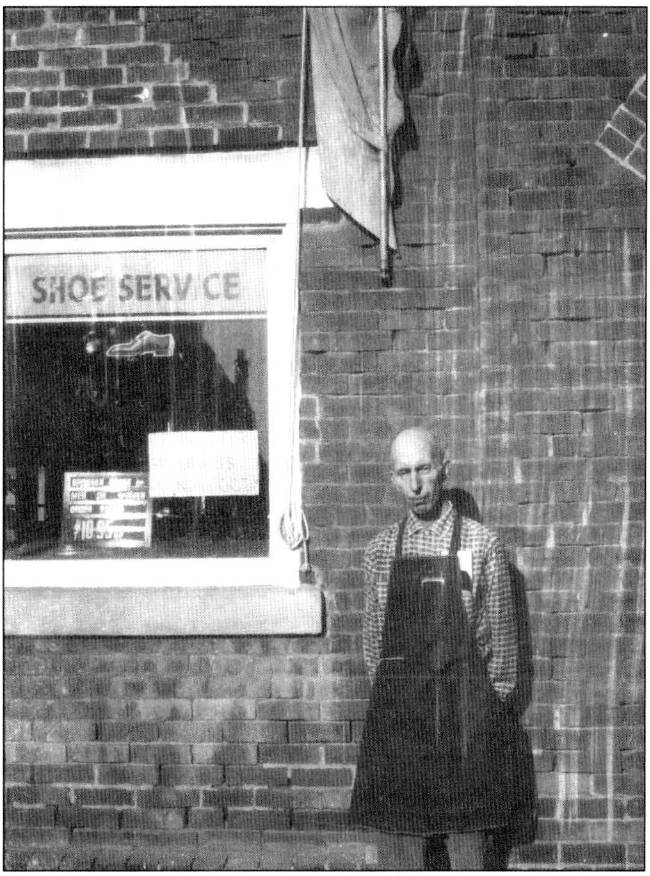

Ivan Scott of Scott's Shoe Repair is standing outside his shop on south Green Street. The shoe repair business was located in back of the Hunter building on the southwest corner of Main and Green Streets. Scott also served for a time as a park superintendent in Brownsburg.

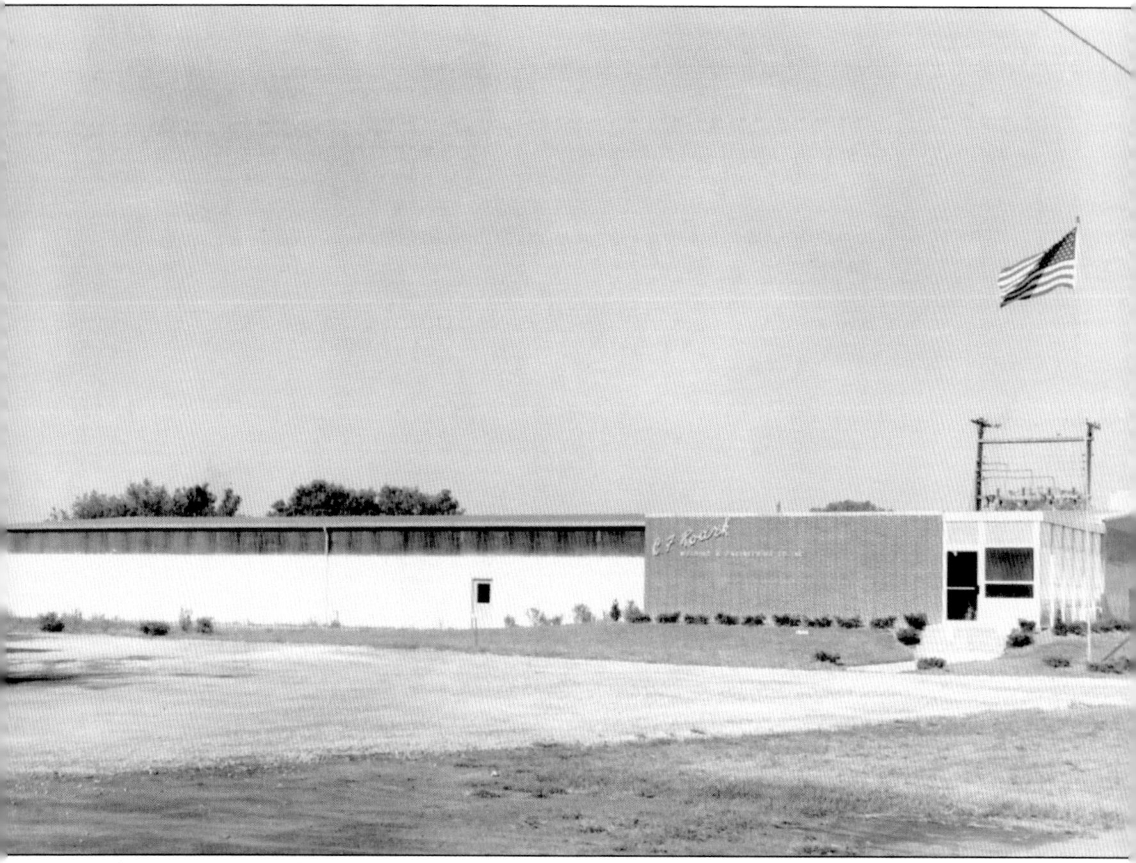

This very recognizable business in the community is C.F. Roark Welding & Engineering Company. Located at 136 North Green Street, the photograph captures the building shortly after construction in the early 1960s. Roark's spot on the west side of north Green Street is the same location that had been previously occupied by the Brownsburg Canning Company before it was torn down by the fire department as part of an exercise. C.F. Roark Welding & Engineering Company received, among other awards, the Outstanding Contractor Award in 1990 from the Aeronautical Systems Division at Wright Patterson Air Force Base. The business was commended at the time for the quality of work that they did and for doing it right each time. No doubt that tradition has continued as the business still operates in the same location today.

Four

CHURCHES AND CEMETERIES

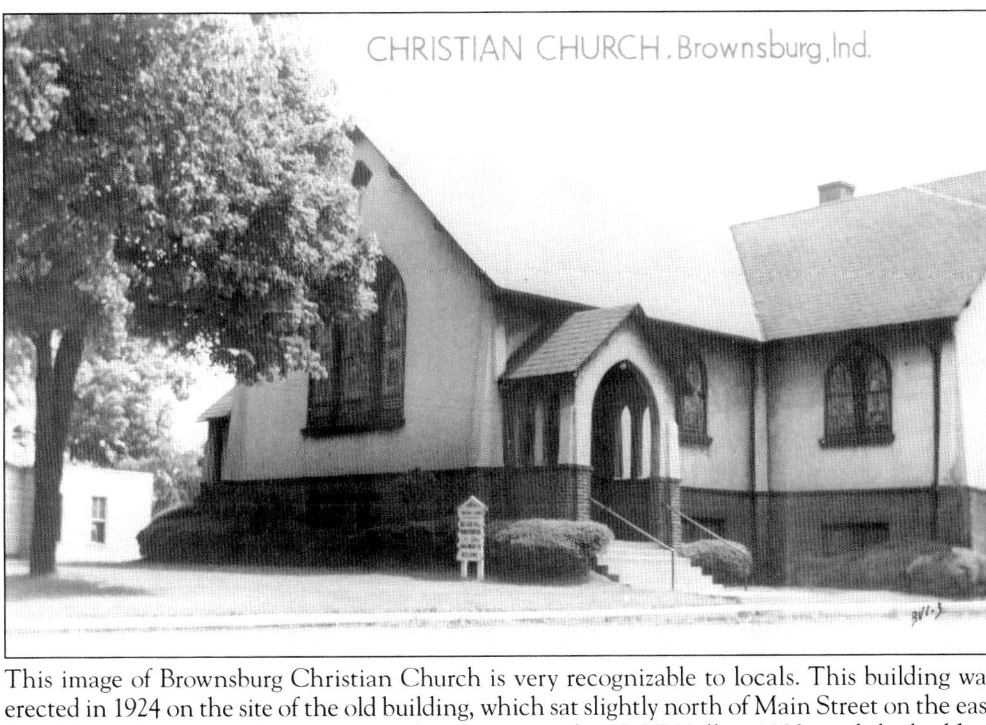

This image of Brownsburg Christian Church is very recognizable to locals. This building was erected in 1924 on the site of the old building, which sat slightly north of Main Street on the east side of Green Street. Members moved the services to the IOOF Hall in 1923 until the building was complete. Today, the location is part of the parking area and grassy lawn of the Brownsburg Municipal Buildings. (Courtesy of Roger A. Zimmerman.)

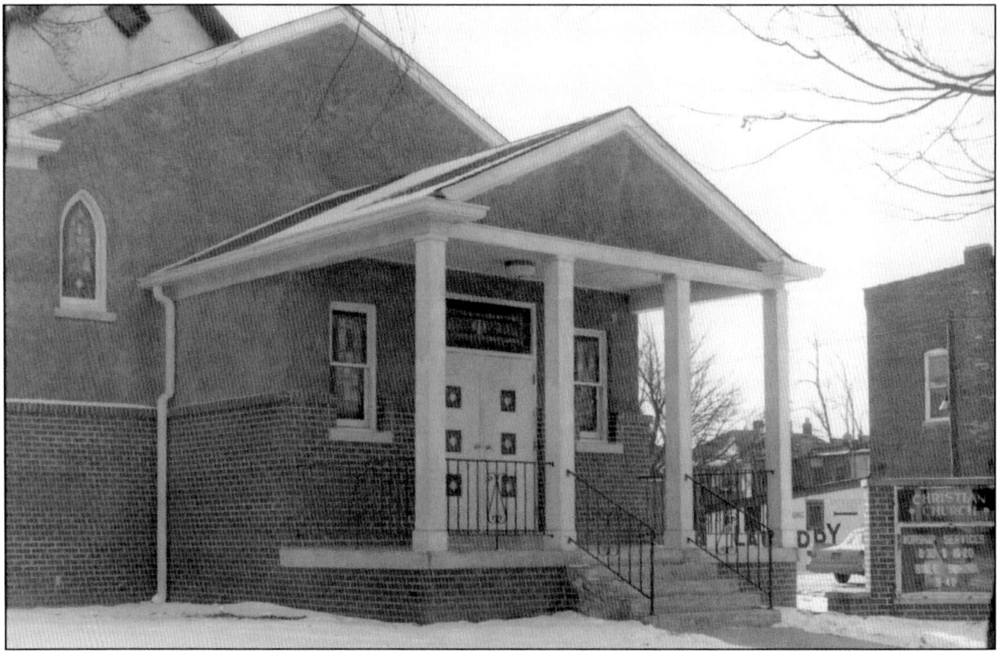

The Brownsburg Christian Church, established in 1837, has had a long and faithful history to the residents of Brownsburg. This is a photograph of the Brownsburg Christian Church after the Green Street entrance was added. The top of the old building is visible slightly above the entrance, at the top left of the photograph. The back corner of the Knights of Pythias building can be seen at right.

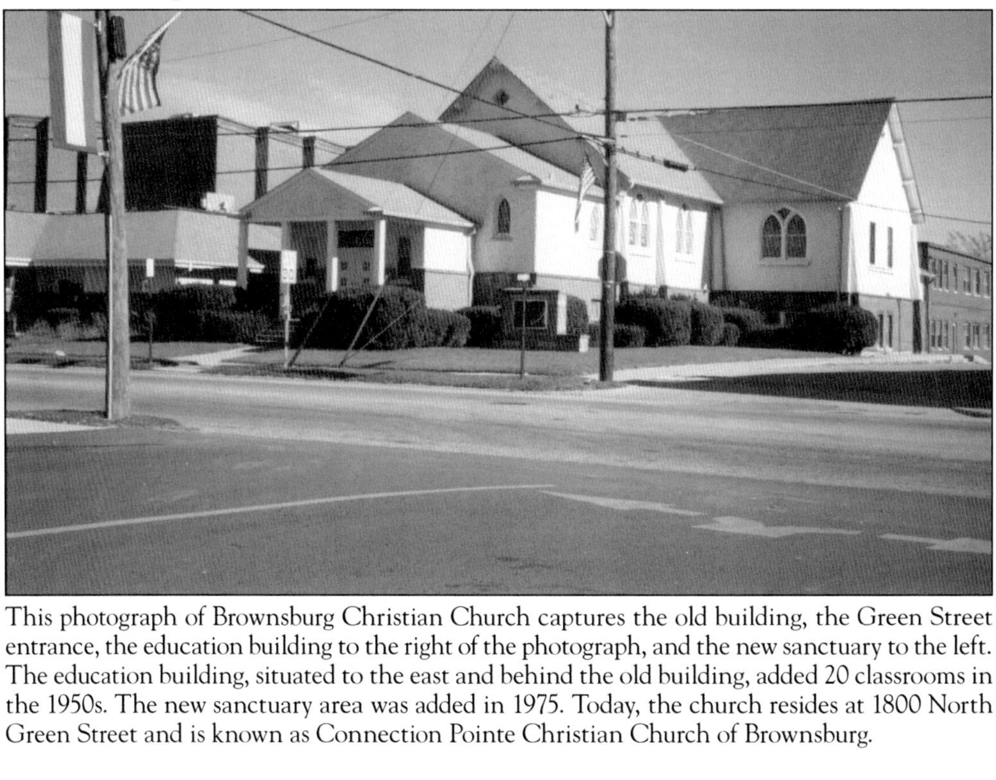

This photograph of Brownsburg Christian Church captures the old building, the Green Street entrance, the education building to the right of the photograph, and the new sanctuary to the left. The education building, situated to the east and behind the old building, added 20 classrooms in the 1950s. The new sanctuary area was added in 1975. Today, the church resides at 1800 North Green Street and is known as Connection Pointe Christian Church of Brownsburg.

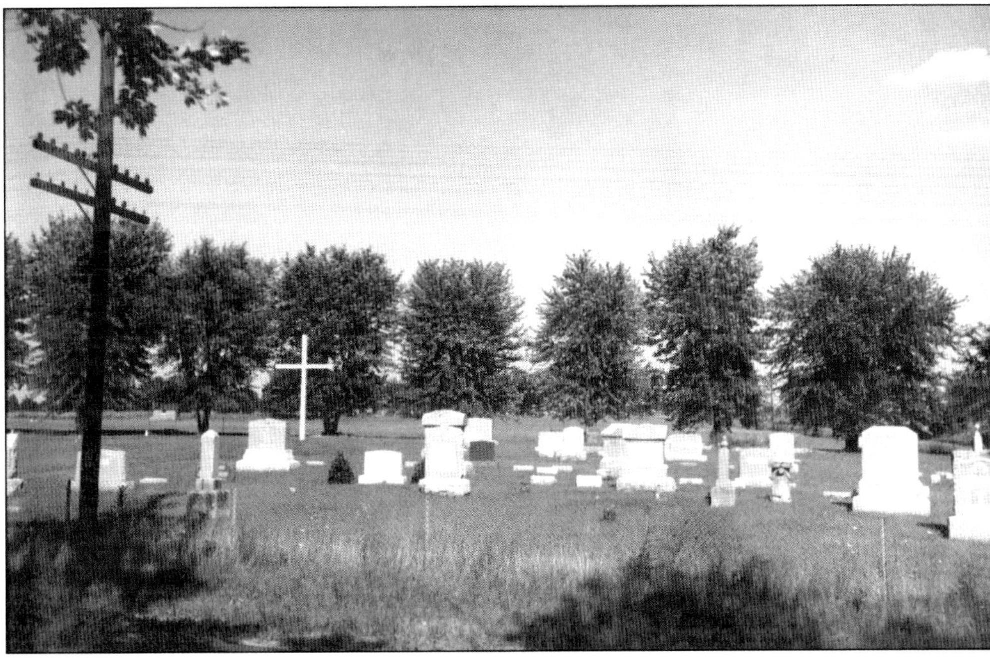

The St. Malachy Cemetery, shown above, is located on the northeast corner of the intersection of SR 267 and 56th Street in Brownsburg. The Brownsburg Cemetery sits seamlessly next to it on the north and east sides. The distinctive white cross in this photograph of the St. Malachy Cemetery can still be seen today from either road.

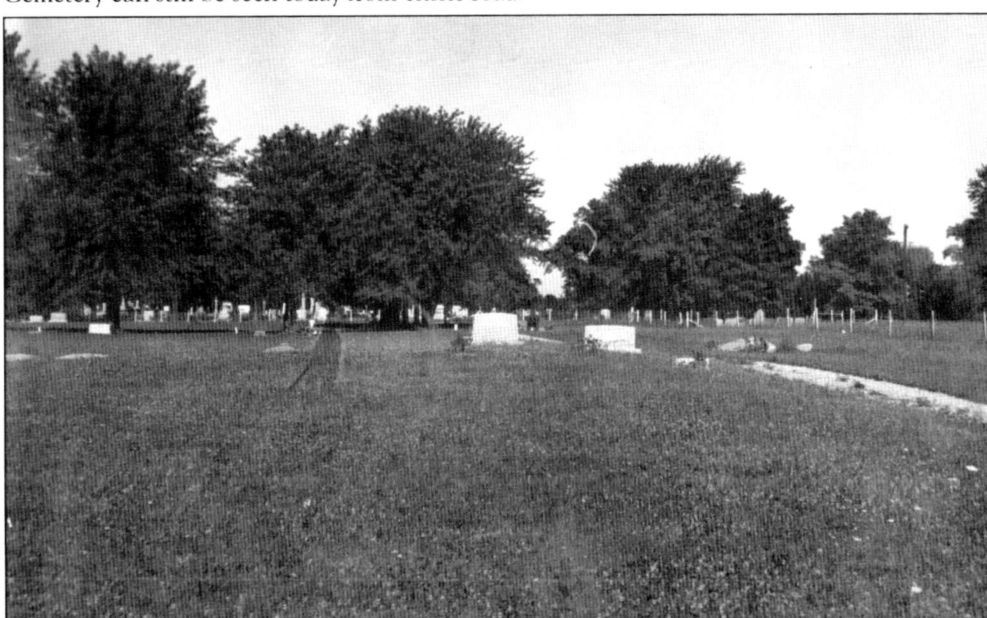

The Brownsburg Cemetery is also situated on the northeast corner of the intersection of SR 267 and 56th Street, farther east of the St. Malachy Cemetery. The cemetery was opened in 1946. In 1984, the remains of Jonathan and Hannah Ward were moved from a pioneer cemetery to Brownsburg Cemetery. The stone, not grave, for Revolutionary War soldier Thomas Harding was also moved to Brownsburg Cemetery in 1992 from Lingeman Cemetery.

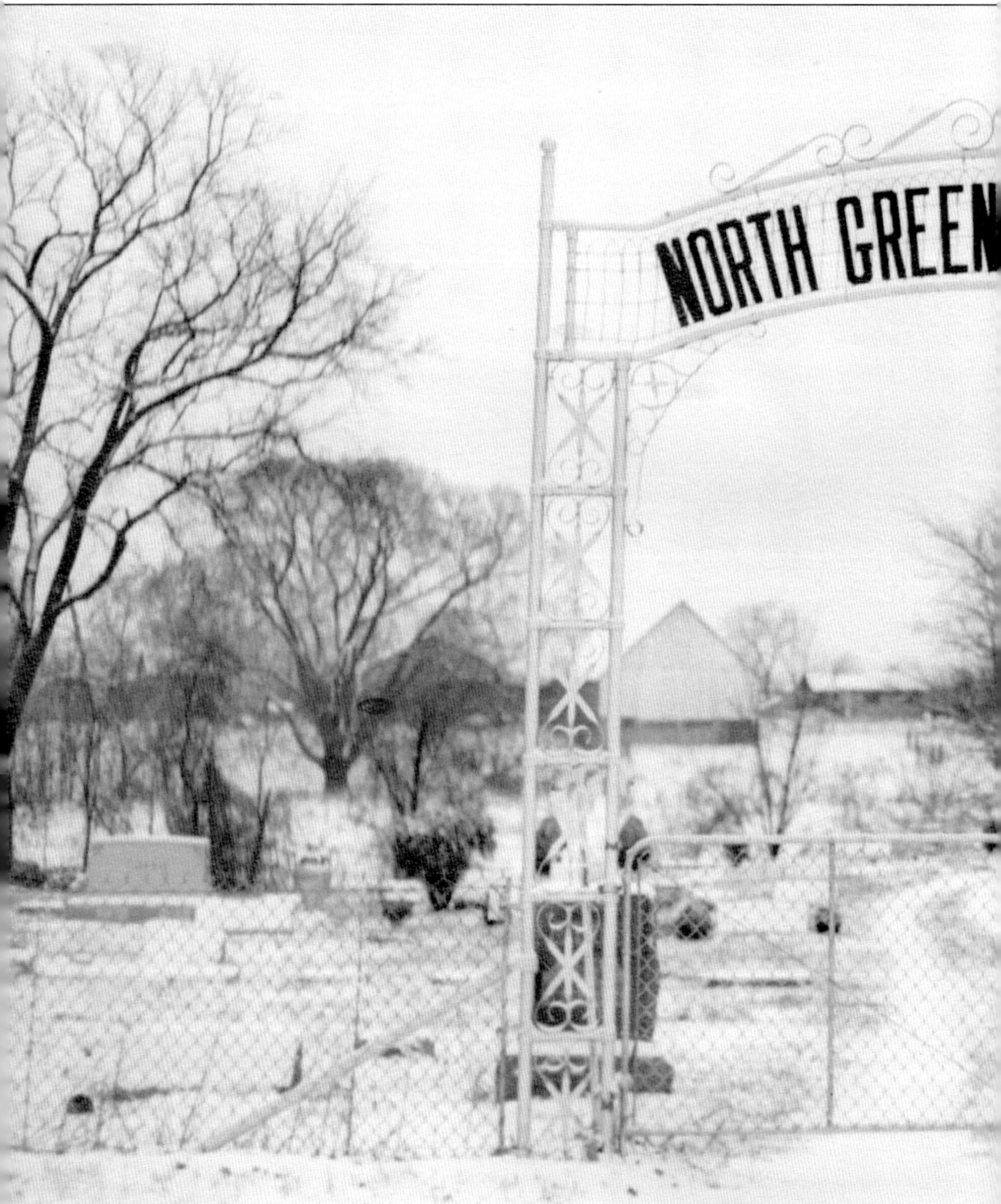

This is a beautiful snowy view of the Greenlawn Cemetery entrance. The name Greenlawn was given to the cemetery in homage to landowner Morton Green. This cemetery is on the west side of SR 267 north of 56th Street. The Greenlawn Cemetery association was incorporated in spring 1897. In April 1911, a petition circulated requesting that the town board extend sidewalks from town to the cemetery, as many times the conditions of the street were impassable. The *Brownsburg*

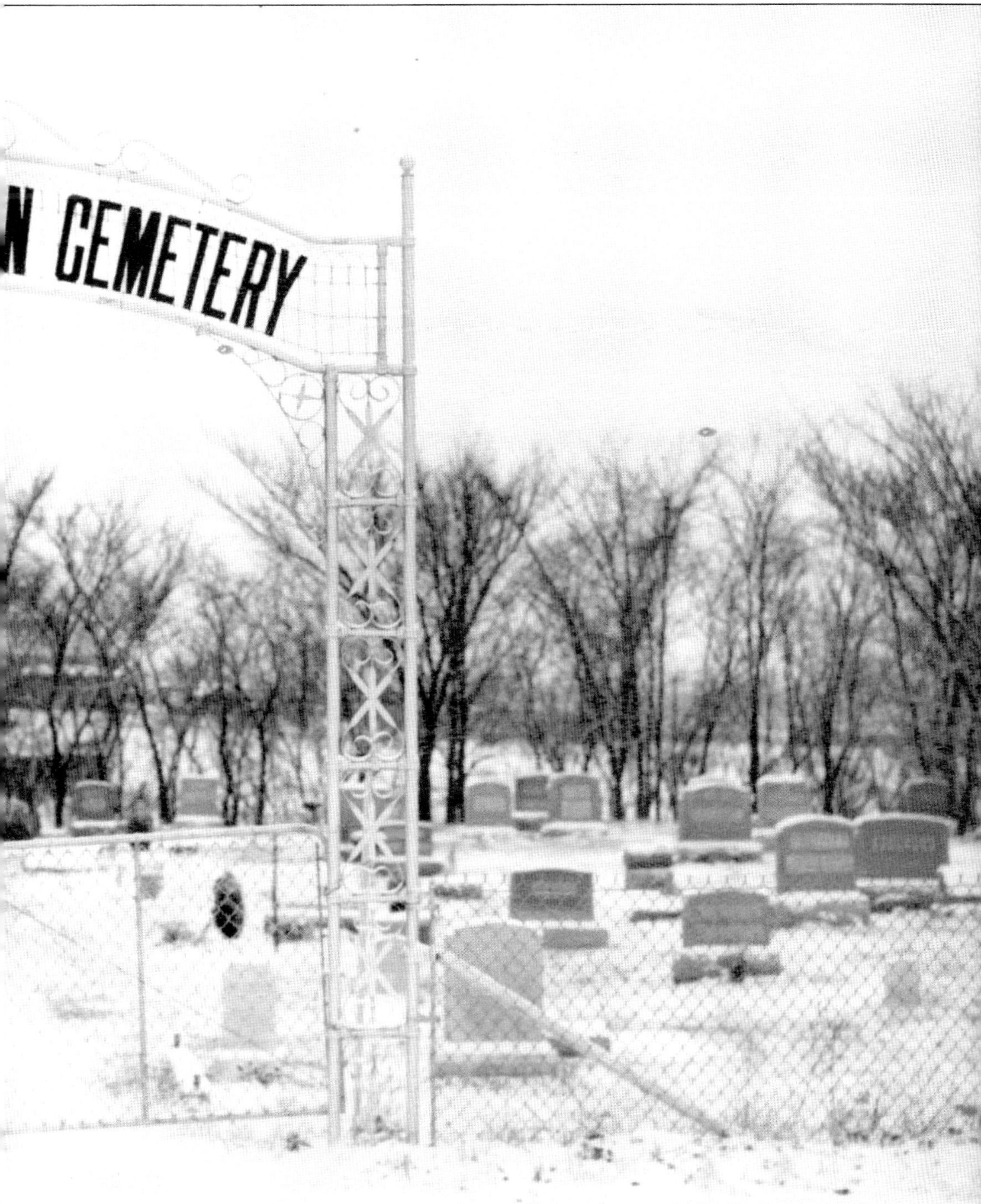

Record at the time called the public's attention to the "obnoxious habit" that had developed among young people using the cemetery as a loafing rendezvous on Sunday afternoons. Many of the important figures to Brownsburg's history are buried in this cemetery. The older graves are mostly in the southern section.

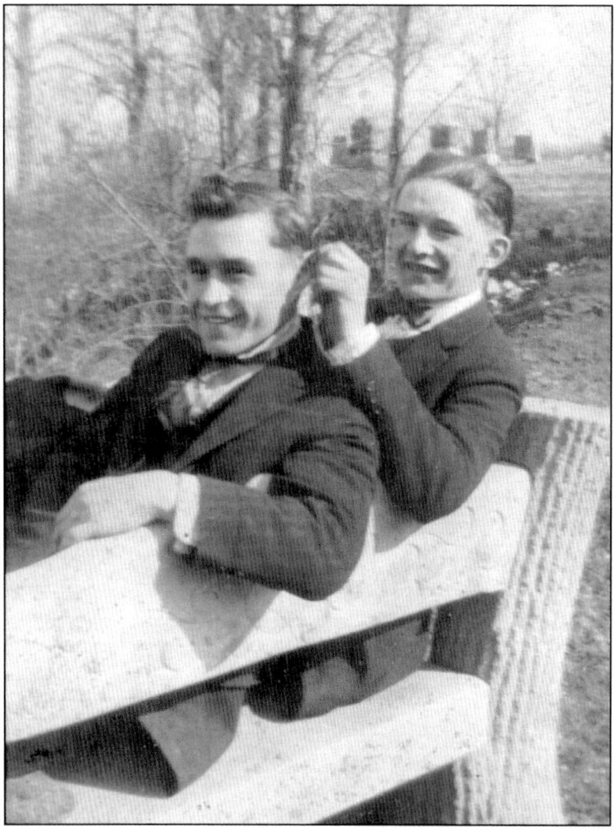

Perhaps these two young men are an example of what the *Brownsburg Record* mentioned regarding loafing. The unidentified young men are sitting on a stone bench at the grave of Lemuel and Mary Menefee. Although the bench has since collapsed, its remnants and the surrounding graves are still present.

This is another view of the Greenlawn Cemetery along SR 267 facing south. The fence of the cemetery has been damaged. Graves are well maintained. The majority face east as in the tradition of burying the dead to face the direction of the resurrection or the rising sun. Most of these graves have an identifying tombstone, though graves of Quakers, Native Americans, and the poor were sometimes marked with fieldstones.

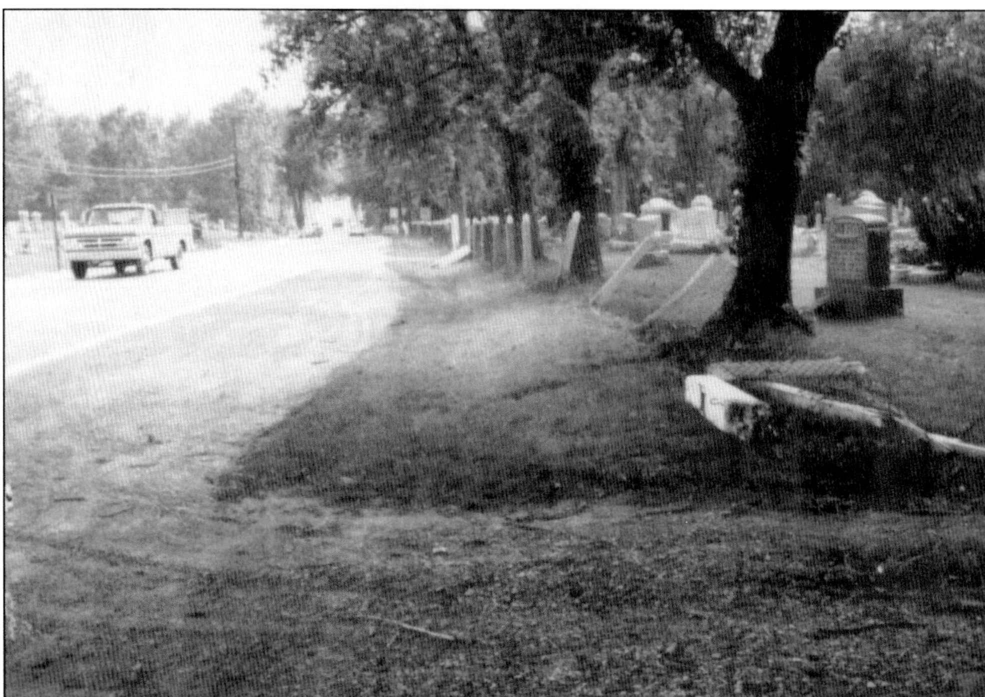

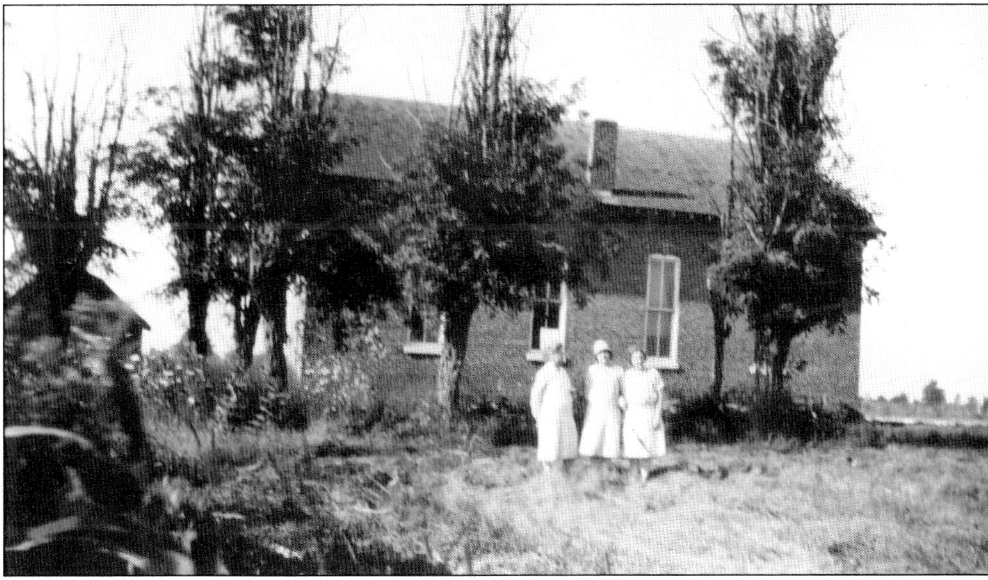

The words "church at Squankum" are scrawled in ink on the back of this 1928 photograph. Pictured are three women standing in front of the structure indicated as the old church also known as Bethesda Missionary Baptist Church. The old building collapsed in 1929 when some eager young men took it upon themselves to dig out the basement for expansion.

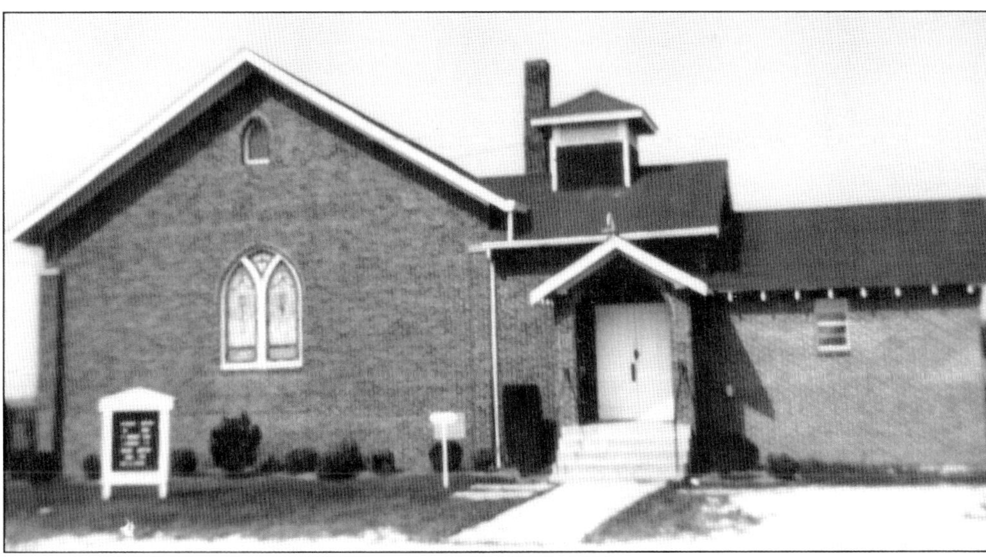

This photograph of Bethesda Missionary Baptist Church was taken in the 1950s. The building prior to this one had been built in 1883 and collapsed in 1929. Services after the collapse were held in the old frame schoolhouse nearby. The church, also known as "Squankum," rebuilt a few months later.

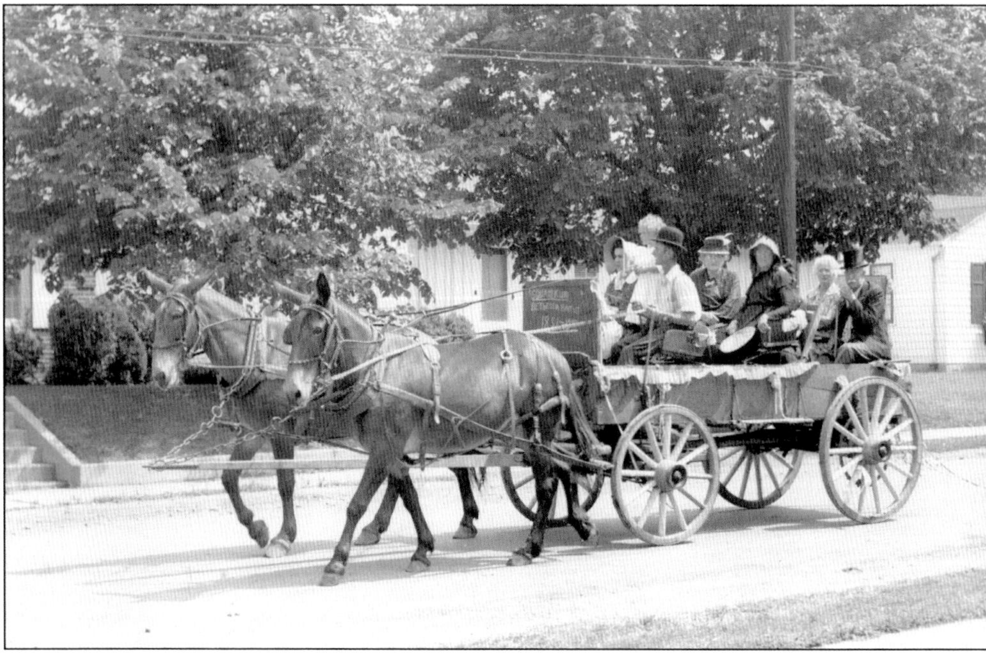

The sign on the front of this wagon appears to say "Squamkum, Bethesda Baptist, 1851–1948." The spelling of the word "Squamkum" is an interesting variation of the spelling "Squankum." This photograph was taken in 1948. The long legacy of the Bethesda Baptist Church, which continues today, had not yet been written.

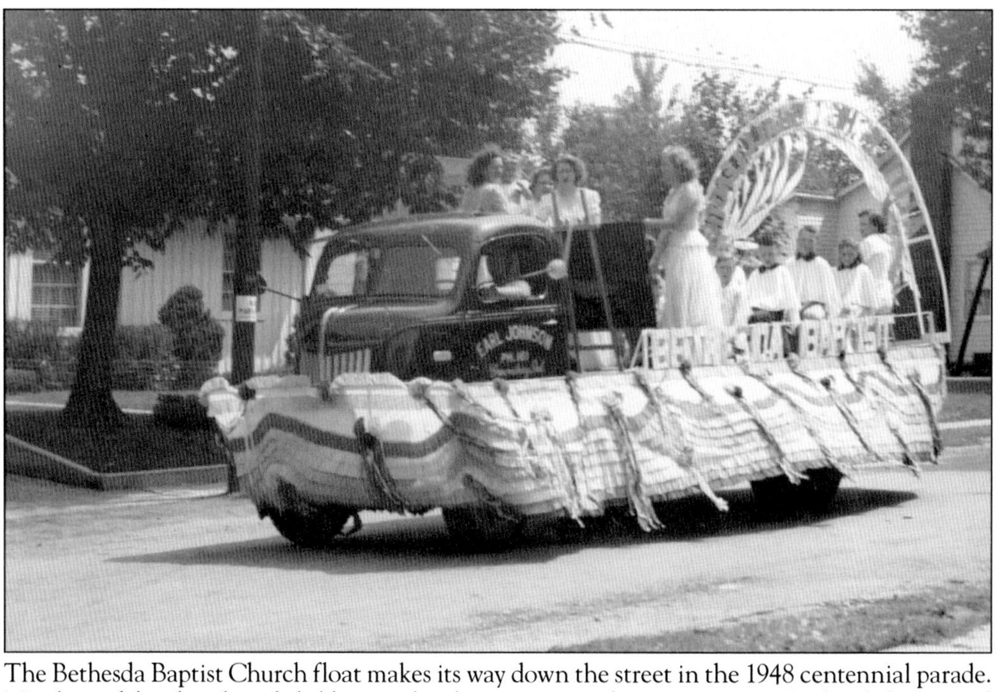

The Bethesda Baptist Church float makes its way down the street in the 1948 centennial parade. Members of the church and children in the choir represent the congregation. Bethesda has served the community not only through the church but through the education of students at Bethesda Christian Schools at 7950 North County Road 650 East.

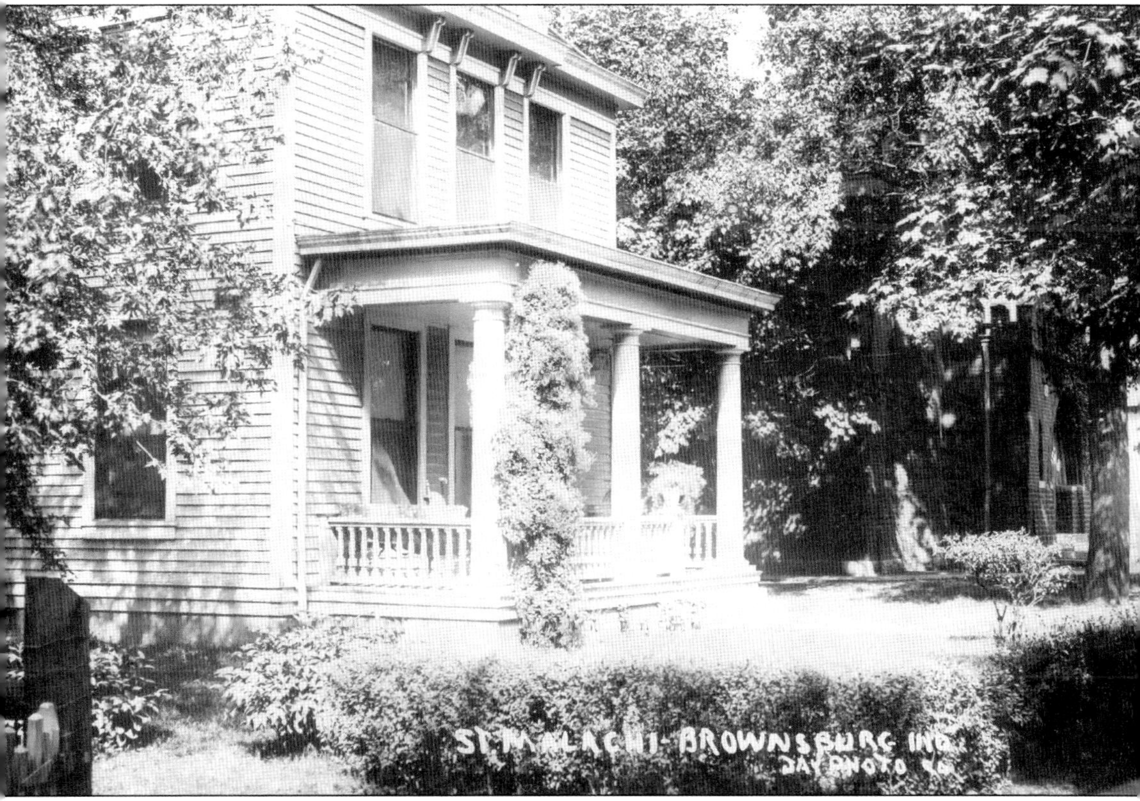

This sunny photograph was taken of the St. Malachy Catholic Church parish house. The Gothic-style church can be seen through the trees on the right of the photograph. The house sits to the south of the church and at the corner of Lucas Drive and north Green Street at the entrance to Arbuckle Acres Park. Also sometimes referred to as the rectory, some documents indicate the house was built in 1900 and some indicate that it was built sometime during the period of the dedication of the Gothic-style church around 1904. In 1954, the house was still the residence of Fr. Edward Bauer and later became a residence for the Sisters of Providence when they came to staff the new St. Malachy School. The house is still located at 224 North Green Street and has been remarkably restored.

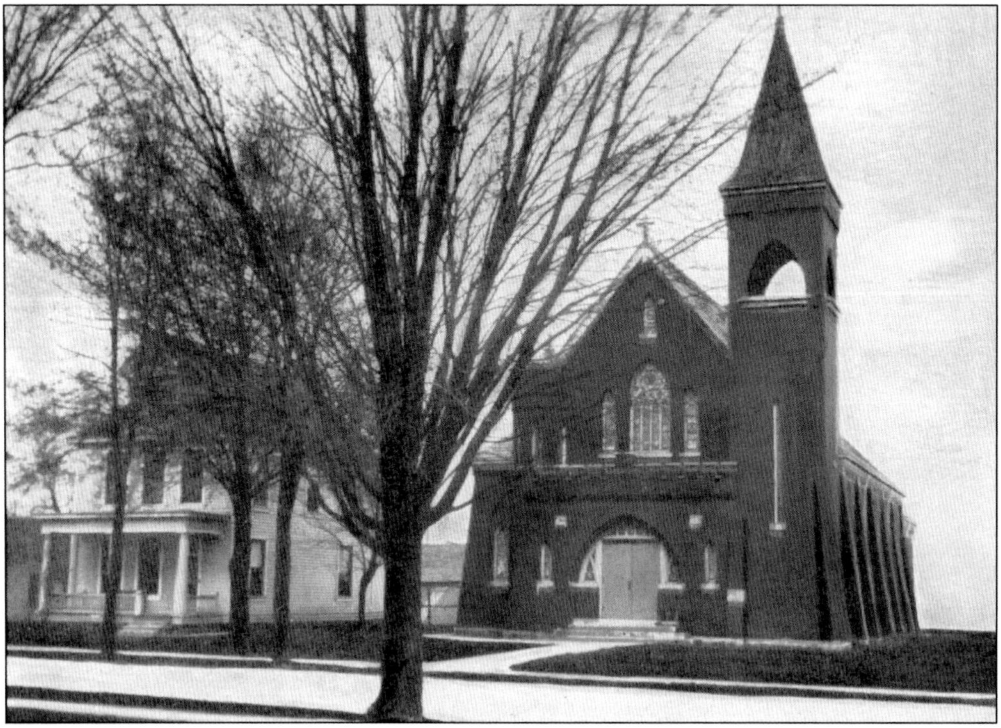

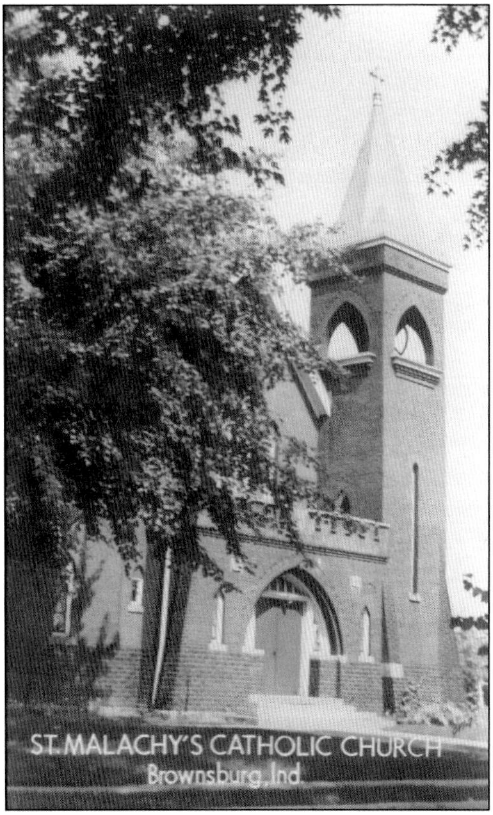

These two photographs capture the stunning Gothic-style beauty of the St. Malachy Catholic Church. The above photograph shows the parish house and church on the west side of north Green Street with still barren surroundings around them. The history of the St. Malachy parish begins with a group of Irish settlers who continued to grow in numbers and faith. In 1867, a formal attempt was made to create a congregation and start a building fund. In 1869, a modest chapel housed the parishioners. The cornerstone for the church shown below was laid in 1903. The Celtic Gothic architecture sealed the church's place as one of the most impressive churches in Hendricks County. The church was eventually sold and repainted. It has been home to numerous businesses throughout the years and is still at this location at 228 North Green Street.

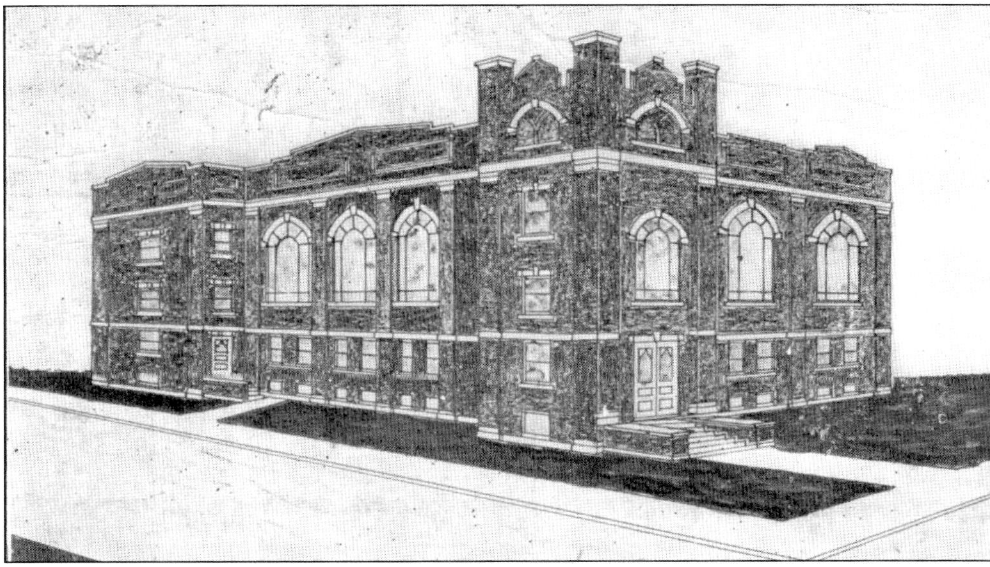

The Methodist church in Brownsburg was organized in 1828 under Pastor Joseph Tarkington. The congregation originally met in the red schoolhouse near where the water tower south of Main Street and east of Green Street used to sit. Over the years, the congregation grew and moved to additional locations. A 1920 postcard view above shows the sketch of the proposed Methodist church in Brownsburg. In 1923, the stately brick building on the corner of east Main Street and north Jefferson Street (then Christian Street) was built. The similarity between the two buildings was well maintained, with some noticeable differences in the windows and entryways. On September 30, 1928, the membership voted to adopt the name Calvary United Methodist Episcopal Church. Today, the building at 204 East Main Street still stands.

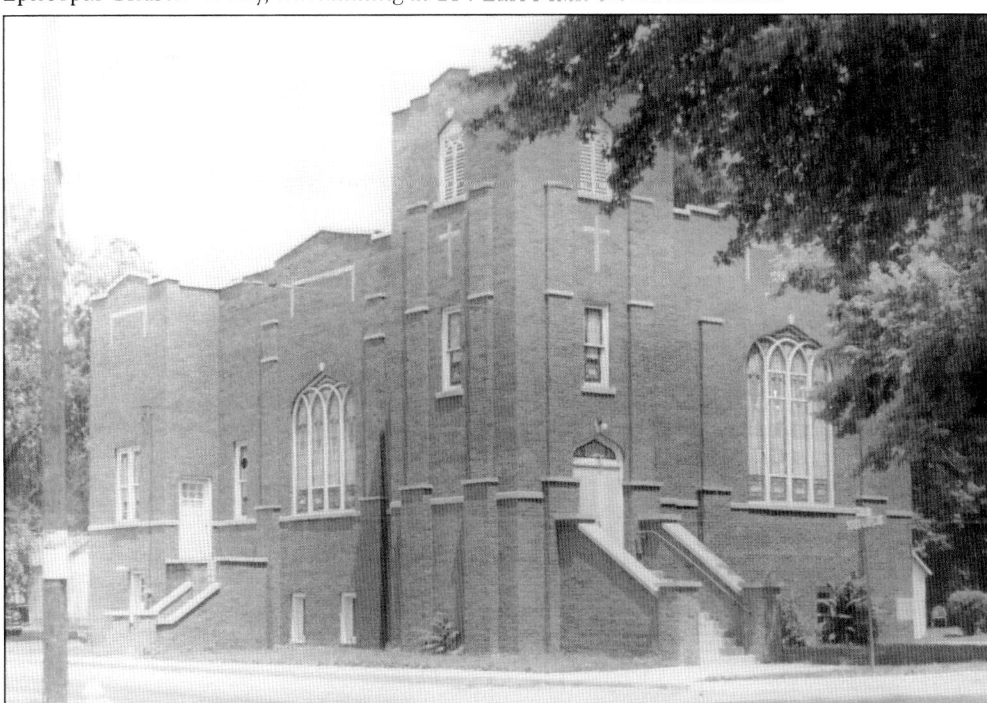

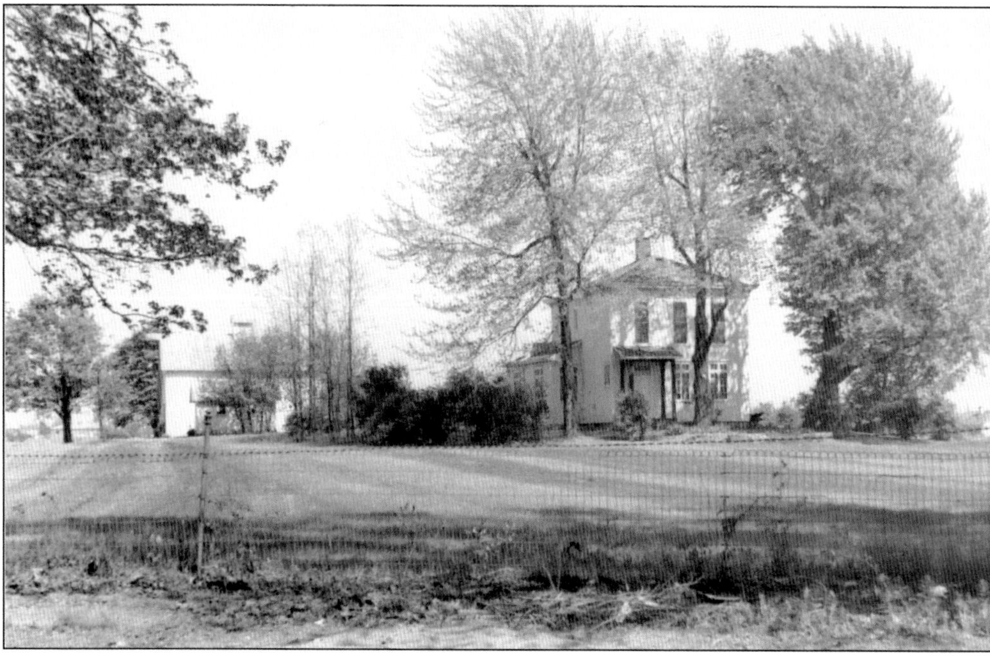

The striking farmhouse seen in this photograph was that of Joseph F. Sheetz; it was located on south Green Street at the northeast corner of Green and Tilden Streets. The property was purchased by Calvary Methodist Church from Sheetz's wife, Bertha, who died in 1992. Sheetz and his wife are buried in Brownsburg Cemetery.

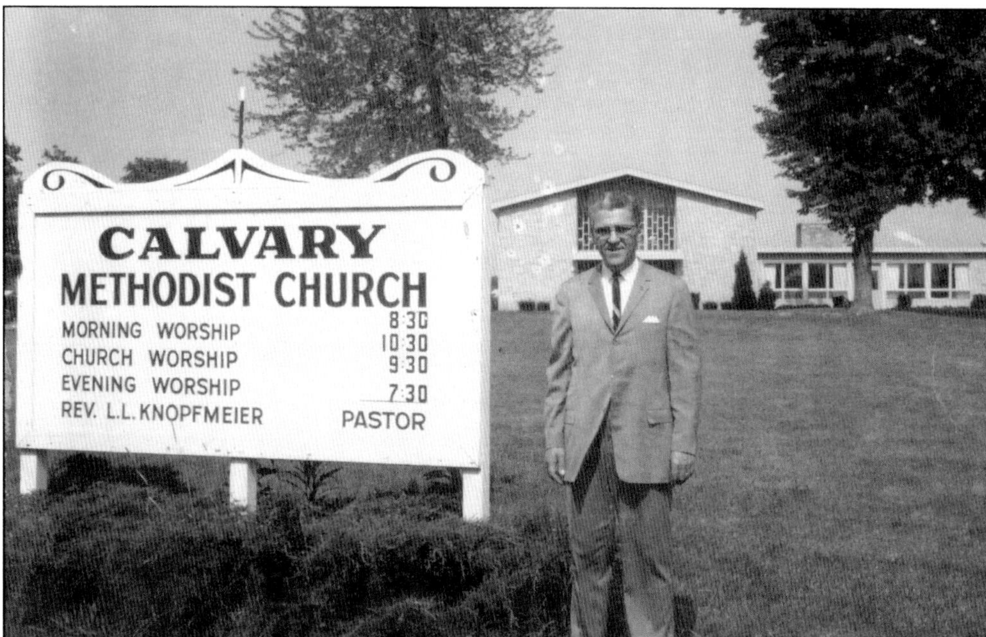

Identified on the photograph, Rev. Lester Knopfmeier stands in front of the Methodist church built on the former location of the Sheetz farm. Today, the church building is gone, and this location is occupied by a business. Calvary Methodist Church is currently located in a new home at 575 West Northfield Drive.

Five

Schools and Sports

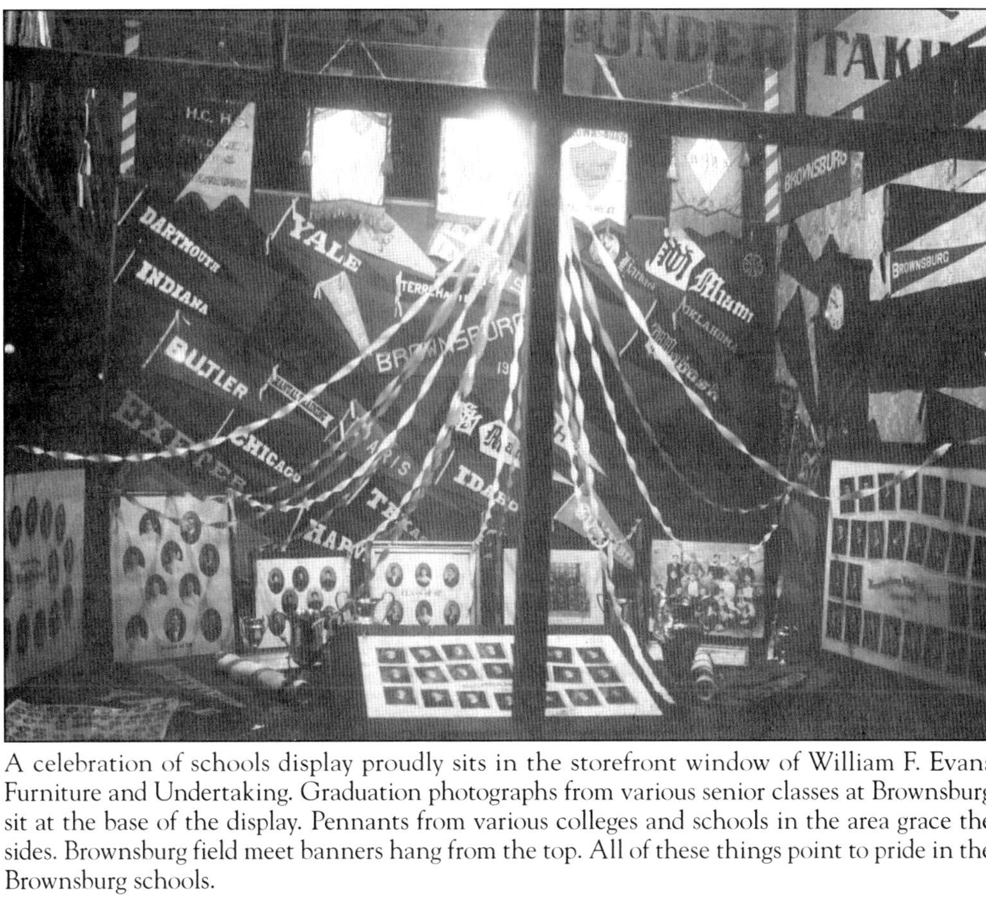

A celebration of schools display proudly sits in the storefront window of William F. Evans Furniture and Undertaking. Graduation photographs from various senior classes at Brownsburg sit at the base of the display. Pennants from various colleges and schools in the area grace the sides. Brownsburg field meet banners hang from the top. All of these things point to pride in the Brownsburg schools.

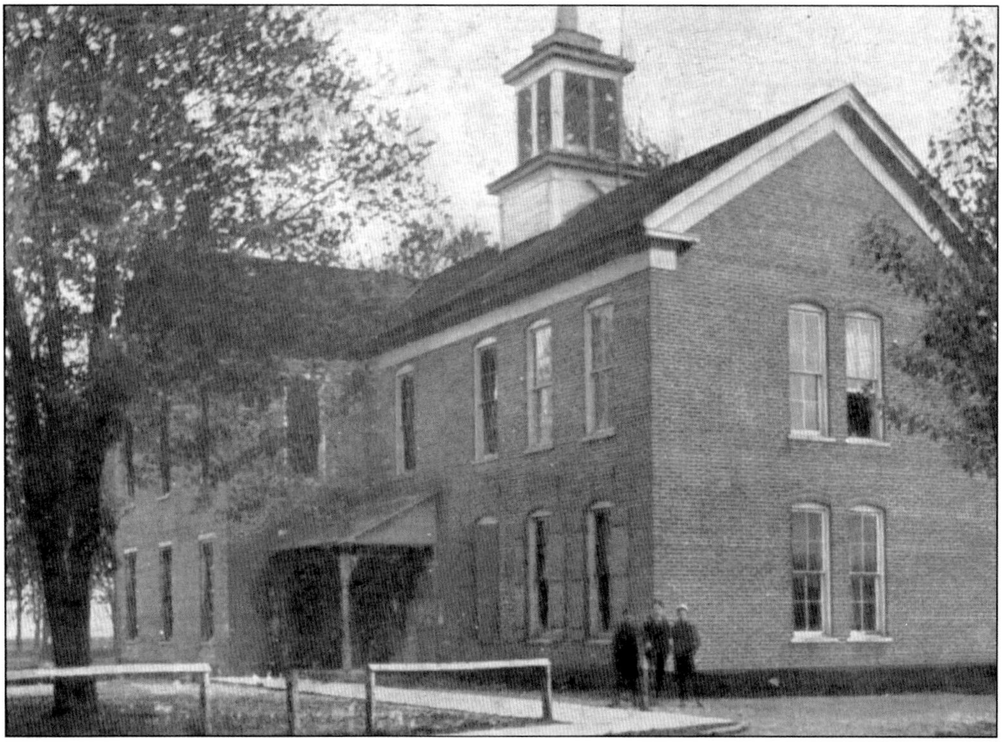

A 1903 postcard labeled "'old' school house" showcases the Brownsburg school located on the southeast corner of College Avenue and School Street. In 1890, prior to the addition and repairs being done on the building, the *Brownsburg Record* implored the school board to install lights of some kind to help avoid accidents, collisions, and trysts at the location. The school was built to accommodate multiple grades of schoolchildren.

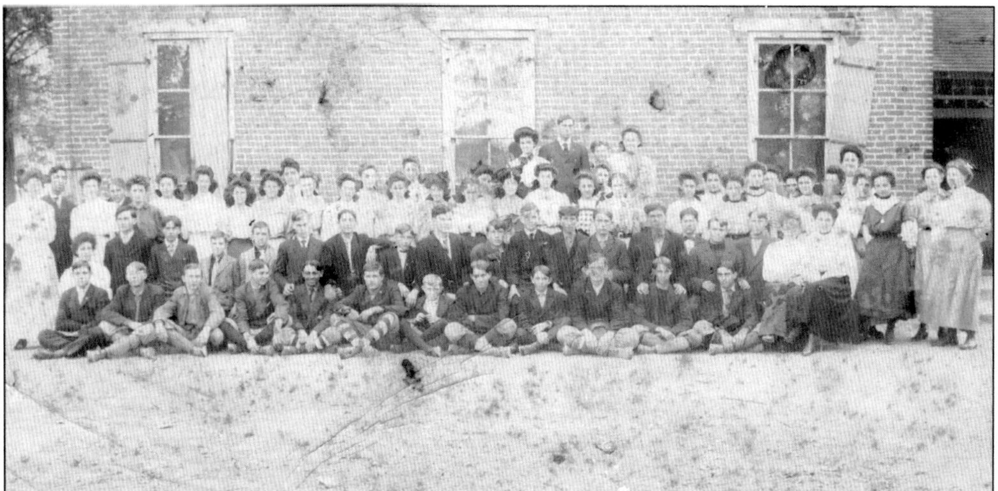

These children pose for a class photograph in front of the grade school building in town. The covered doorway can be seen to the right of the photograph, and a young educator, George Reitzel, is standing to the far left. The schoolhouse had become a valuable and important part of the first steps of education in the community. The building was torn down and replaced with a new grade school in 1908.

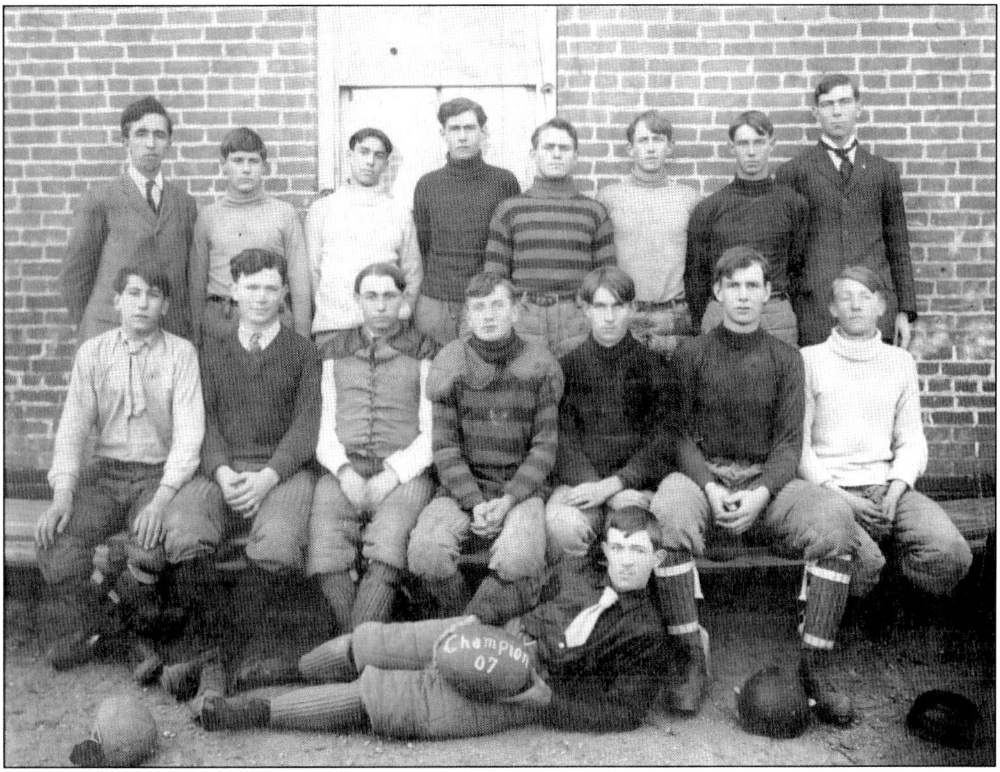

The 1907 Brownsburg football champions are pictured from left to right: (first row) Urban Salmon; (second row) John Symmonds, Chester Edwards, Chester Neal, Russell Nevitt, ? Gilbert, Irvin Herdrich, and Herman Garner; (third row) Coach George Reitzel, Ray Ottinger, Sam Patterson, Earl Reed, Roger Lingeman, Leslie Lingeman, Roy Smith, and Oscar McDaniel.

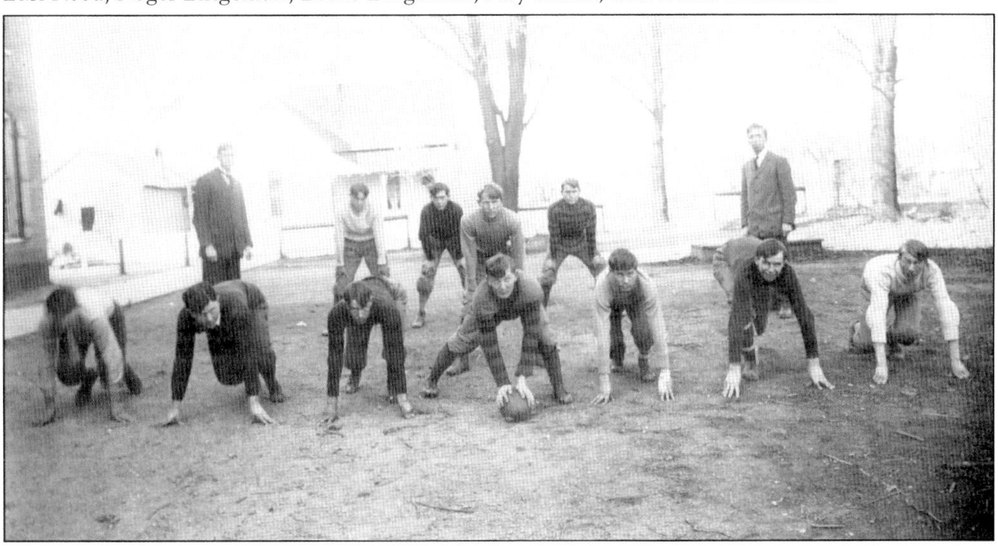

The 1907 Brownsburg football champions are pictured practicing. This photograph of the young men was taken in the school yard in front of the Brownsburg school on the corner of College Avenue and School Street. The view is facing west toward School Street. Although it has been remodeled since this photograph was taken, the white house in the background still exists today.

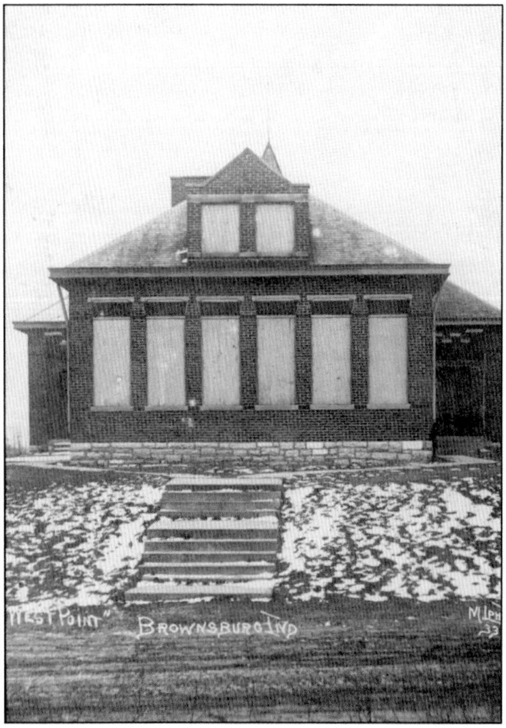

The West Point School sits boarded up on a hill slightly west of Brownsburg on the south side of Crawfordsville Road (US 136) in this postcard dated 1915. Designed initially as a township high school, children would walk the distance to the location. The school was eventually abandoned, and in November 1921 fire destroyed the building. Today, this location is 285 West Main Street.

Posing outside of the West Point School, Brownsburg basketball team members are, from left to right, (first row) Adna Harris, Robert Dozier, and Urban Salmon; (second row) Leslie Lingeman, Ray Ottinger, Roger Lingeman, and Russell Nevitt; (third row) coach George Reitzel, Herman Garner, Earl Reed, Sam Patterson, and Oscar McDaniel. Reitzel, a well-respected teacher and coach, was also elected superintendent of schools in 1920.

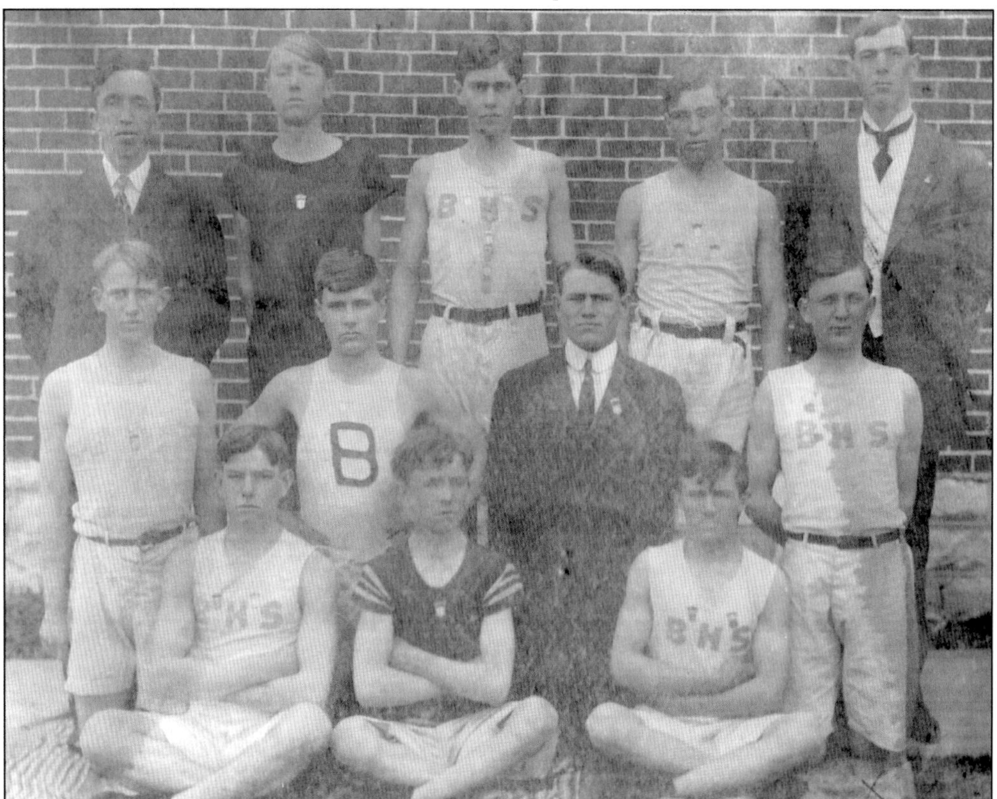

Part of managing the growing educational needs of the townships included organizing district schools in several locations so that children would not have to walk more than two miles to school. One-room schoolhouses solved this problem and were cheaply and numerously built. These photographs of the Watson School were taken in 1928. The school stood on the east side of SR 267 south of Maloney Road near the area of Bethesda Cemetery. In the above photograph, are, from left to right, unidentified, Nora Johnson, and Everett Turner. In the photograph below, Everett Turner stands in the doorway of the school. Although it is in bad shape, the flagpole on the roofline at the front of the building can be seen still standing proudly.

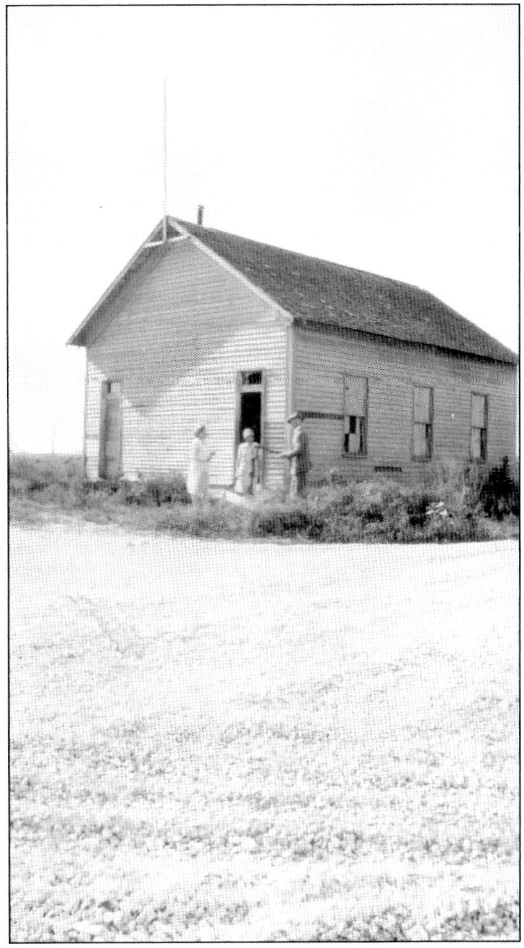

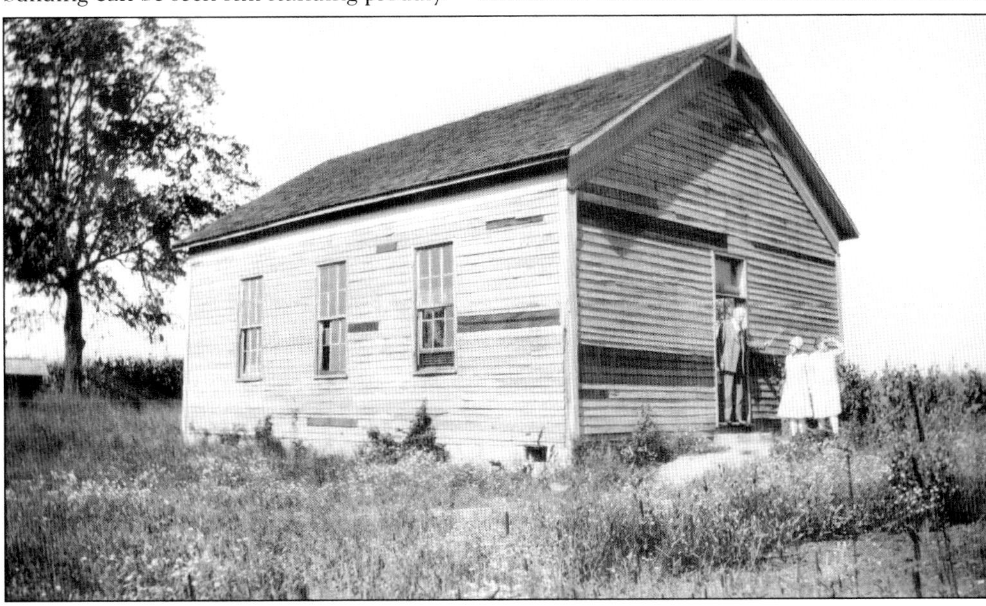

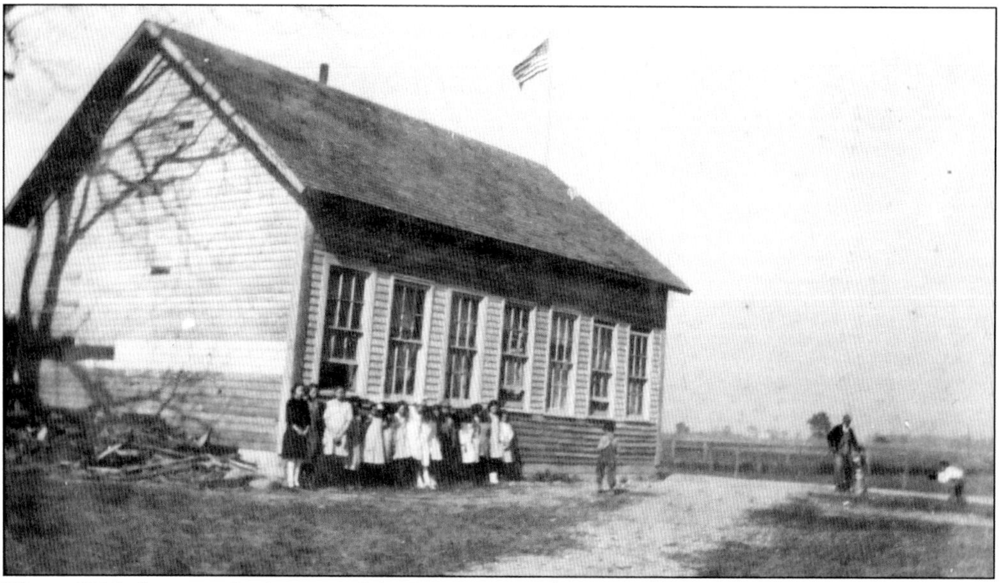

The c. 1920 photograph above is of the Brown Township School. All eight grades were taught in the same building. Below, schoolchildren pose for the camera in the doorway of the school. The students are, from left to right, (first row) Imelda Fahay, Catherine Garner, Eloise Hopkins, Michael Lee, Ann Pollock, Bill Feeney, Mary Elizabeth Lee, Thomas Duffy, Marie Quinn, Eddie Eaton, and Edna Mae Eaton; (second row) Thomas Fahay, Hoyt Hamilton, James Mayo, Earl "Jack" Eaton, Joseph Fahay, Martha Hession, Mary Catherine Duffy, Mary Hession, Delia Fahay, and Frances Hopkins; (third row) Bill Hopkins, Bernard Maloney, Marion Mayo, Joseph Feeney, Martin Feeney, Edward Fahay, Howard Hopkins, and Margaret Fahay; (fourth row) Martin Fahay, Earl Smith, Martin Hogan, Mildred Hamilton, ? Pollock, Thelma Eaton, Marie Earl, Elizabeth Hession, and teacher Genevieve Maloney; (fifth row) Ernest Hamilton, Sheila King, and Ellen Maloney.

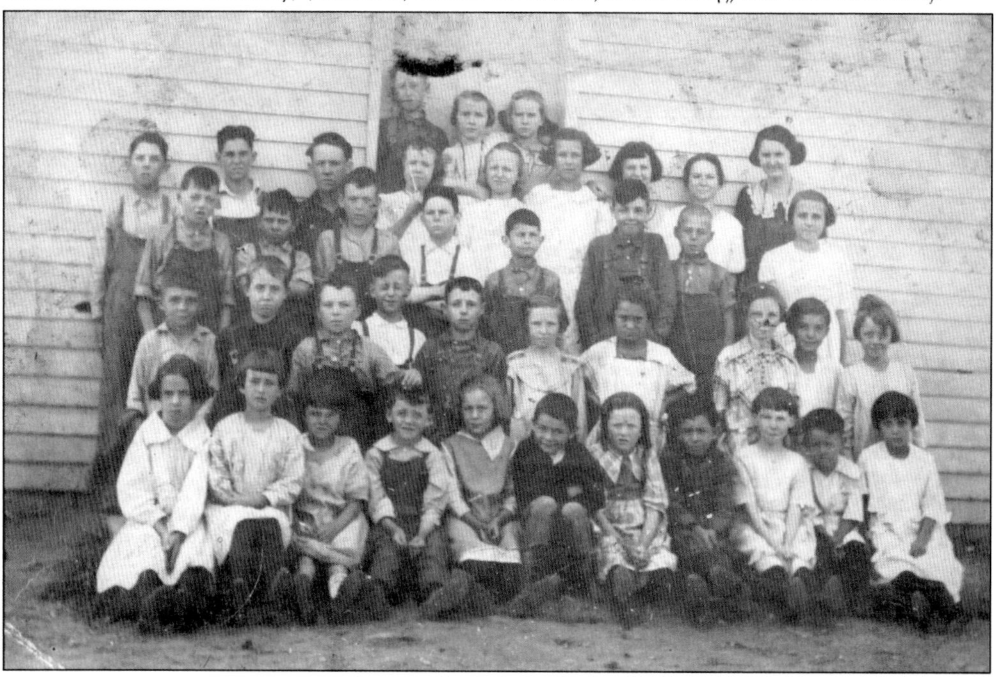

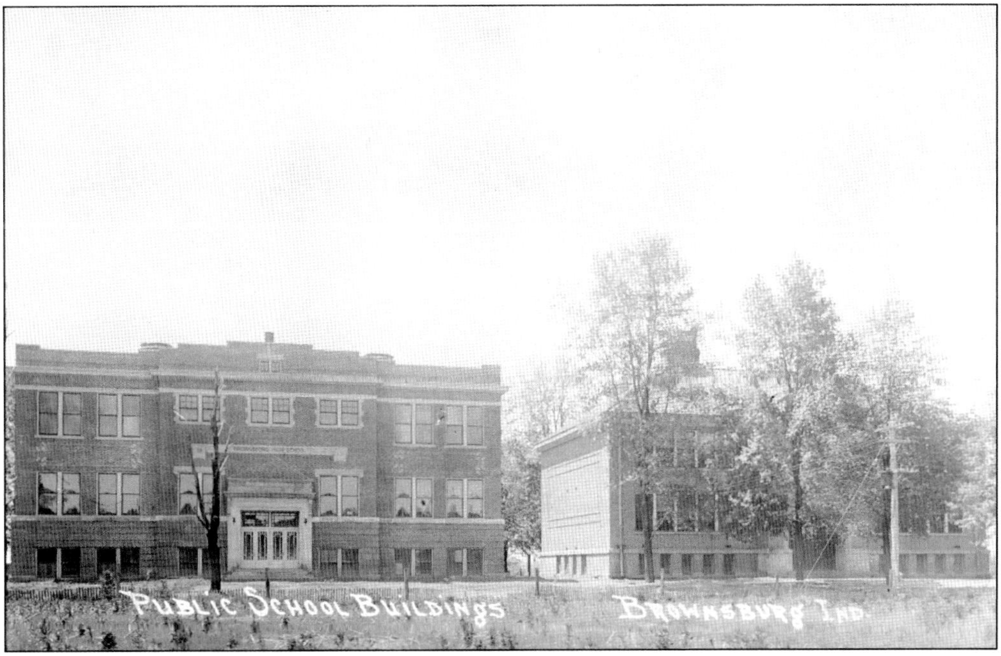

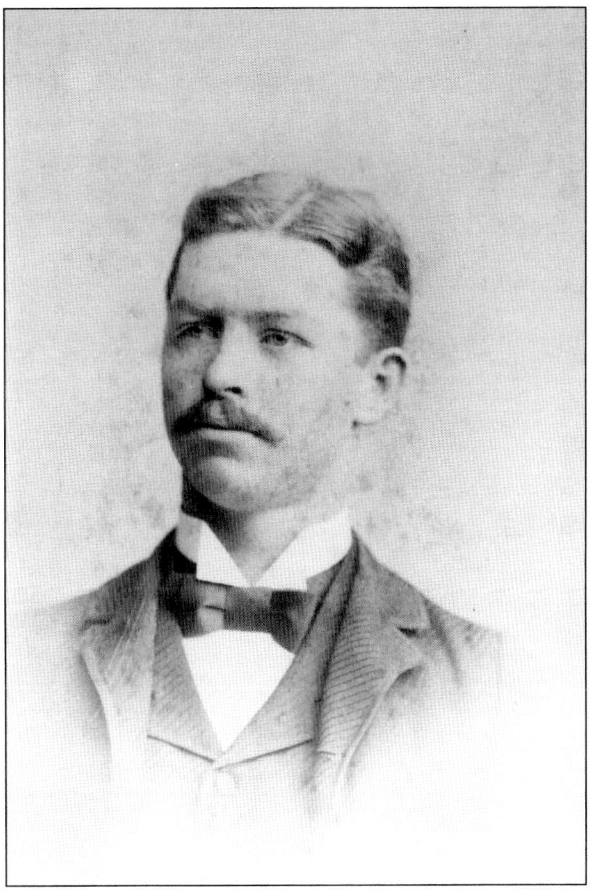

These majestic buildings stood side by side on the southeast corner of College Avenue and School Street. The photograph was taken from College Avenue facing the south. The school on the right is the grade school or Lincoln Township School. Constructed in 1908, it served the community for nearly 60 years before it was torn down. The Brownsburg High School, on the left of the photograph with large ornate white doors, sat east of the grade school. It was constructed in 1915 under the trusteeship of Horatio Brown. The dashing man pictured at right is Horatio Brown, the great-grandson of James B. Brown. It may be said that there are few who contributed more to the community at this time, than Horatio. He helped preside over construction of the Brownsburg Public Library just two years later. (Below, courtesy of Laura Thomas.)

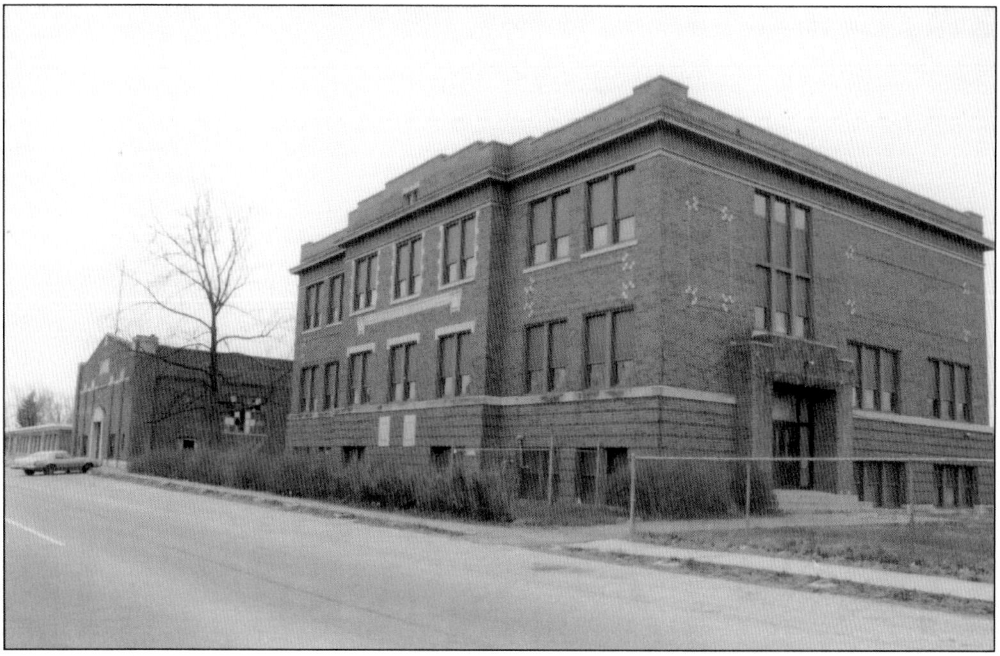

This view of Brownsburg High School on College Avenue is unique in several ways, capturing the location of the community building (or gymnasium) and elementary school to the east of the high school. A careful observer will note that the white ornate front doors have been removed from the old high school.

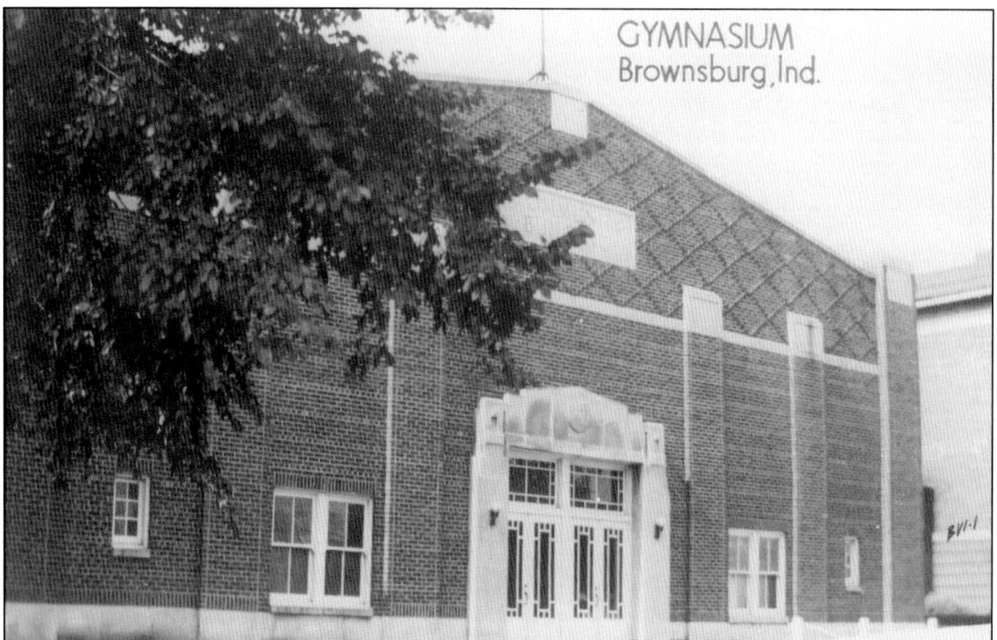

The push for a community building is documented as early as 1923. Built in 1928, it was packed to the rim at its 1929 dedication. The first basketball game played in the facility against Pittsboro served Brownsburg a loss 32 to 22. Interestingly enough, it seems that the ornate white doors that used to grace the high school next door, have now appeared on the front of the community building.

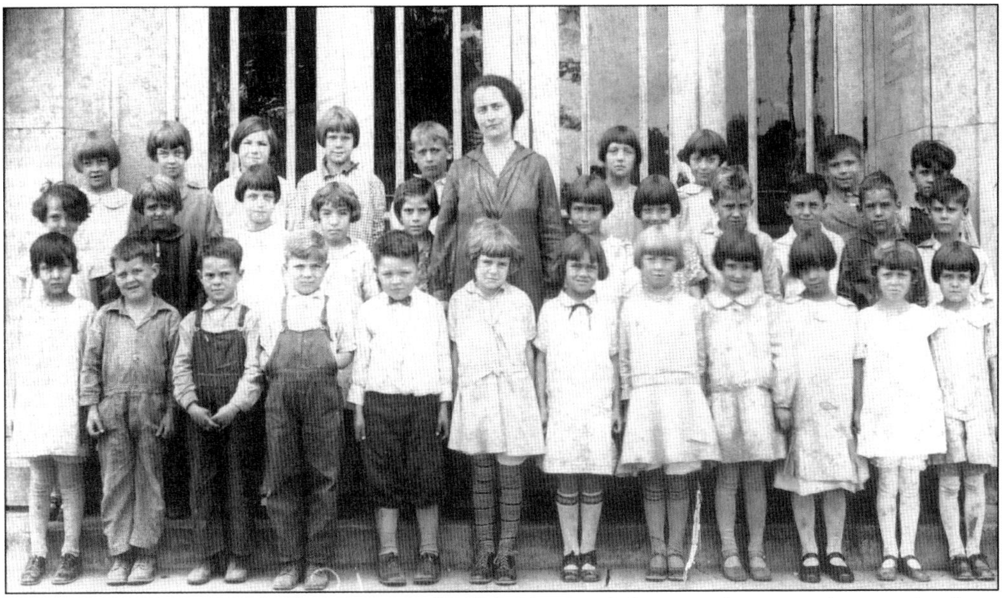

This undated photograph of a group of schoolchildren and their teacher was taken on the front steps of the high school building constructed in 1915. The ornate doors are still in place, and it can be assumed that the photograph was taken between 1915 and 1928. On each side of the entrance, the stones bearing the names of the trustee, advisory board, architect, and contractor can be seen.

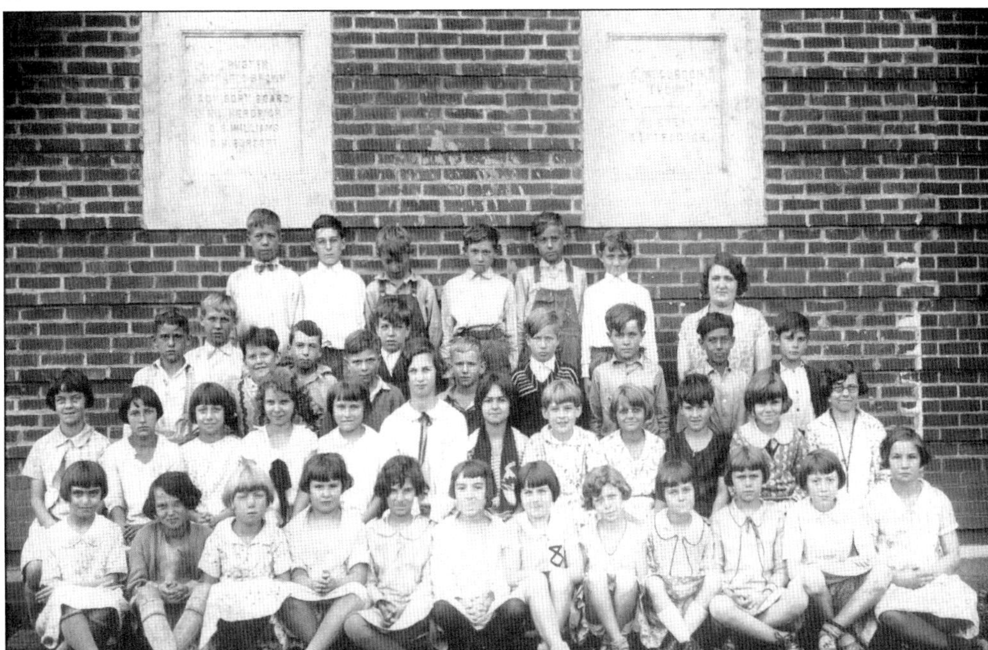

In this photograph, schoolchildren and their teacher pose for the camera at the bricked-up front of the Brownsburg High School. The stones bearing the name of trustee Horatio Brown, the advisory board members, the architect, and the contractor have been moved to the front of the building where the doors used to be. The outline of the old doors can be seen in the brick.

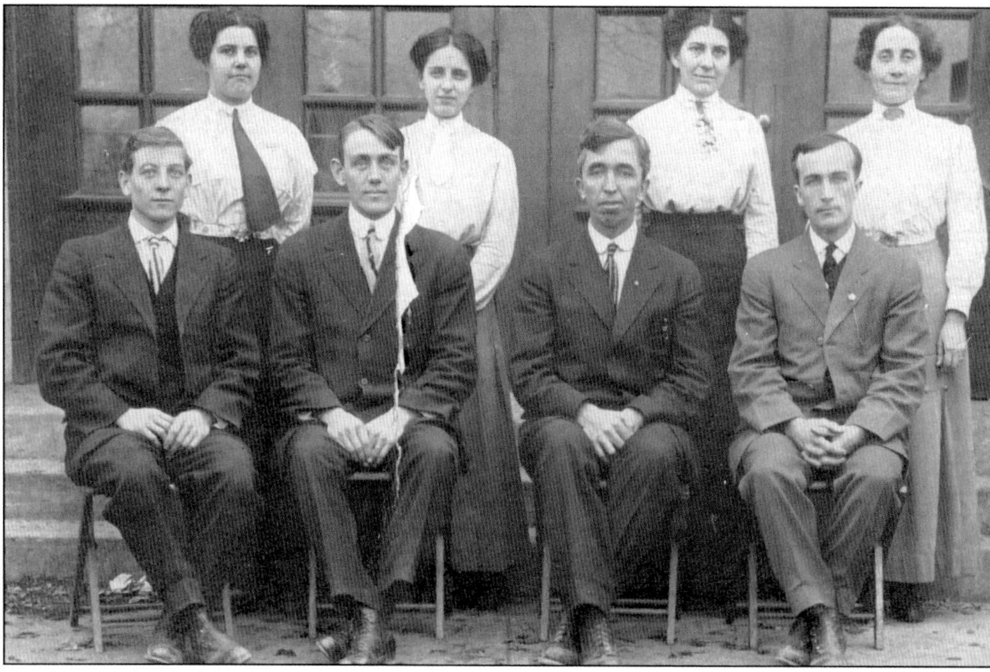

Faculty members of the Brownsburg Public Schools are photographed around 1912 in front of the Lincoln Township Public School. The staff members are, from left to right, (first row) unidentified, R. Lingeman, George Reitzel, and Ernie Gray; (second row) Nell Carter, unidentified, Kate Walsh, and Ottie Roberts.

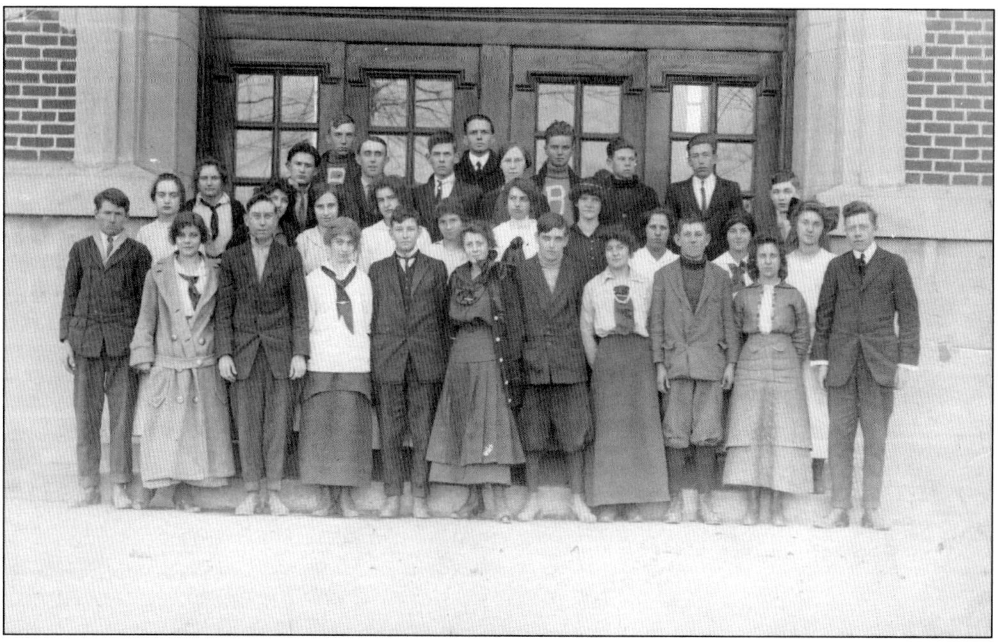

These smartly dressed high school freshmen pose for their 1914–1915 class picture. During the same year that these students started their high school experience, Brownsburg athletic teams began to be featured regularly in meets held for all of the schools in the county.

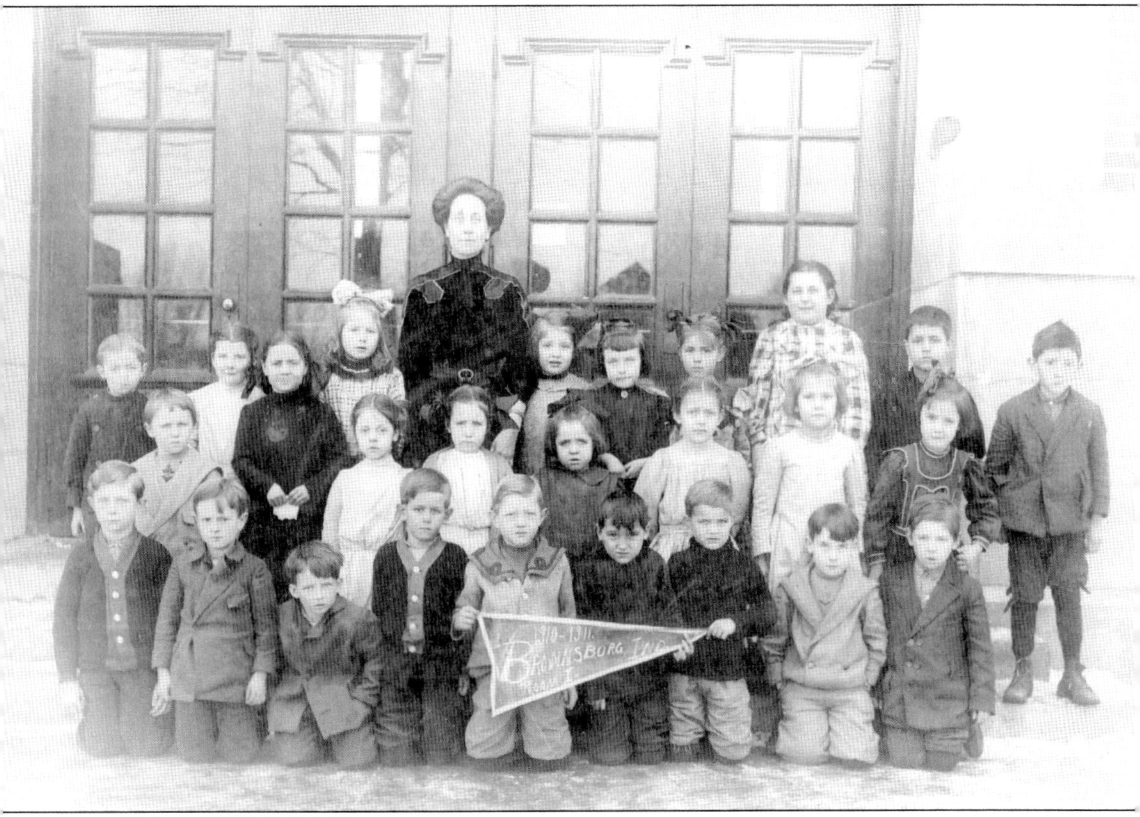

These adorable children are posing for their class picture on the steps of the Lincoln Township Public School located on the southeast corner of College Avenue and School Street. Holding their pennant for 1910–1911, it is possible they are gathered here with teacher Mary Ottie Roberts. Roberts was a direct descendant of William Harris, who platted the town of Brownsburg. She graduated from Brownsburg High School in 1891 and attended Indiana State Teachers College. An article in the *Brownsburg Record* at the time lamented that teachers were not paid enough for the profession. Those that dedicated their lives to it ought to be compensated for their preparations. Regardless of the pay, Mary Ottie Roberts taught in the public schools for several years. She left the public school system to become the first librarian for the town at the new library in September 1918 until 1944. Ottie was a well-loved and active member of the community.

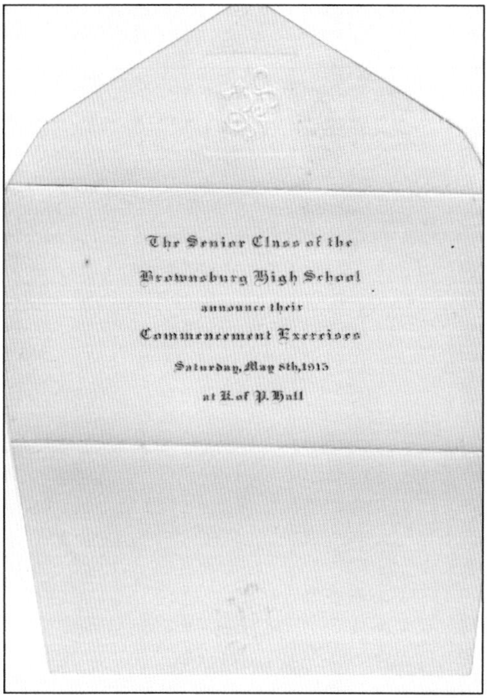
The Senior Class of the
Brownsburg High School
announce their
Commencement Exercises
Saturday, May 8th, 1915
at K. of P. Hall

The class of 1915 announced their graduation in style. The baccalaureate sermon was given May 2, at the Christian Church by Rev. M.W. Lyons. Commencement exercises followed about a week later on Saturday, May 8. The commencement was held at the Knights of Pythias Hall. This well-preserved announcement belonged to student Jalie Thornburgh. (Courtesy of Roger A. Zimmerman.)

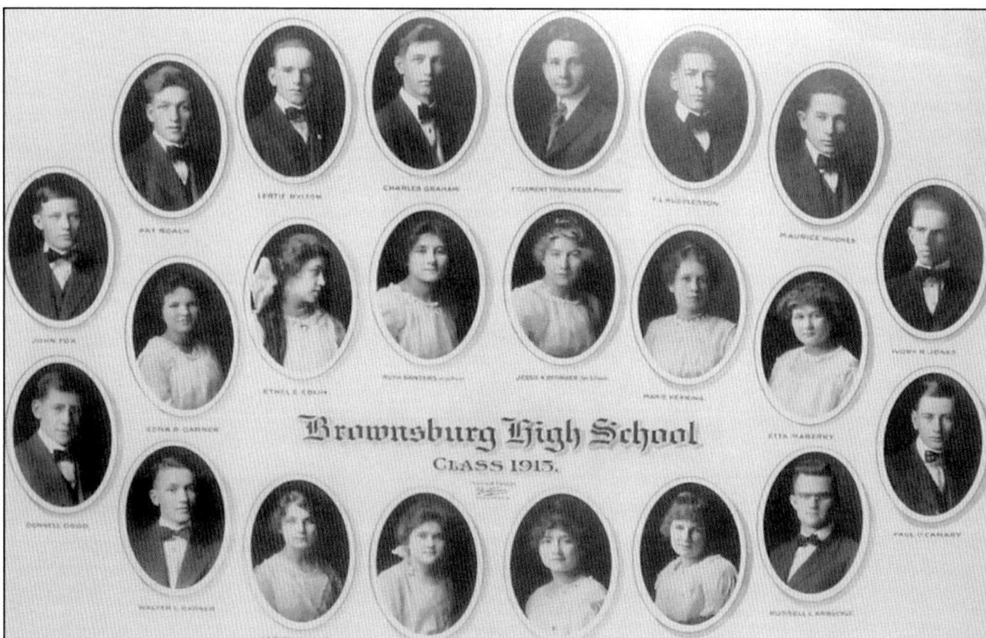

Members of the 1915 graduating class are, from left to right, (top arc) John Fox, Pat Roach, Lertie Hylton, Charles Graham, F. Clement Trucksess (president), F.L. Huddleston, Maurice Hughes, and Ivory R. Jones; (middle arc) Edna B. Garner, Ethel E. Eblin, Ruth Sanders (vice president), Jessie K. Ottinger (secretary treasurer), Marie Herring, and Etta Maberry; (bottom arc) Donnell Good, Walter L. Garner, La Ruth Henson, Cordis L. Gentry, Jalie Thornburgh, Edna C. McKeown, Russell L. Arbuckle, and Paul O. Canary.

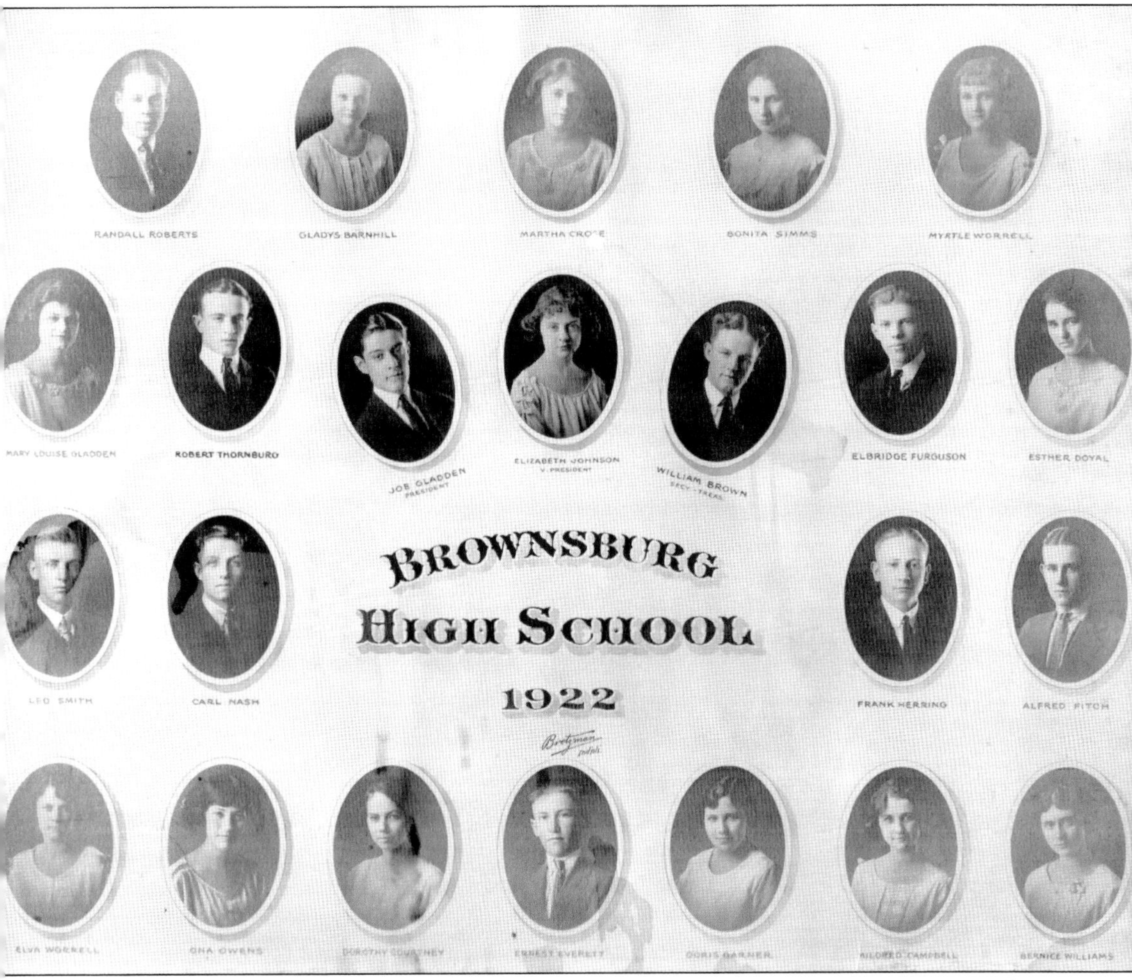

Pictured are the graduating students of 1921–1922. In April 1922, the senior class presented its class play before their graduation day. The play, *Assisted by Sadie* was given in the high school auditorium, and tickets were sold for 25¢ at Hollett and Harmon's Drugstore. The class chose a play intertwining mystery, adventure, humor, and romance. Students promised that the plot would keep the patrons in a constant state of wonder.

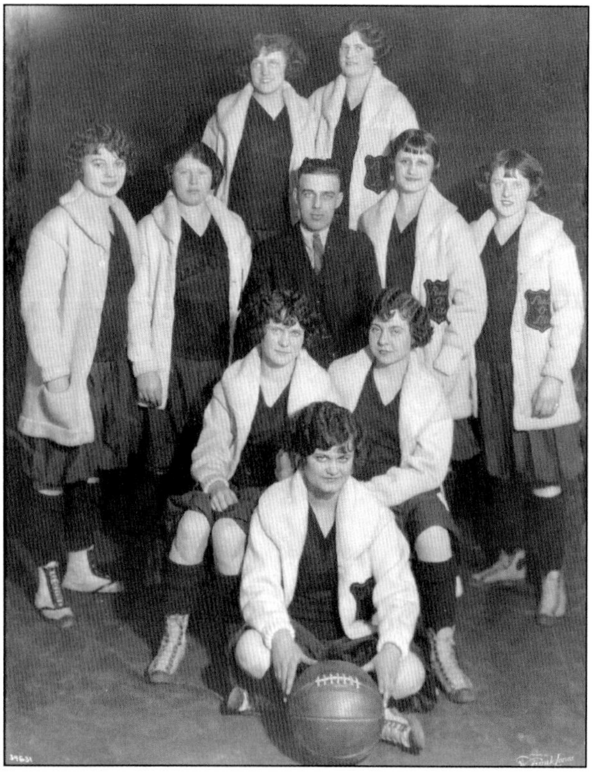

This group of unidentified young women were members of a Prest-O-Lite basketball team. In December 1923, the Brownsburg Prest-O-Lite girls' basketball team played the YPC girls' team from Indianapolis at the Speedway Community House. The Brownsburg team was made up entirely of Brownsburg alumni girls, and it was thought to be the fastest team in the state.

These students are standing in front of the high school building located on the west side of Stadium Drive. The building was constructed in 1957 around the corner from the buildings on College Avenue. Although it has been repurposed, the building is still owned by the Brownsburg School Corporation.

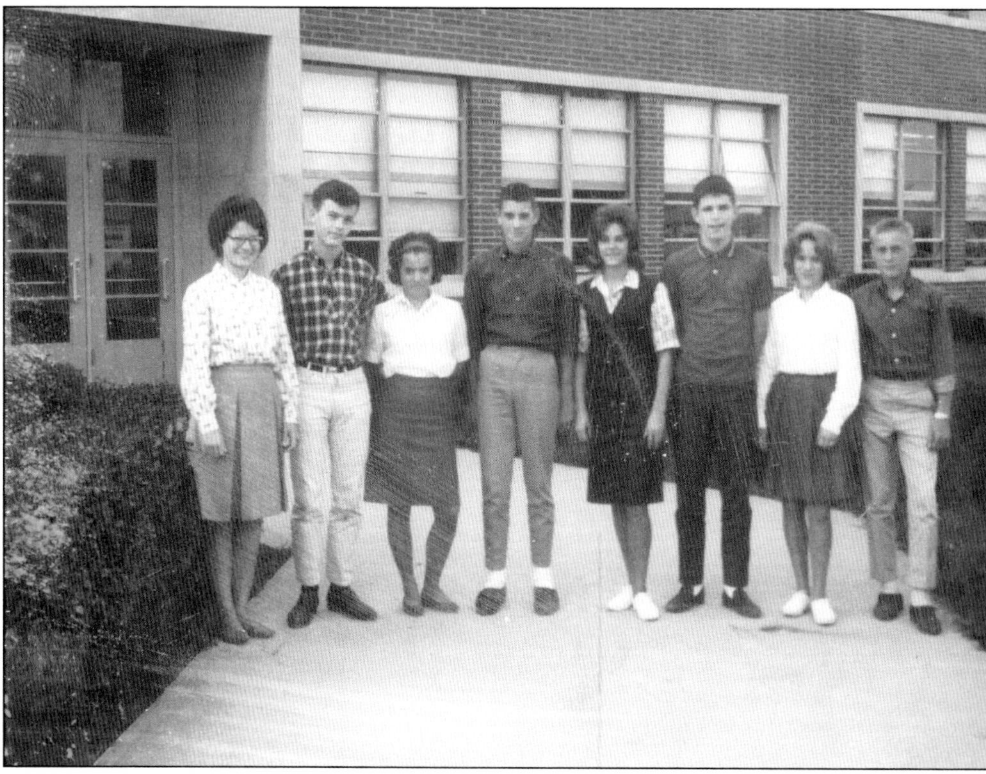

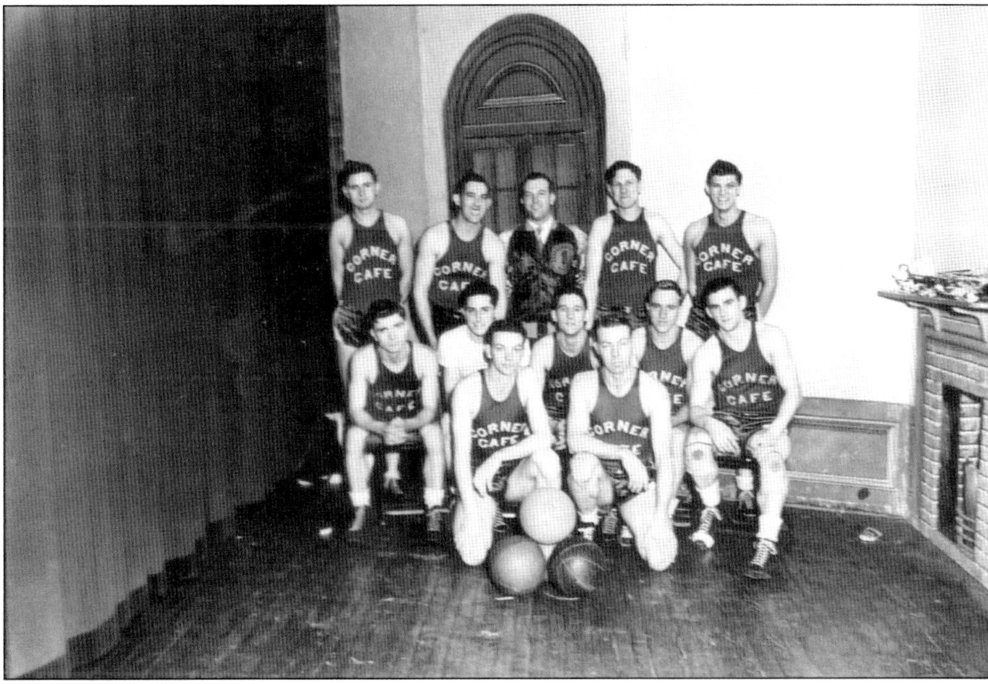

A group of young men pose in their Corner Café basketball attire in this undated photograph. The Corner Café was previously located on the southwest corner of Main and Green Streets in the old Hunter Bank Building. It is possible that the photograph was taken inside the building.

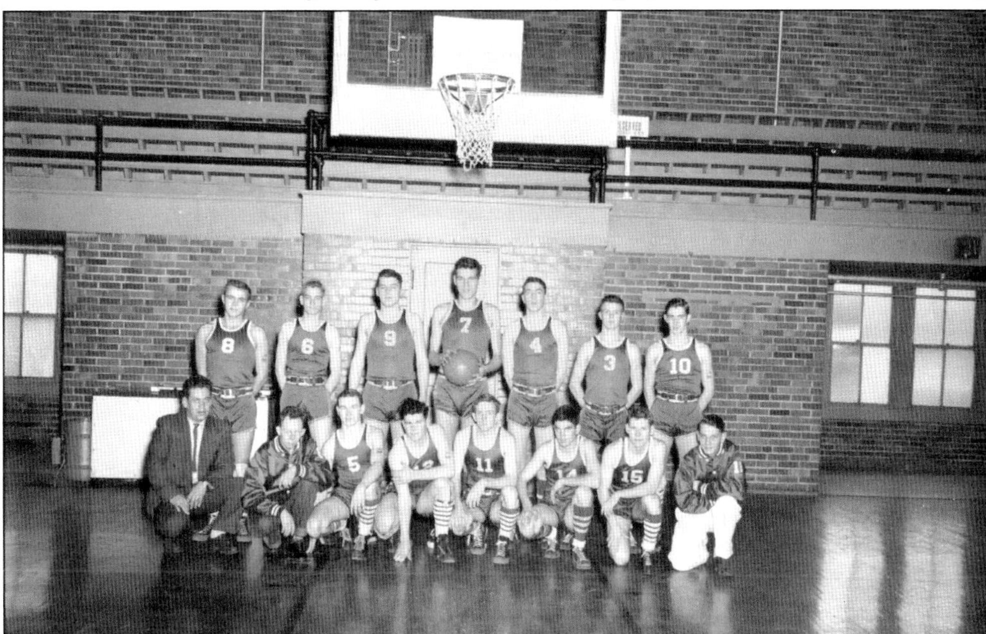

The men's basketball team of 1946–1947 is lined up in the College Avenue Gym. The men identified from the photograph are, from left to right, (first row) coach Glenn Steele, M.E. Smith, Tom Haulk, Bob Ruse, Wayne Hott, ? Poole, Tom McClarnon, and Dick Wilson; (second row) Art Wilson, ? Hodge, Jack Schenck, George Litteral, Don Garner, Don Ottinger, and Tom Ballard.

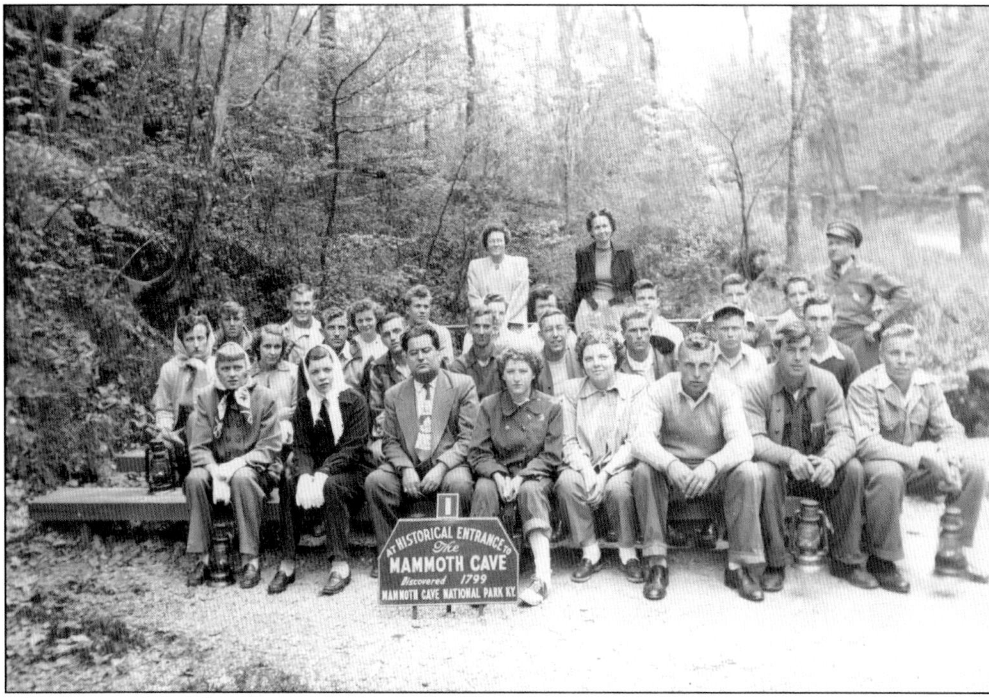

The senior class of 1948–1949 takes a moment for a picture on their senior class trip. Their destination was the Smoky Mountains, and one of the stops along the way was a visit to Mammoth Cave. The class is shown here with their classmates, chaperones, tour guide, and other visiting tourists. (Courtesy of Laura Thomas.)

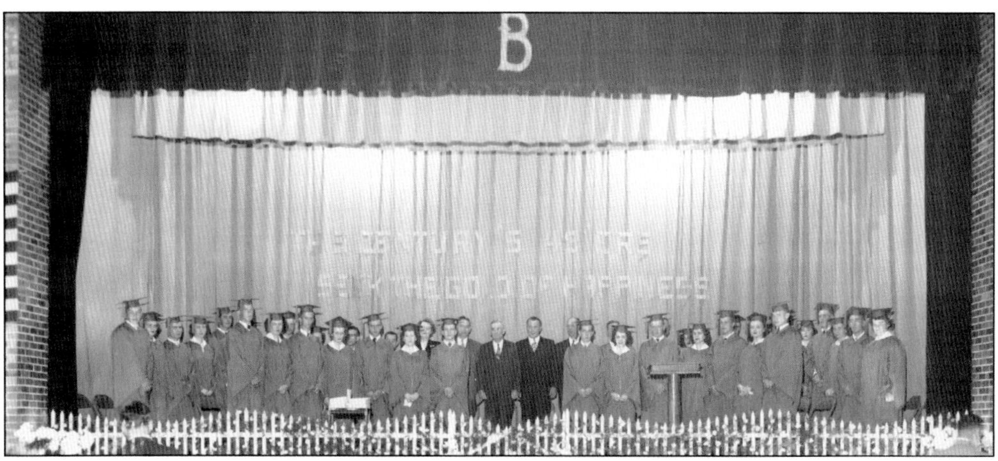

The 1949 Brownsburg High School graduating class made it to the big day and proudly stands in caps and gowns. The motto of the class can be seen hanging on the curtain in the background, "This Century's 49'ers Seek the Gold of Happiness." It was a play on words in 1949 referring to the gold rush in 1849, 100 years prior. (Courtesy of Laura Thomas.)

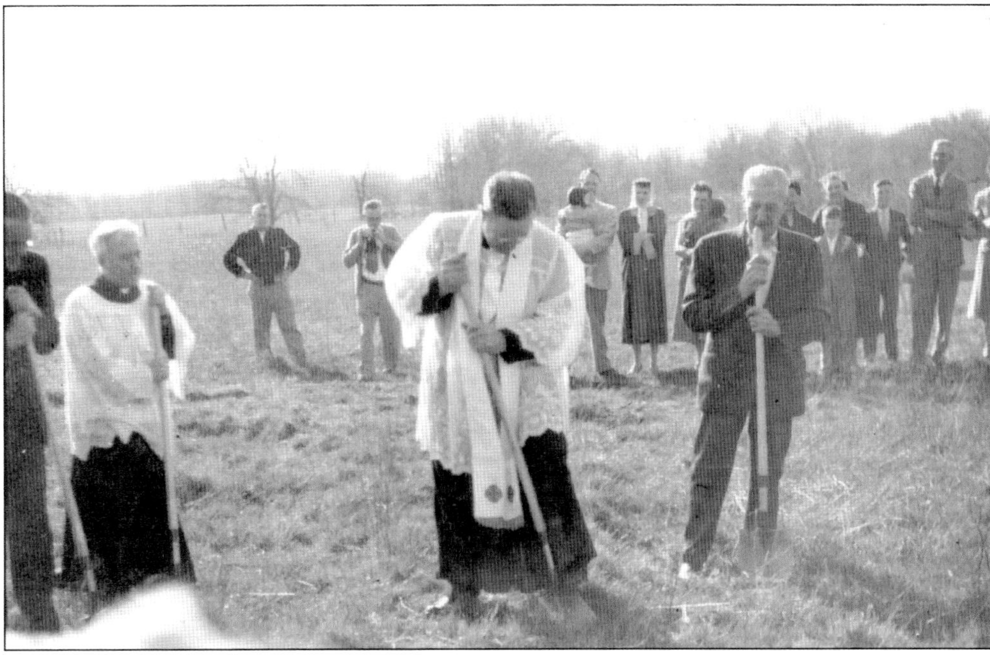

Ground-breaking ceremonies for the new St. Malachy Catholic School took place in the spring of 1955. The school, to be located on the west side of north Green Street, near Arbuckle Acres Park, was to contain five classrooms and was anticipated to be opened by August of the same year.

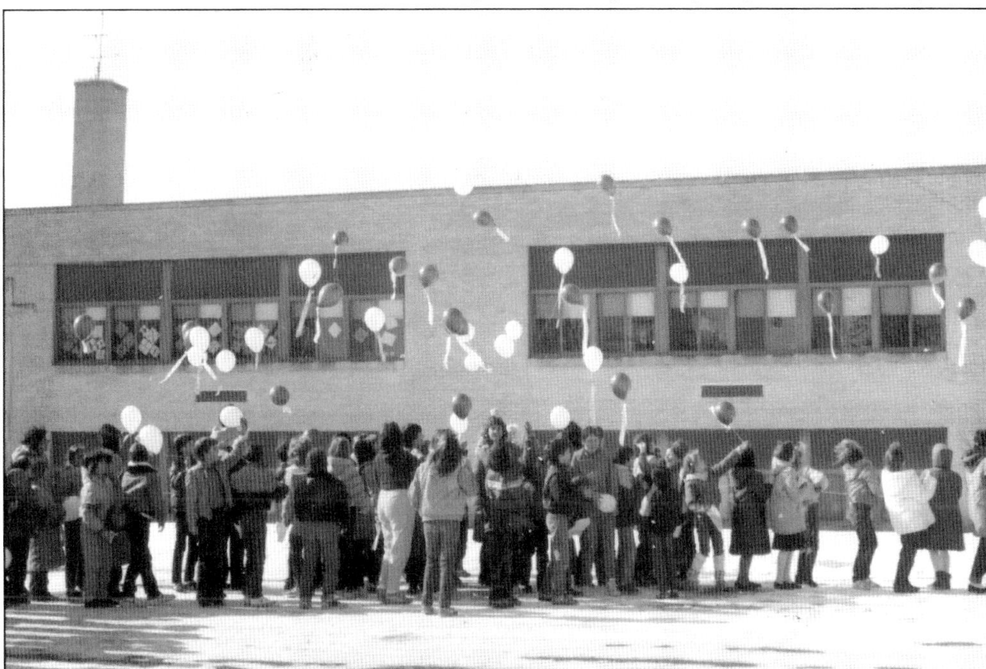

The St. Malachy Catholic School was the first parochial school in Brownsburg. The brand new building opened in August 1955, and in the early 1960s an addition to the original building was made. All eight grades were taught in the building. Pictured here, many years later, the students stand in the parking lot of the St. Malachy Catholic School and release balloons.

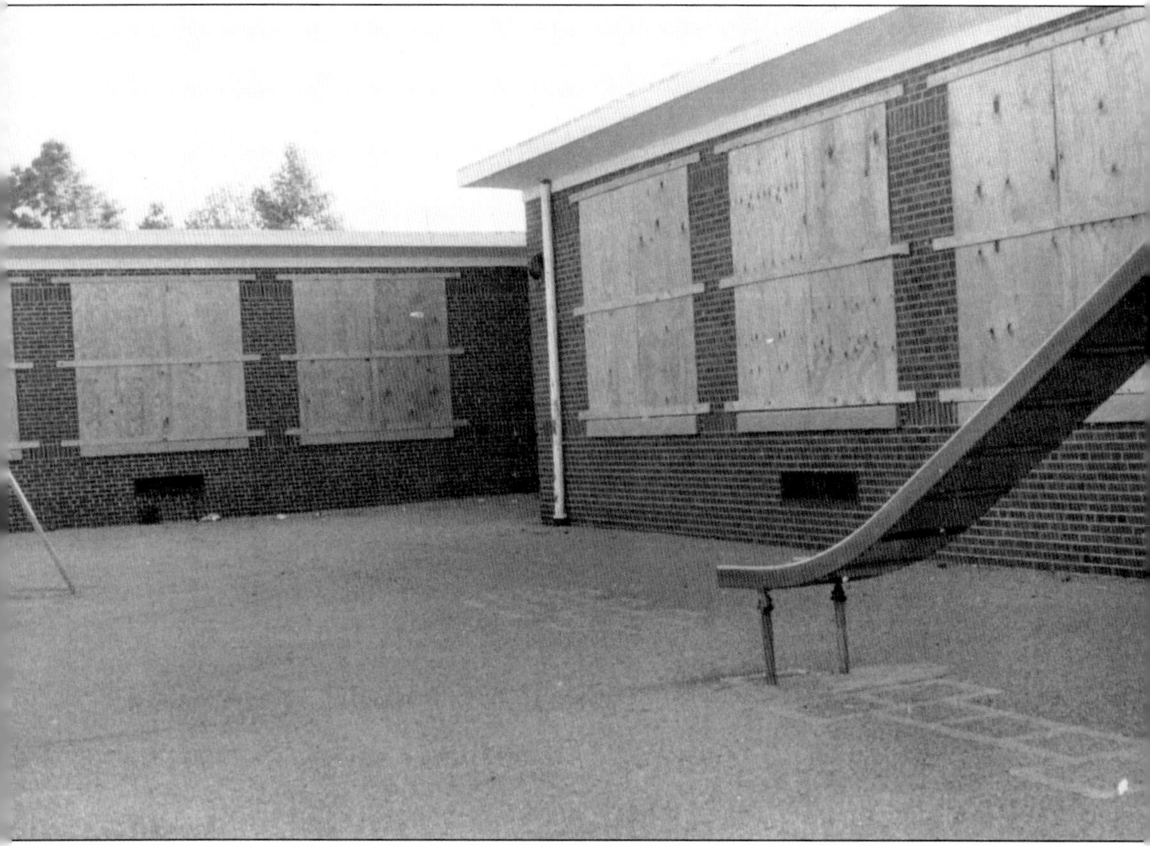

East Elementary School, also sometimes known as College Avenue Elementary, was located just east of the College Avenue Gymnasium near the corner of south Grant Street and College Avenue. The school was built in the early 1950s to help relieve the growing need for additional space to educate students. In the photograph, the window glass has been removed from the old school, and the windows have been boarded up in preparation for demolition. The view is at the back of the building in the playground area. In 1985, suggestions to the school board for saving the property included using it as an office for the chamber of commerce or a nonprofit, vocational workshop, or recycling facility, among others. In the end, the old school along with the gymnasium and former high school to the west could not be saved, and the demolition began in the 1990s to make way for condominiums being built.

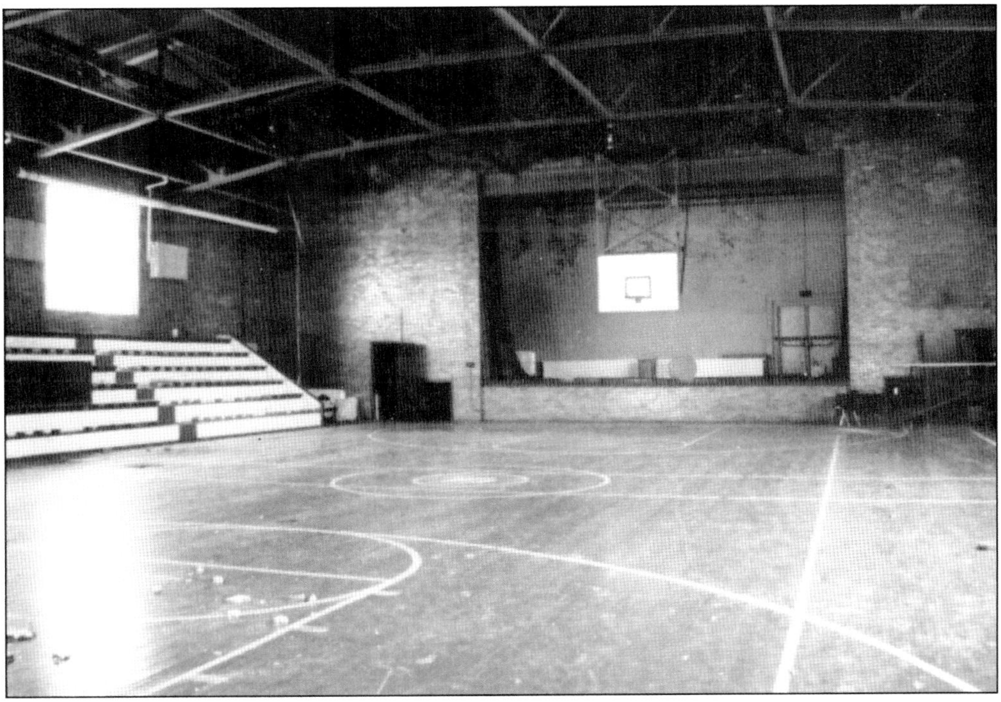

Sometimes it is the simplest of photographs that has the ability to bring back the fondest memories. These two shots taken from inside the College Avenue Gymnasium have captured a unique glimpse of the symbols of Brownsburg pride. The Brownsburg Community Building, or College Avenue Gymnasium, was built in 1928 for approximately $35,000. In addition to sporting events and other school functions, many locals may also remember it as a location for filming of the 1986 basketball film, *Hoosiers*. Actors Barbara Hershey and Gene Hackman were photographed together standing on the Bulldog symbol in 1985 during filming. Efforts were made by the Celebration Square organization to restore the gym and the other school buildings, but a lack of funding prevented their efforts. The grand old gym was put up for sale in 1989. It was torn down to make way for condominiums.

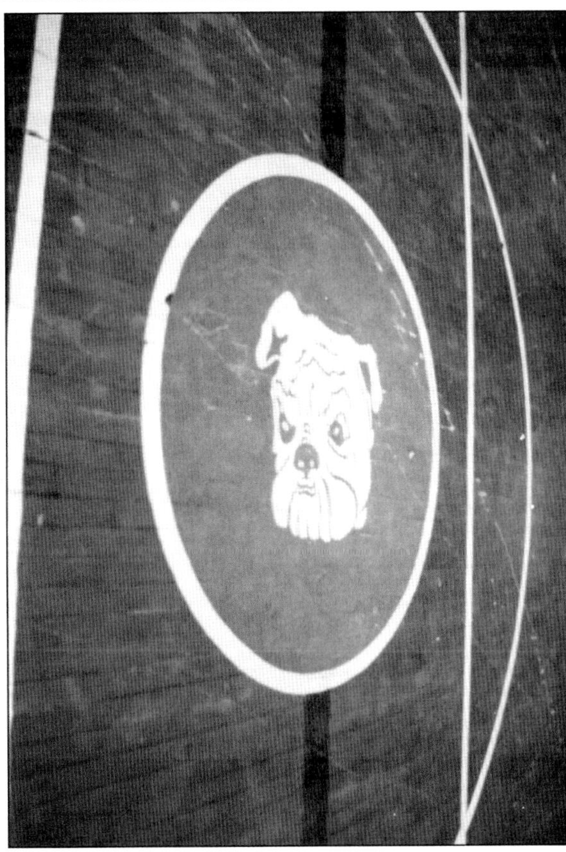

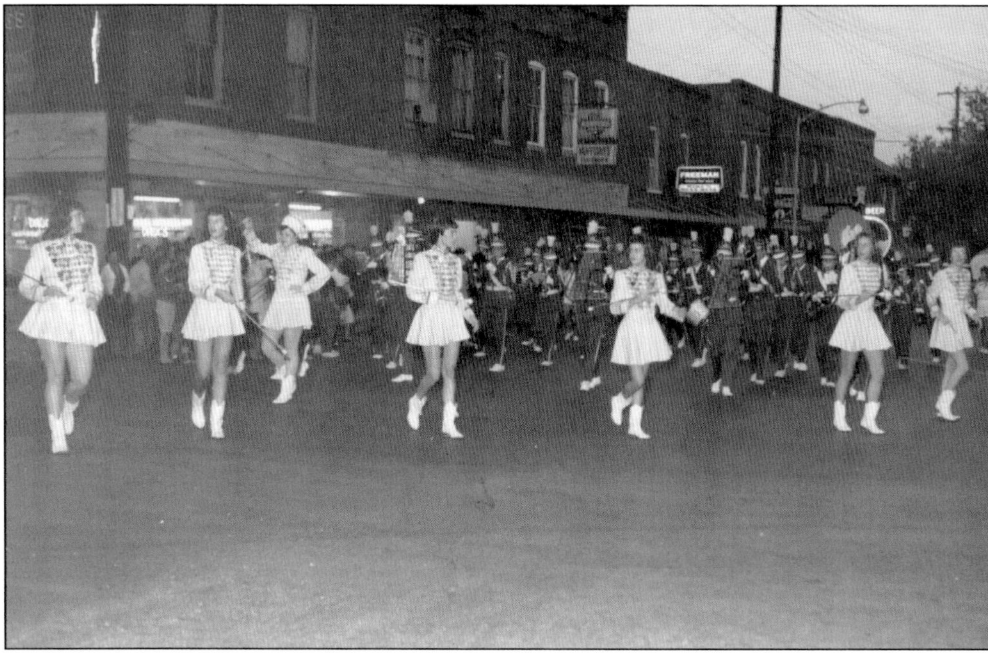

Marching with pride down Main Street, the band here is being led by the batons with the drum majorette in the left portion of the photograph wearing the hat. In the background, the shops of the northeast corner block of Main and Green Streets can be seen. The 1960s photograph was taken as the band turns south onto Green Street.

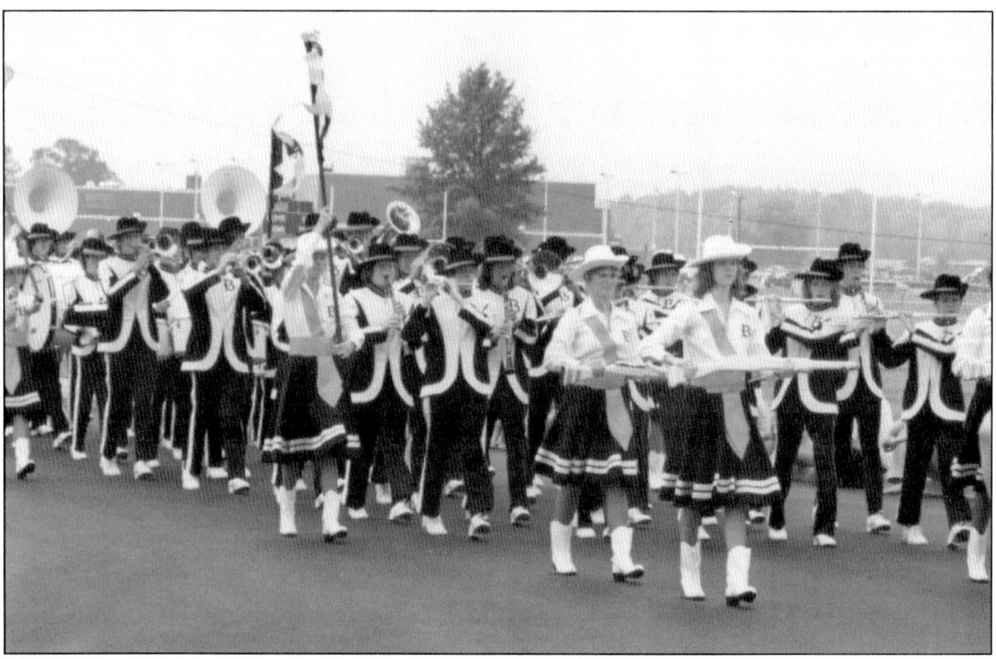

The uniforms have changed, but the pride has not. Continuing the tradition, the marching Bulldogs, led by the flags and rifles, make their way in a parade in this 1981 photograph. The members of the band dedicate their summers to practice in soaring temperatures. With a busy schedule, they reliably represent the town and students. (Courtesy of Mickie Myers.)

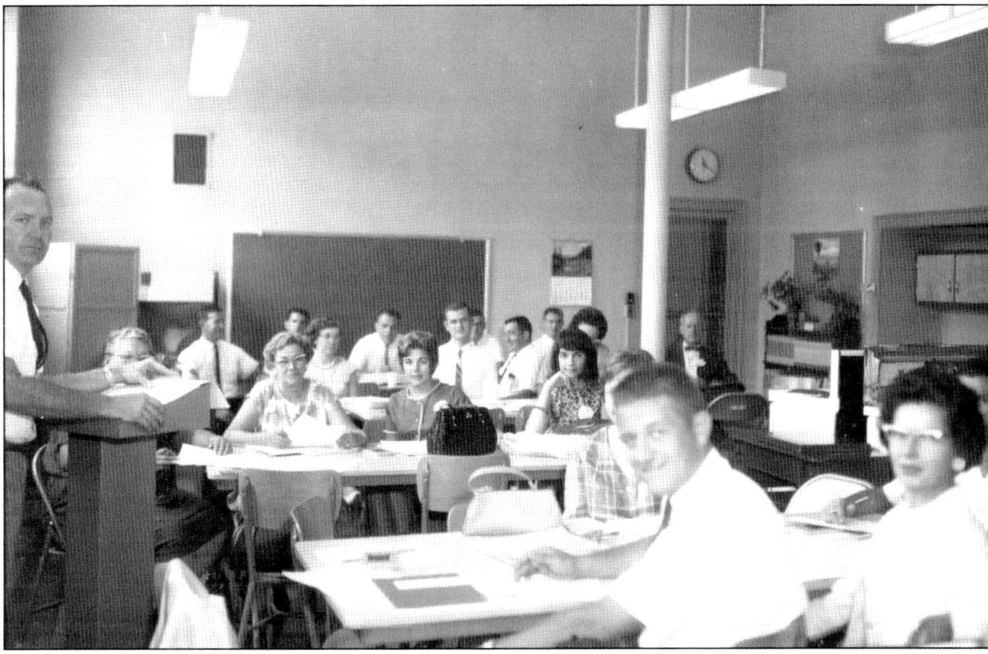

These teachers are ready to start the day at the Brownsburg Junior High School. Conducting the meeting in 1965 is Principal Rilus J. Hill, who attended Central Normal College in Danville and served the Brownsburg Community School Corporation for many years. In 1984, he celebrated his retirement from the Brownsburg School Corporation.

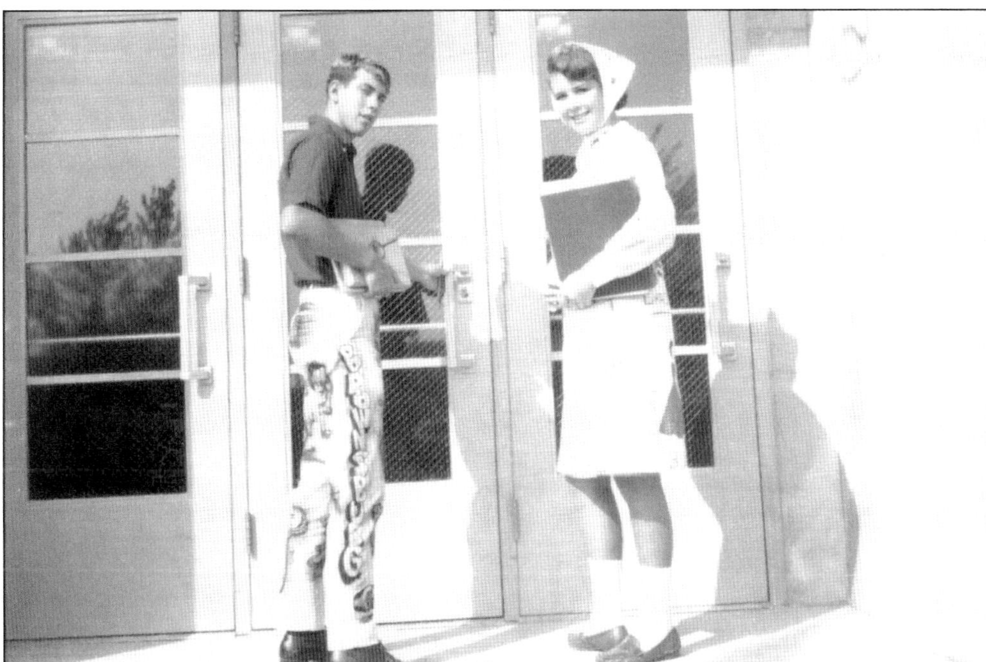

This 1965–1966 photograph was taken in front of the high school located on Stadium Drive. Pictured are two seniors modeling their senior clothing. Brownsburg is clearly marked on the pants, and although not as easy to see, the skirt is marked as well.

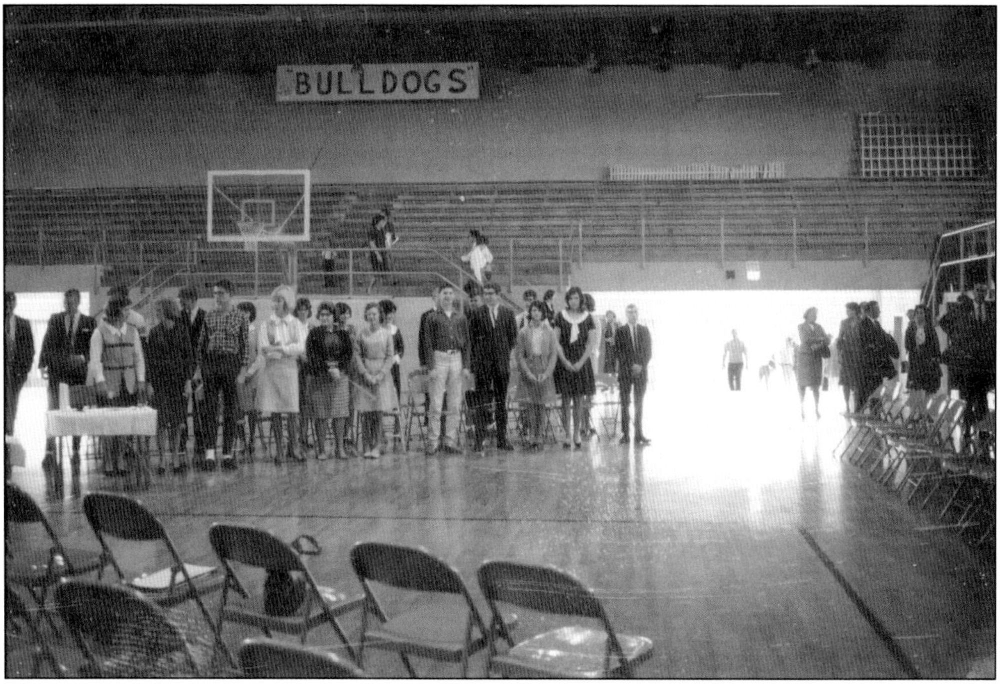

The national honor society participated in initiation in this photograph from 1965. The old varsity gym located on Stadium Drive was the venue for the event. The view is facing west looking through the large entrance doors. The homemade "Bulldogs" sign can be seen at the top.

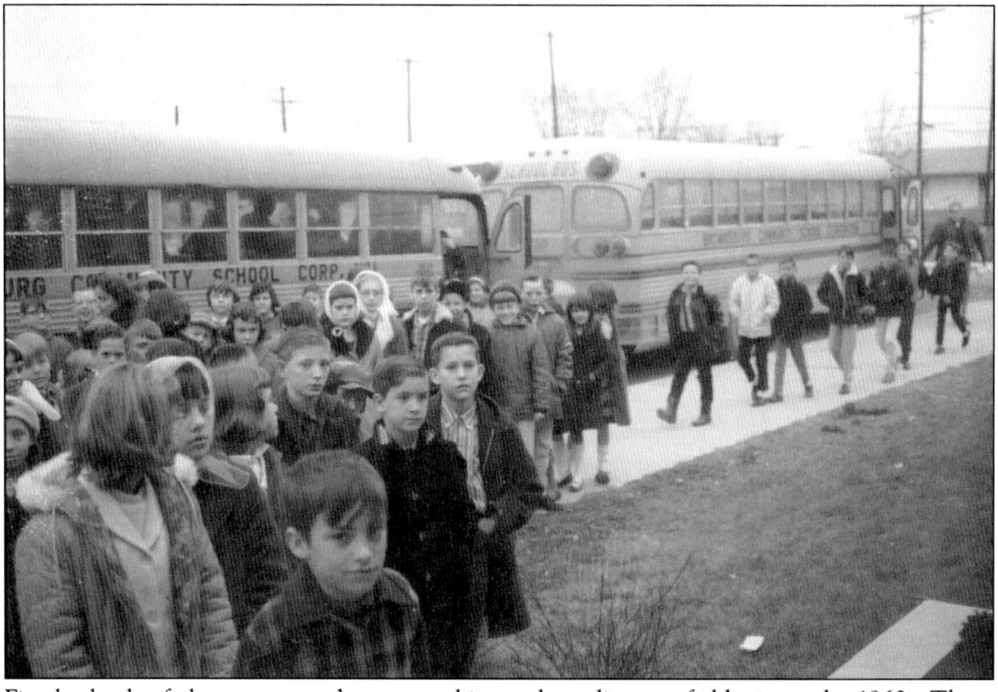

Five busloads of elementary students are taking a short-distance field trip in the 1960s. These students from East Elementary School are unloading at South Elementary School, now Harris Academy at 725 South Green Street. They are arriving to attend a school play.

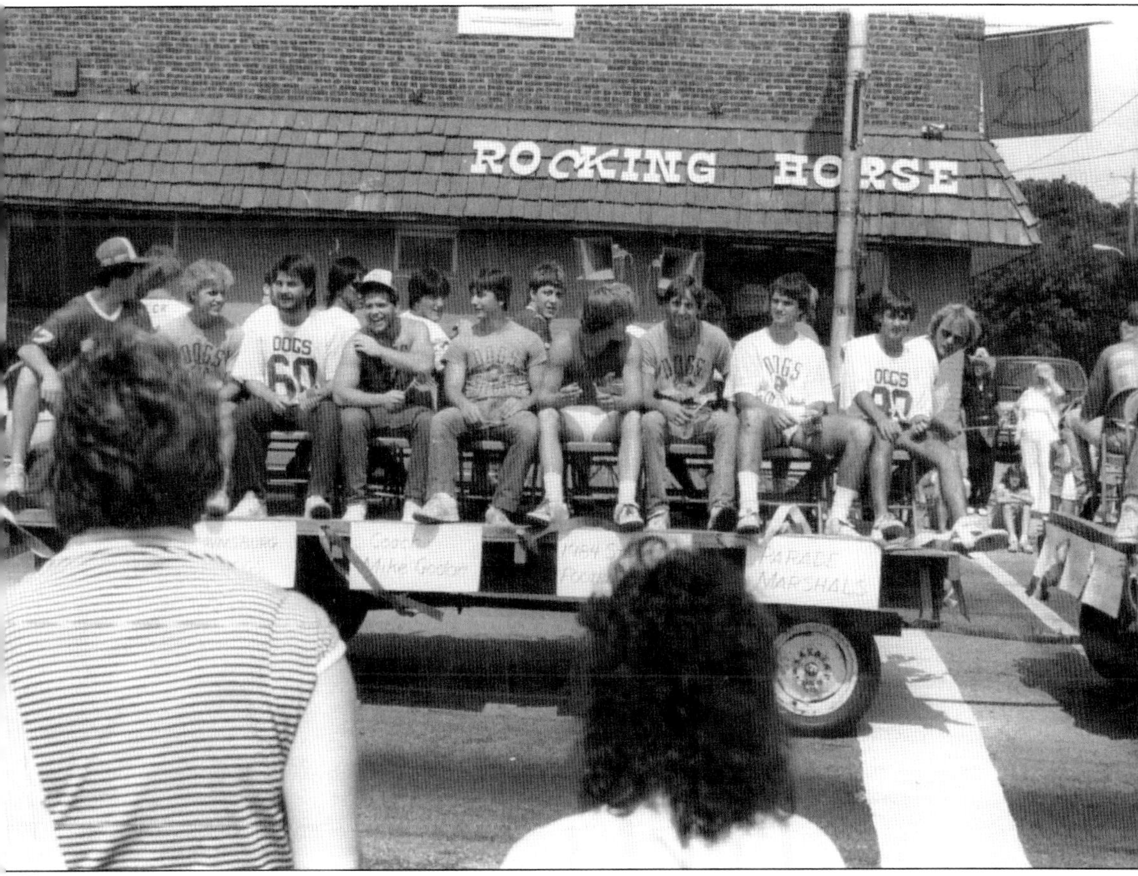

School sports involve teamwork, support, and camaraderie. Continuing a long history of pride in athletics, the young men in this photograph are acting as parade marshals in 1985, representing many years of the football program at Brownsburg. The parade is making its way north on Green Street past the Rocking Horse Pub. The pub was located in the Hunter building on the southwest corner of Main and Green Streets. They were headed for the Lions Club Extravaganza in Arbuckle Acres. Two years in a row the Bulldogs went to the Hoosier Dome and came back to Brownsburg as champions. The Brownsburg Bulldogs won back-to-back state championships in 1984–1985 as Class AAA and 1985–1986 as Class AAAA. In both years, the Bulldogs went undefeated. The young men were coached both times by Mike Godan.

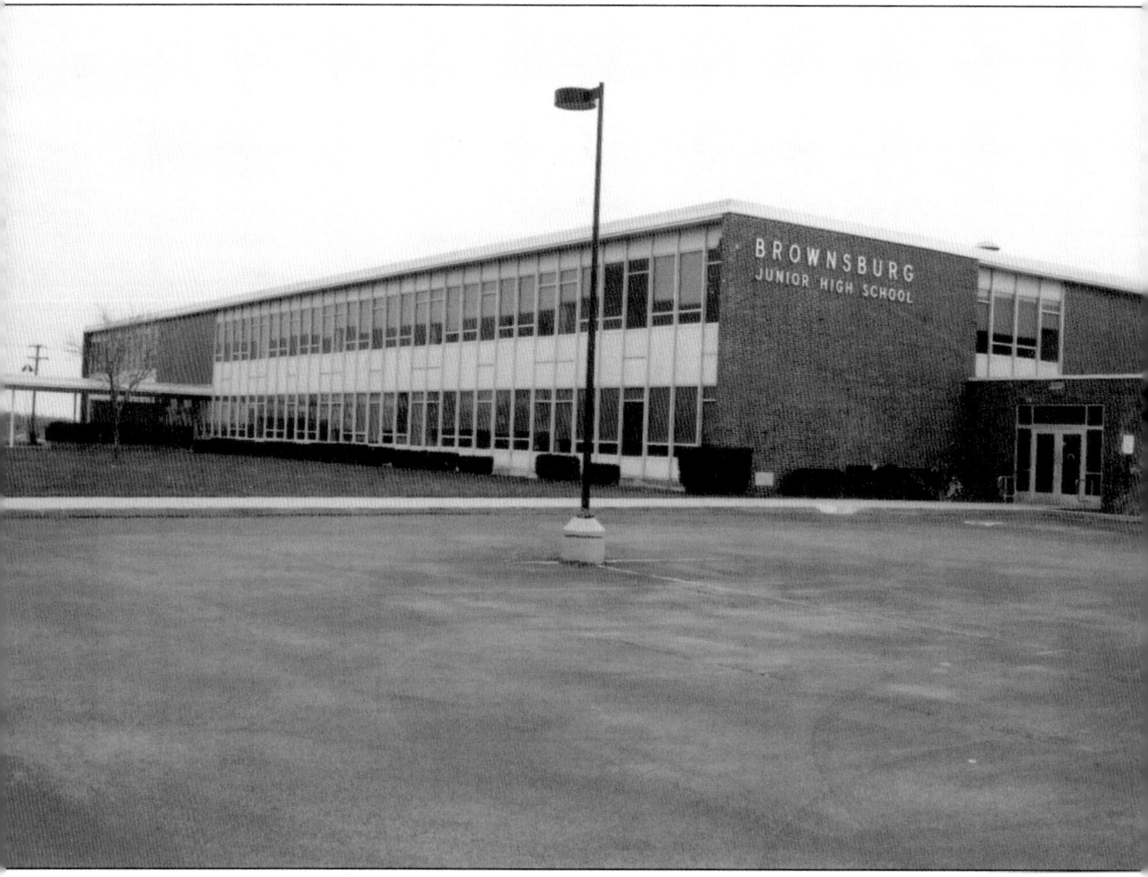

Owing to the growing educational needs of the community, a new junior high school was planned in late 1964. Ground was broken on the $1,800,000 building in February 1965, and the new Brownsburg Junior High School was under construction just south of the varsity gymnasium on Stadium Drive. At the time, the building to the north was used as the Brownsburg High School, and students would have a very close transition between the two buildings. The future athletic field sat just across Tilden Road to the south in a large grassy area. Rilus Hill, the junior high school principal, welcomed the students at the new junior high when the doors opened in the fall of 1966. The building opened to receive approximately 600 students in the seventh through ninth grades. In 1966, the total enrollment for the school corporation sat at 2,540 students.

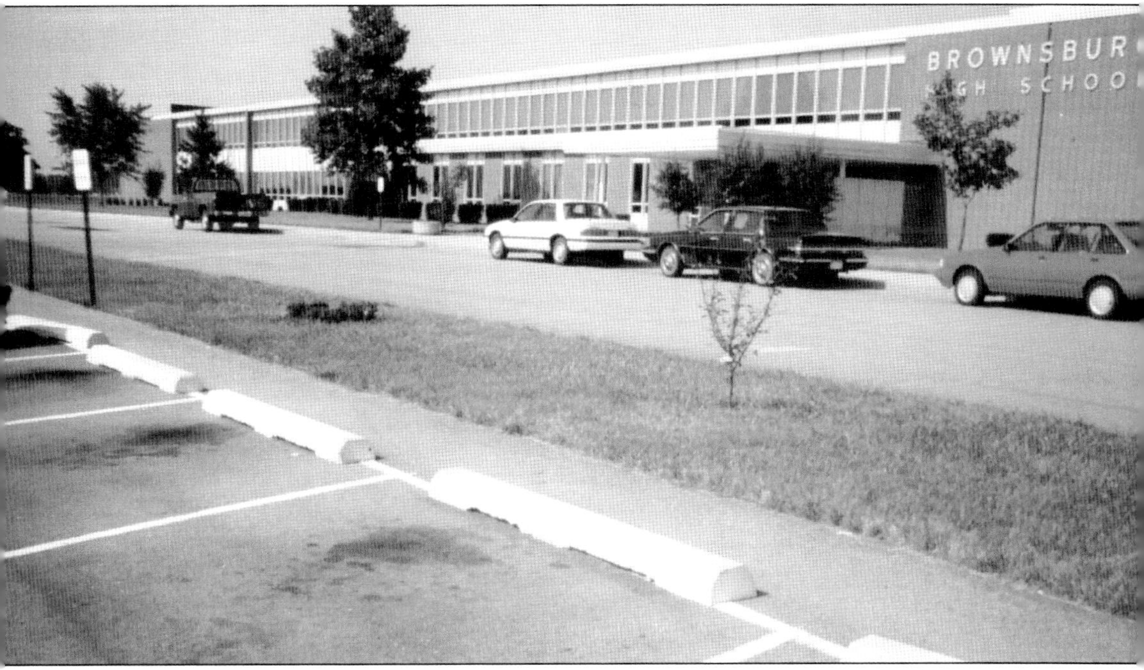

Again, the size of the growing town would warrant the need for more space for students. Under the leadership of superintendent Hubert Haynes, this time the corporation determined that a new high school building was necessary. In 1967, the school board began plans for a new high school building on just over 112 acres at a total cost of $4,270,101.41. Ground was broken on the west side of Odell Street in May 1969 for the building that could house 1,200 students. Construction was underway and the new building was scheduled to be opened in the fall of 1971 with Donald French at the time as the principal. When the new facility was dedicated in October 1971, it had several state-of-the-art classrooms and features. Among some of these classrooms were the Homemaking Family Living Center, Food Lab, and Business Department.

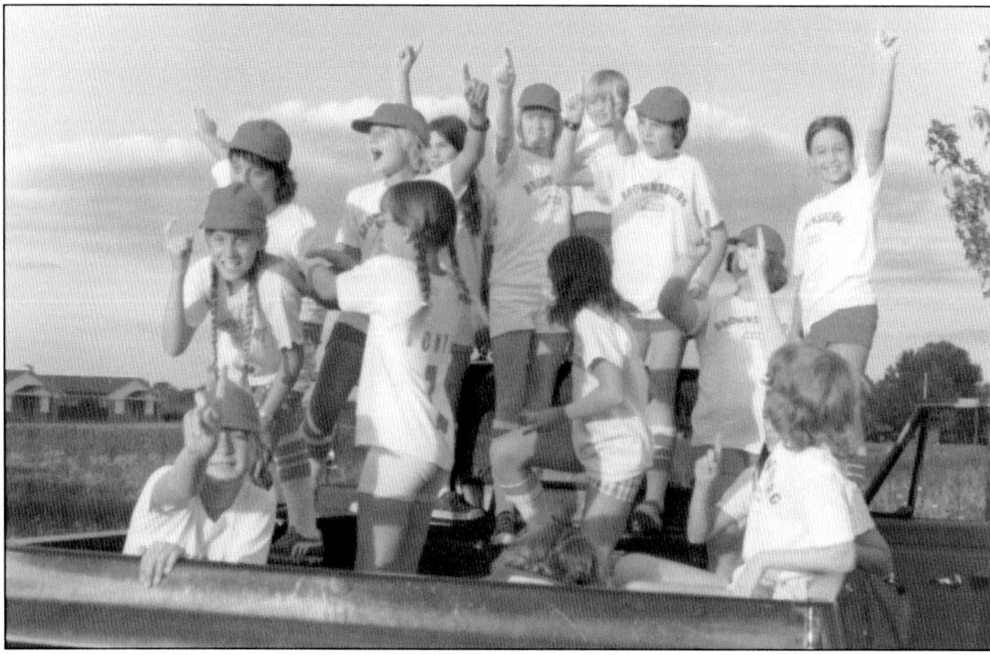

Pure joy and the thrill of the win is priceless on the faces of this young softball team. Playing for the Brownsburg Girls Softball League in 1976, this team, representing the hometown Dairy Queen store, celebrates in the back of a pickup truck waiting for their drive to the ice cream store. The Dairy Queen team won the minor tourney in that year with 12 wins and only 2 losses.

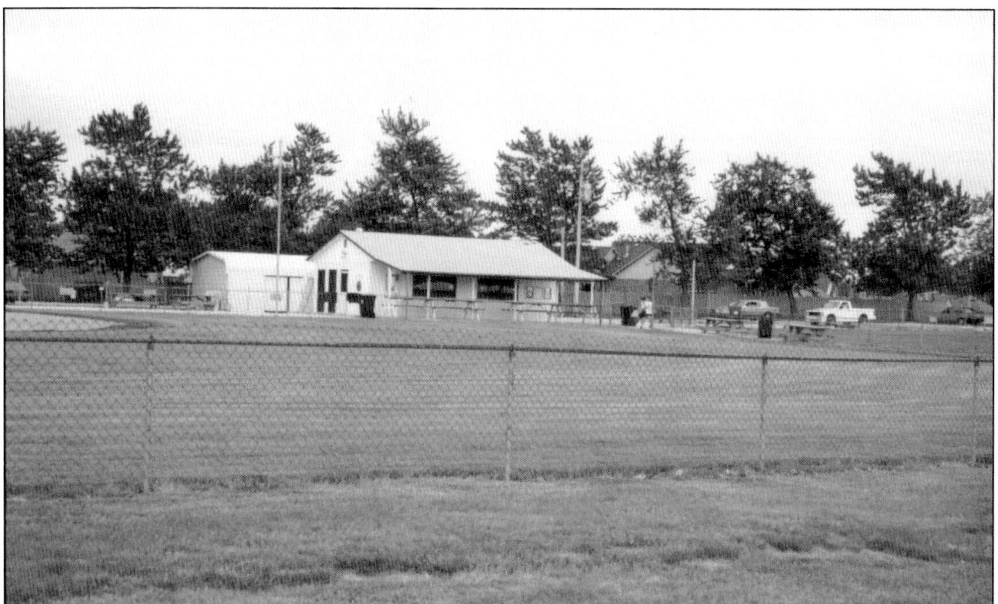

The ball diamonds, at one time more commonly known as Sportsfield Park, have been used for generations. The diamonds and their facilities were updated many times. The Brownsburg Girls Softball League played their games on these fields directly across the road from the Brownsburg High School. Today, the school corporation and the Brownsburg Girls Slo-pitch Corporation both maintain property in the area.

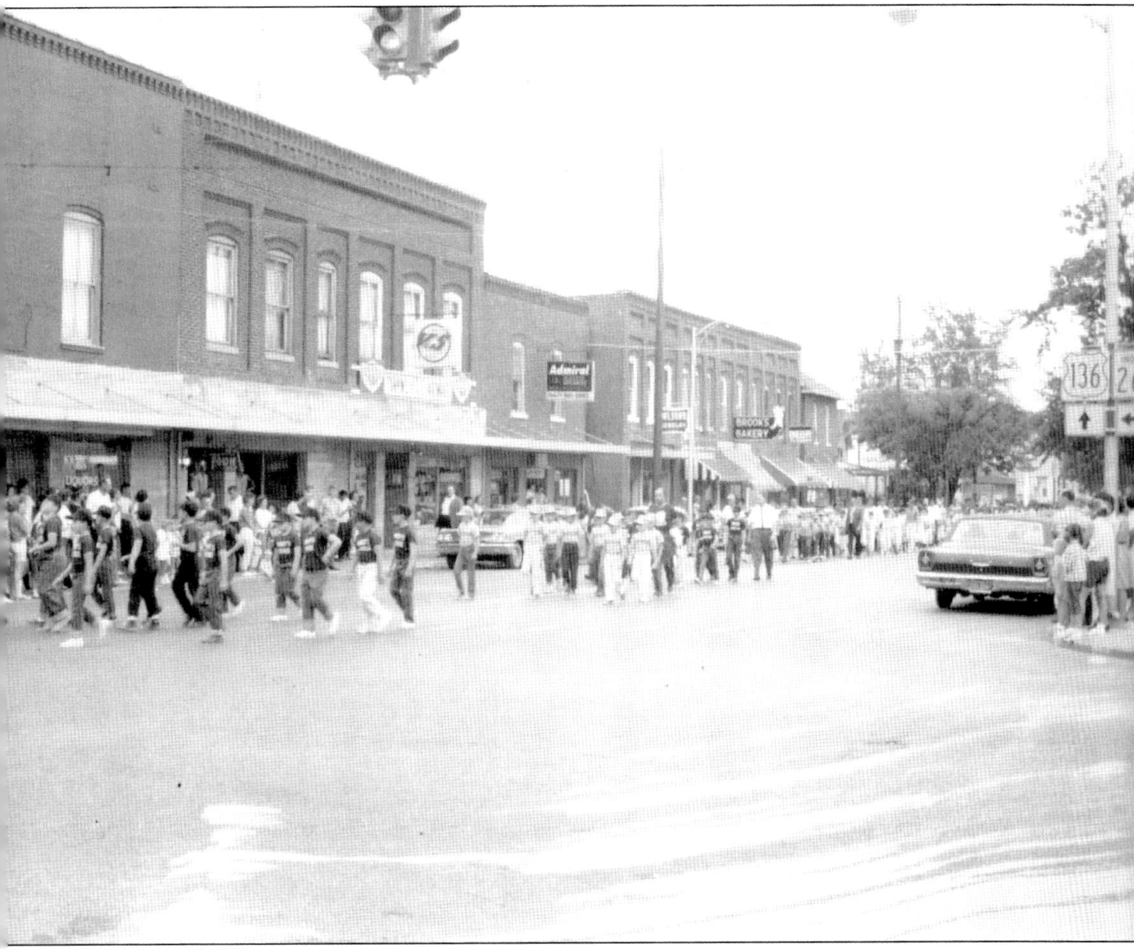

There has been a long history of baseball in the town of Brownsburg. In this photograph, the boys form part of a parade down Main Street past the northeast block of businesses to kick off the 1965 Brownsburg Little League season. Turpin's Hardware, Nelson's Jewelry, Brook's Bakery, among other shops can be seen in the background. In July 1922, Ladoga defeated Brownsburg in the first game opener of a new league. The *Brownsburg Record* at the time accused the Ladoga umpire of winning the game for his team. Records of Brownsburg baseball can be found dating back to as early as 1885. The *Indianapolis Evening Minute News* stated in July 1885 that the Brownsburg Sluggers would be hosting a game against the Indianapolis Standards at Brownsburg. Considering that this mention of a Brownsburg game was 130 years ago, the sport has definitely earned a place in the hearts of the community.

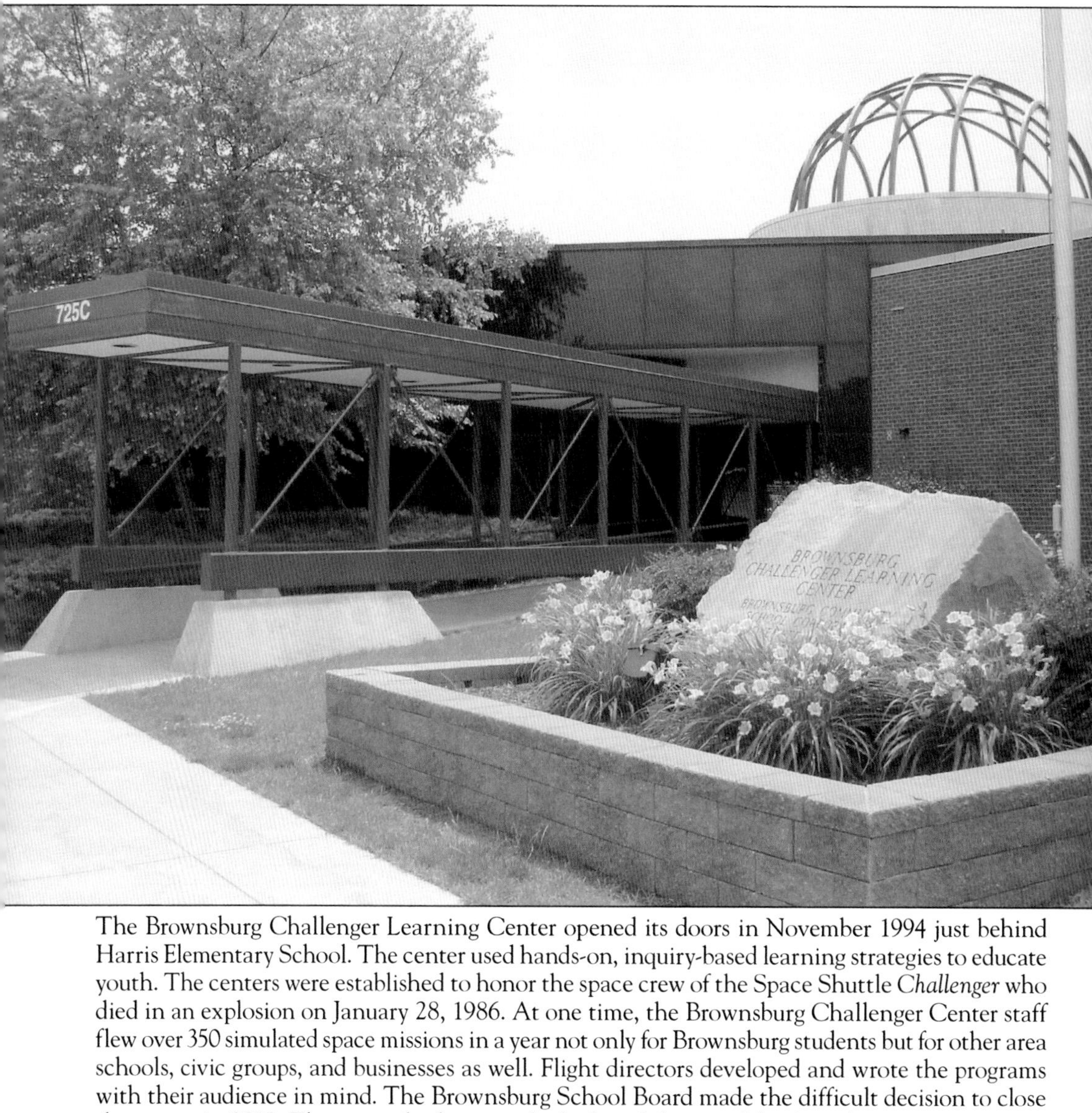

The Brownsburg Challenger Learning Center opened its doors in November 1994 just behind Harris Elementary School. The center used hands-on, inquiry-based learning strategies to educate youth. The centers were established to honor the space crew of the Space Shuttle *Challenger* who died in an explosion on January 28, 1986. At one time, the Brownsburg Challenger Center staff flew over 350 simulated space missions in a year not only for Brownsburg students but for other area schools, civic groups, and businesses as well. Flight directors developed and wrote the programs with their audience in mind. The Brownsburg School Board made the difficult decision to close the center in 2012. The center had incurred a budget deficit, and funding the program was not feasible. It was felt that the funds should be directed into the classrooms.

Six

COMMUNITY AND SERVICE

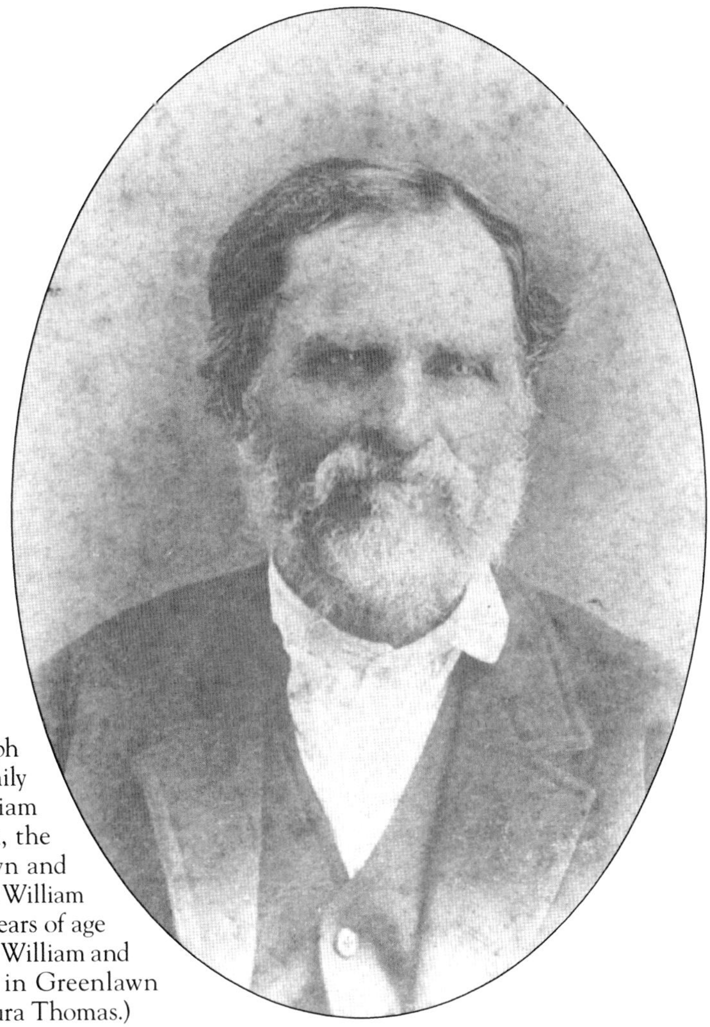

This is a very early photograph from the James B. Brown family line. Pictured here is William R. "California Bill" Brown, the grandson of James B. Brown and the father of Horatio Brown. William died in March 1905 at 76 years of age at his home near Clermont. William and his wife, Lucy, are buried in Greenlawn Cemetery. (Courtesy of Laura Thomas.)

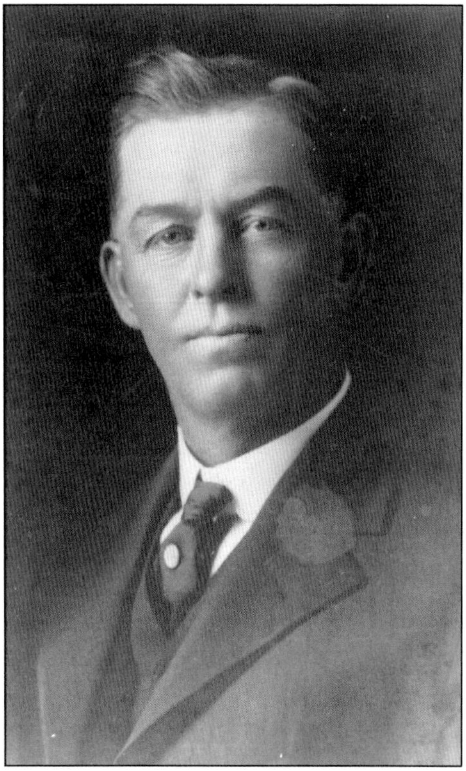

This polished gentleman is Horatio S. Brown. Horatio was born in 1868 and died in 1943 and his heart was for community. Horatio can be credited with overseeing the building of the Brownsburg High School in 1915, serving on the board of the new Carnegie Library from 1916 to 1918, and working with banks among other accomplishments. He and his wife, Addie, are buried in Clermont Cemetery. (Courtesy of Laura Thomas.)

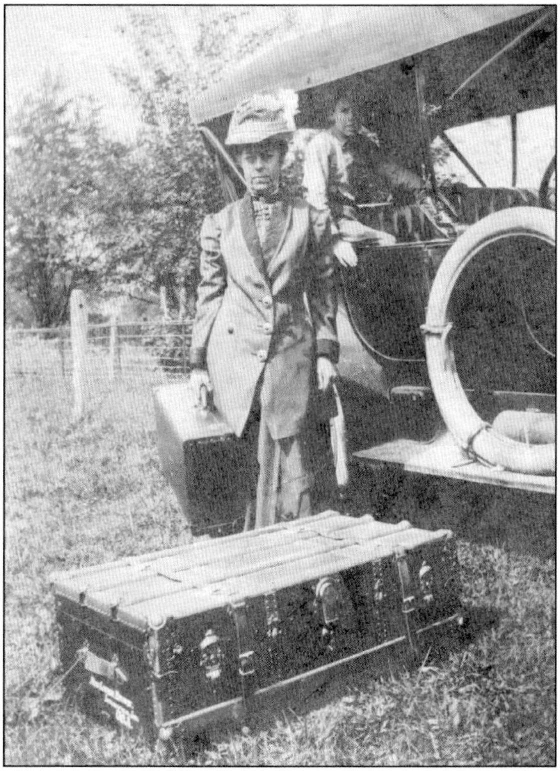

Either coming or going in this photograph is Elizabeth "Lizzie" Brown (Moore), the daughter of William R. Brown and sister of Horatio Brown. Born in 1865, Lizzie died in 1925 and was buried in Greenlawn Cemetery. In this photograph, Lizzie is standing next to a motor car possibly belonging to her brother-in-law Dr. John L. Marsh. (Courtesy of Laura Thomas.)

Ida F. Brown Marsh (right) was another child of William R. Brown, sister to Horatio and Lizzie. Ida married Dr. John L. Marsh (left) and was his second wife. Dr. Marsh was a well-respected citizen of Brownsburg. He practiced medicine in the community, which viewed him as a counselor, physician, and friend. John and Ida Brown Marsh are buried in Greenlawn Cemetery. (Courtesy of Laura Thomas.)

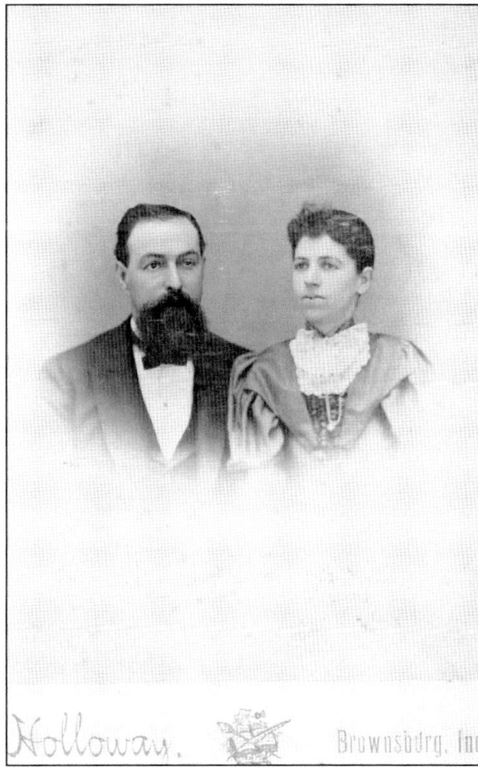

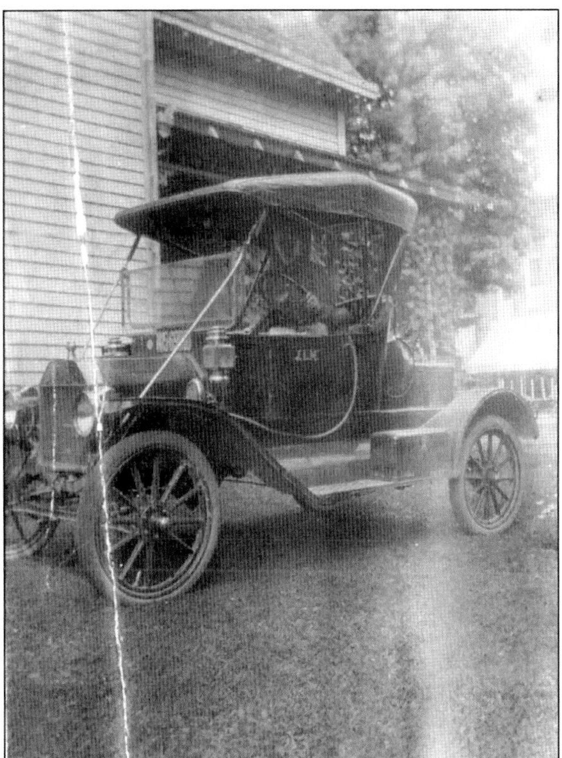

Although the photograph is faded and worn, it is a priceless view of an old motorcar. On the door of the car are the initials J.L.M., for John Leonard Marsh, who established his residency in Brownsburg as the doctor in 1881. Dr. Marsh and Lizzie Brown were brother- and sister-in-law. This is likely the same vehicle that is pictured behind Lizzie on the previous page. (Courtesy of Laura Thomas.)

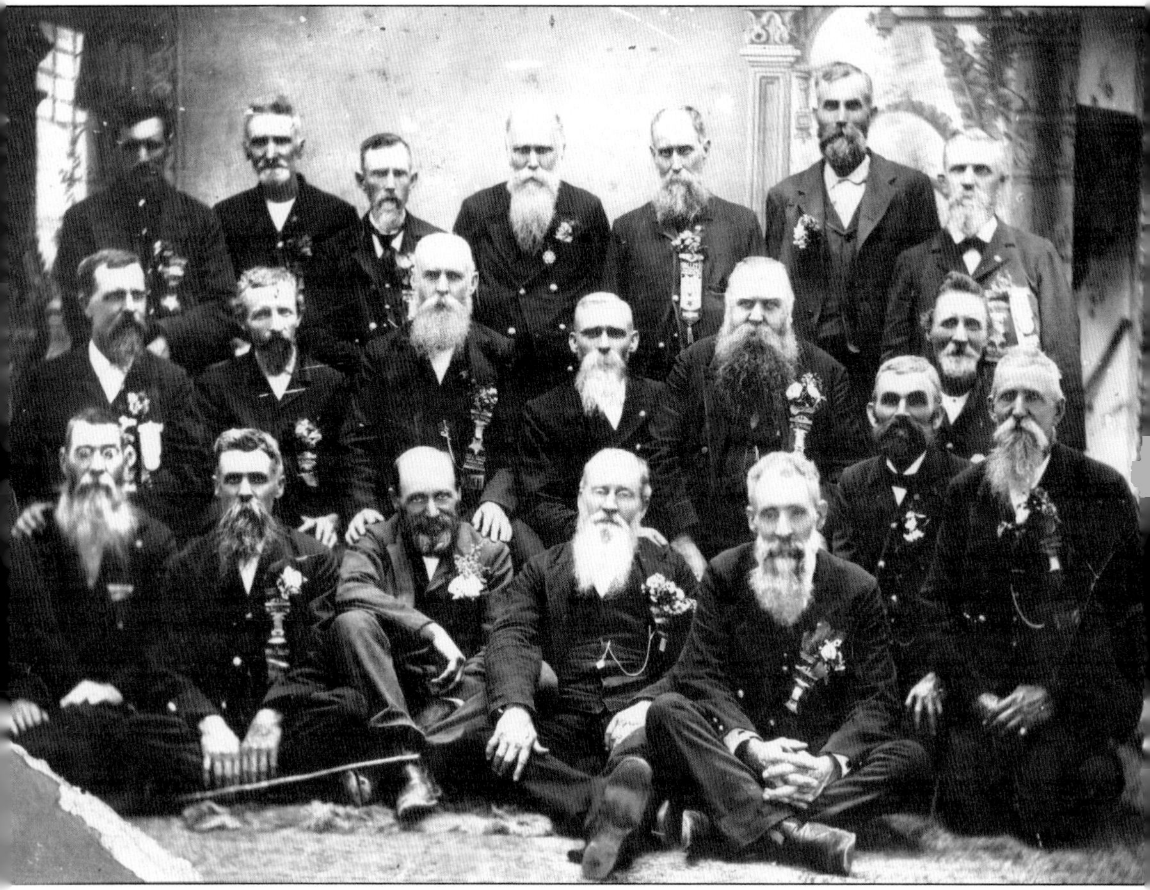

Brownsburg veterans of the Civil War gathered for a group photograph around 1890. The men are, from left to right, (first row) John W. Dewey, Grandison Eaton, Aaron Crouch, W.F. Dinwiddie, Henry Turpin, John Button, and John Ridgeway; (second row) Jim Hollett, Charles Harmon, Preston Tyler, Isaac W. Gray, Charles Tyler, and John A. Arbuckle; (third row) Horace Cook, Bill Gray, Gilbert Wilson, Jim Dobson, Tom Jolly, Oliver James Voorhies, and Bill Ellis. The names of the men were matched with the records of the enlistees from Brownsburg, Hendricks County, Indiana, of Civil War veterans. The majority of the men served with the 79th Indiana, and most were also privates. Jim Hollett, an engineer from Brownsburg, served as the bugler for the 9th Indiana Calvary. Many of the men turn up in later documentation as part of the Grand Army of the Republic, Hollett, Brownsburg Post No. 242, mustered in 1883. The post was named after a fellow soldier in the 79th Indiana, John A. Hollett. The men are wearing "in Memoriam" ribbons on the left chest for John A. Hollett.

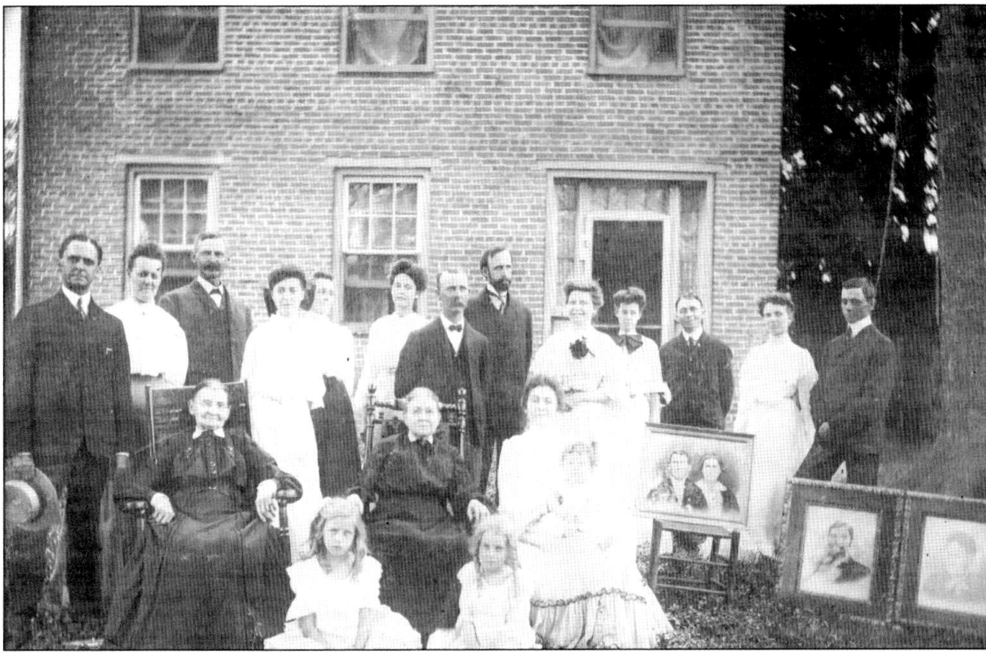

This photograph of Ruah Hopkins, her children, grandchildren, and three great-grandchildren was taken at the old Hopkins home approximately 2.5 miles north of Brownsburg. The date is August 1904. George Andrew Johnson is standing in the center of the photograph with the bow tie and moustache.

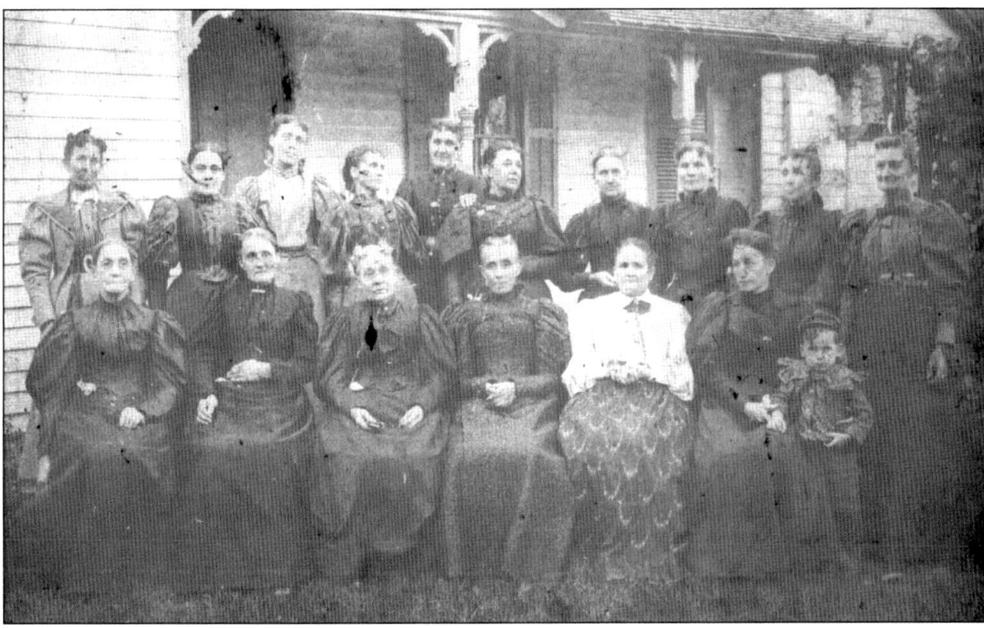

These Brownsburg ladies posing around 1904 are, from left to right, (first row) Elizabeth Hunter, unidentified, Molly Gray, two unidentified women, Florence Webb, and Neal Webb; (second row) Lorinda Roberts, Ollie Miller, unidentified, Fanny Hopkins, Mattie Ridgeway, Jane Hunter Frank, Mrs. Davidson, Mary Hunter, Julia Hunter Hunt, and Jane Dinwiddie. Many of their names will be recognized, as they were pillars of the community.

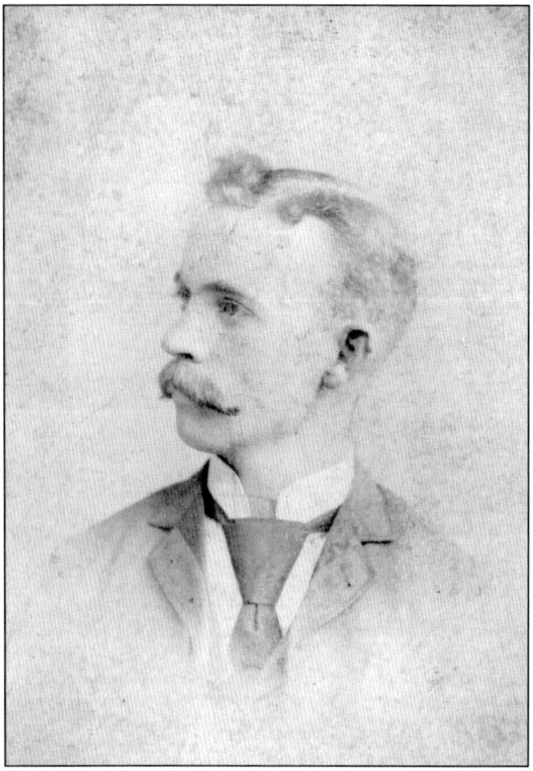

George Andrew Johnson was a great contributor to the community of Brownsburg by serving as a newspaperman, lawyer, and notary. This formal photograph captures the entrepreneurial "Andy," the husband of Nora Belle Hopkins Johnson, around 1900. He died in 1939 at the age of 72.

Larry Wynne, the owner-operator of the Brownsburg Lawn and Garden Center, stands by one of his tractors in this 1965 photograph. Wynne is standing on west Main Street. The Shell gas station and corner of the very recognizable brick Italianate home on the south side of the street are visible in the background.

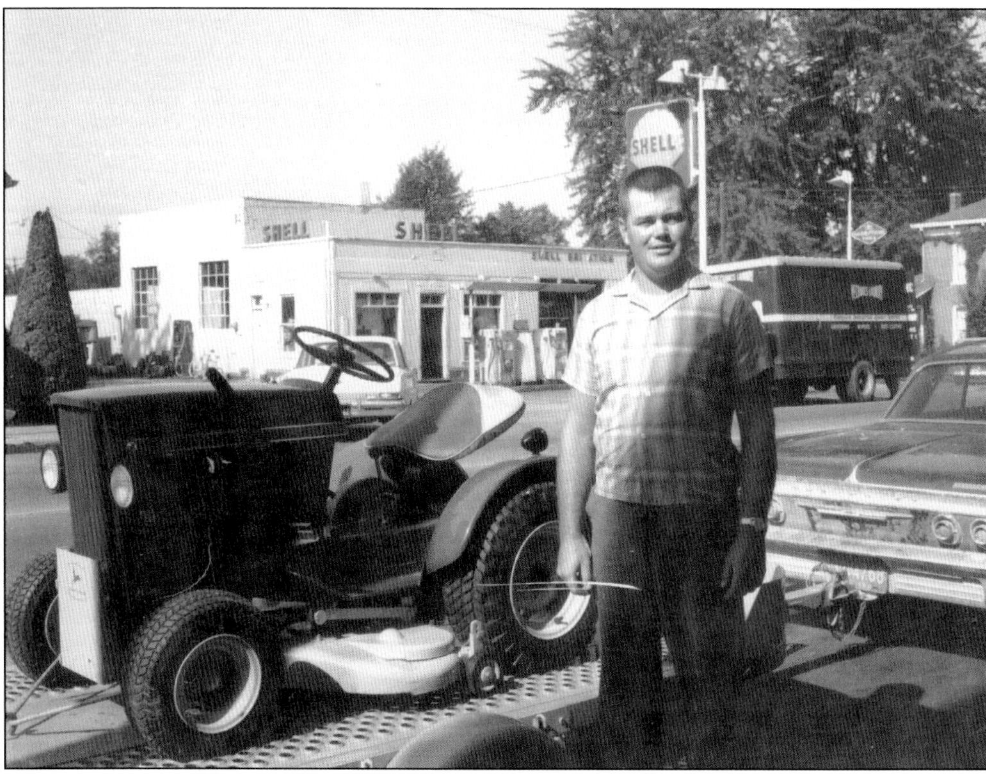

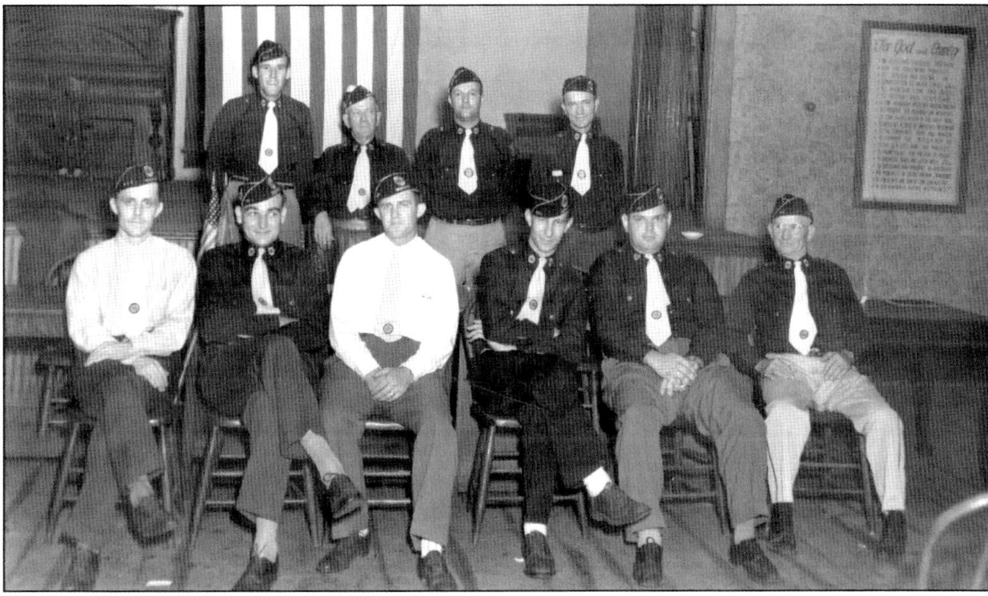

The American Legion is a patriotic veterans' organization devoted to helping communities. The charter for the American Legion Lincoln Post No. 331 in Brownsburg was granted in 1921 with Pat Roach as the first commander. The photograph above captures the men of the legion in front of the large American Flag and the "For God and Country" motto. In the 1948 picture below, the Legion Color Guard leads the band down Main Street heading east for the centennial parade. The Hunter Building can be seen in the center background. Although long gone, the buildings in the foreground comprised the southeast corner of Main and Green Streets. The American Legion Post No. 331 is currently located at 636 East Main Street.

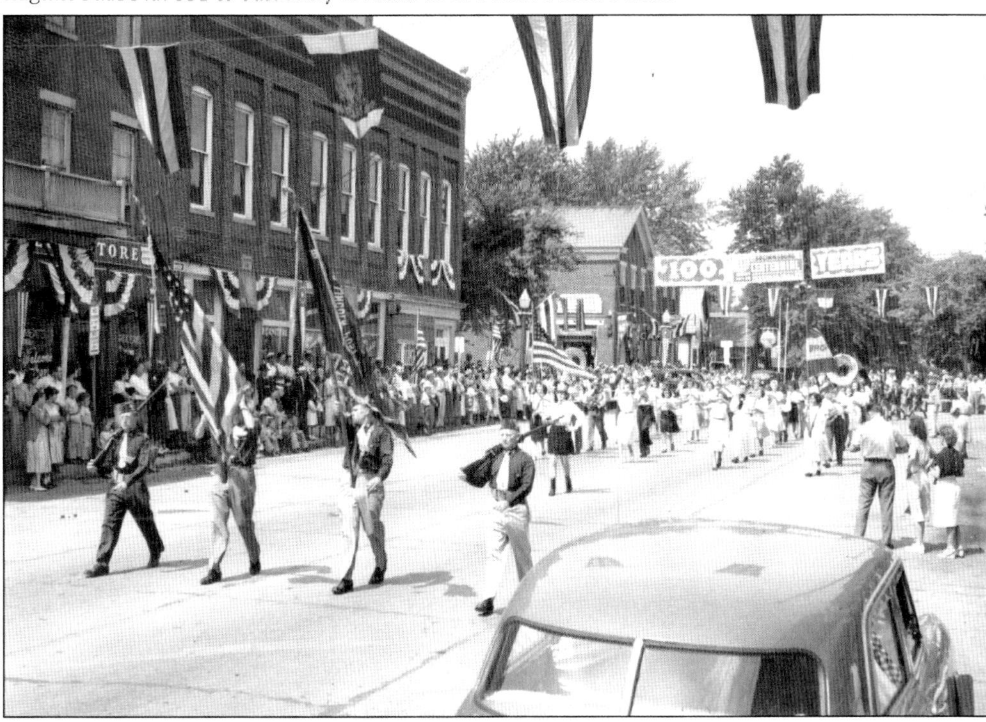

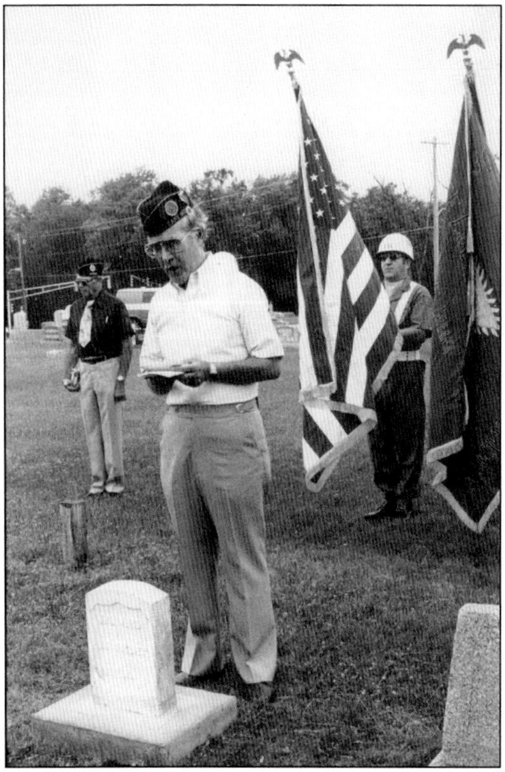

In 1984, the gravestone of Revolutionary War soldier John Ward was moved to Brownsburg Cemetery. Legion chaplain of Post No. 331, Vernon Brown, delivers a message honoring the veteran of the war with England to honor his contribution to the country.

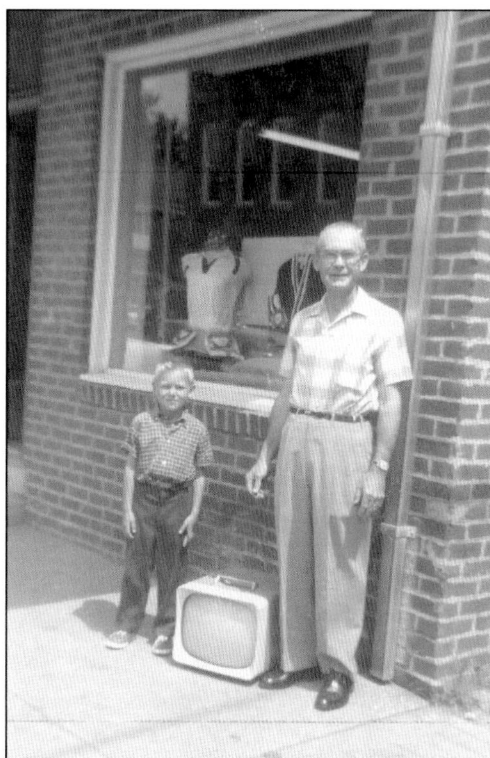

Mike Wilson (right), owner operator of Mike's Men's Wear, stands outside the building at 18 East Main Street. The shop held its formal opening in June 1956 carrying name brand men's clothing. The building, formerly used by W.F. Evans, was remodeled by moving the central stairway to the back and adding flooring and windows.

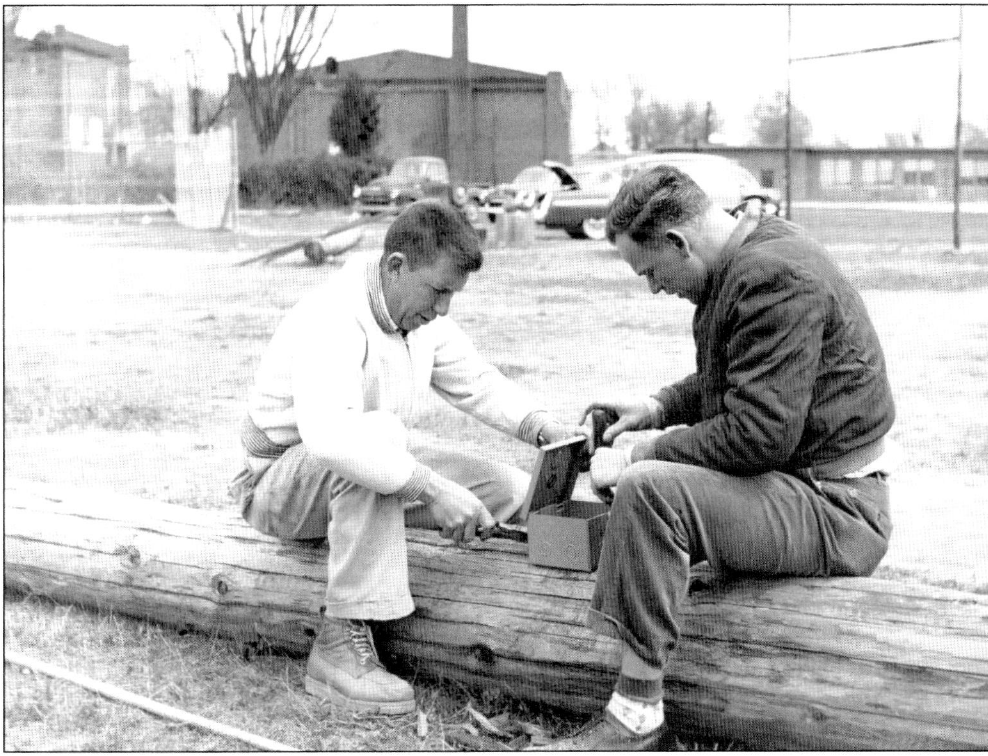

It looks as if the ball field is getting new lights. The two men in the photograph seem to be completing the wiring for lights behind the College Avenue Gymnasium. The photograph was taken from the field behind the three buildings. College Avenue (also known as East Elementary School) can be seen on the right, and the old high school building is seen on the far left.

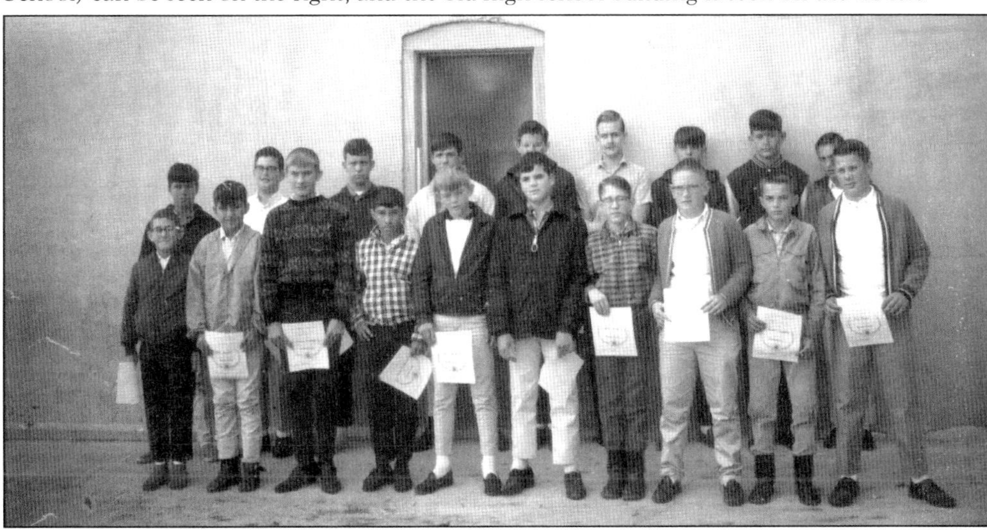

The Brownsburg School patrol boys received awards from the Optimist Club in 1965. The members are, from left to right, (first row) Merle Moore, Bob Burkett, Ronnie Hensley, Gilbert Minton, Jack Shoulders, Mark Schwartzel, Bob Tracey, Bruce Holmes, Robert Carpenter, and Danny Moore; (second row) Gary Catt, ? Schreier, Richard Evans, David Helmer, Dave Downing, Bob Croy, Ray Herring, John Patterson, and Danny Cox.

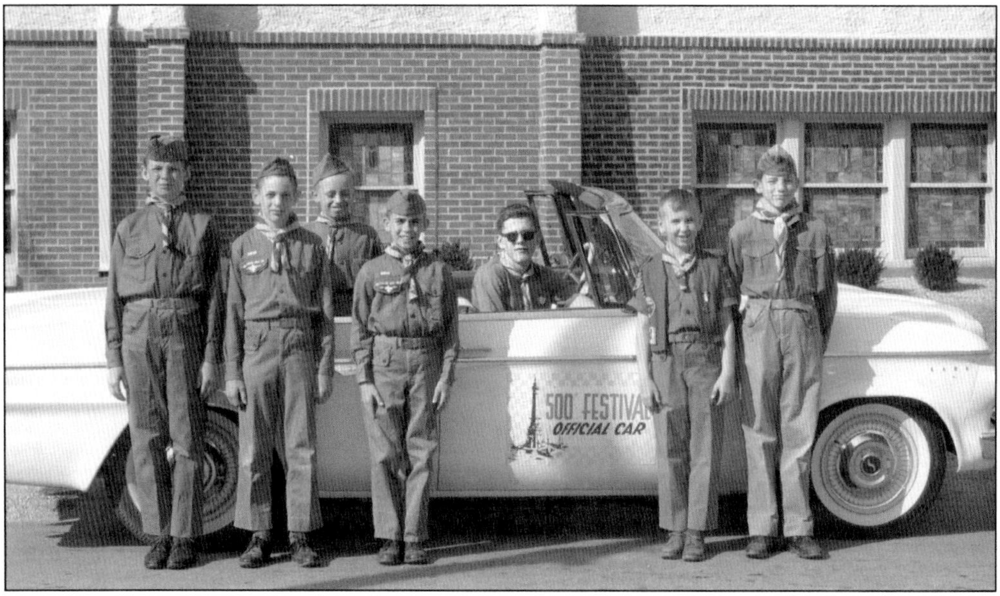

The Studebaker Lark made the rounds as the official pace car of the 1962 Indianapolis 500. Pictured here in 1962, the members of Boy Scout Troop No. 393 pose proudly in front of the car. The distinctive glass windows and exterior of the Brownsburg Christian Church can be seen in the background.

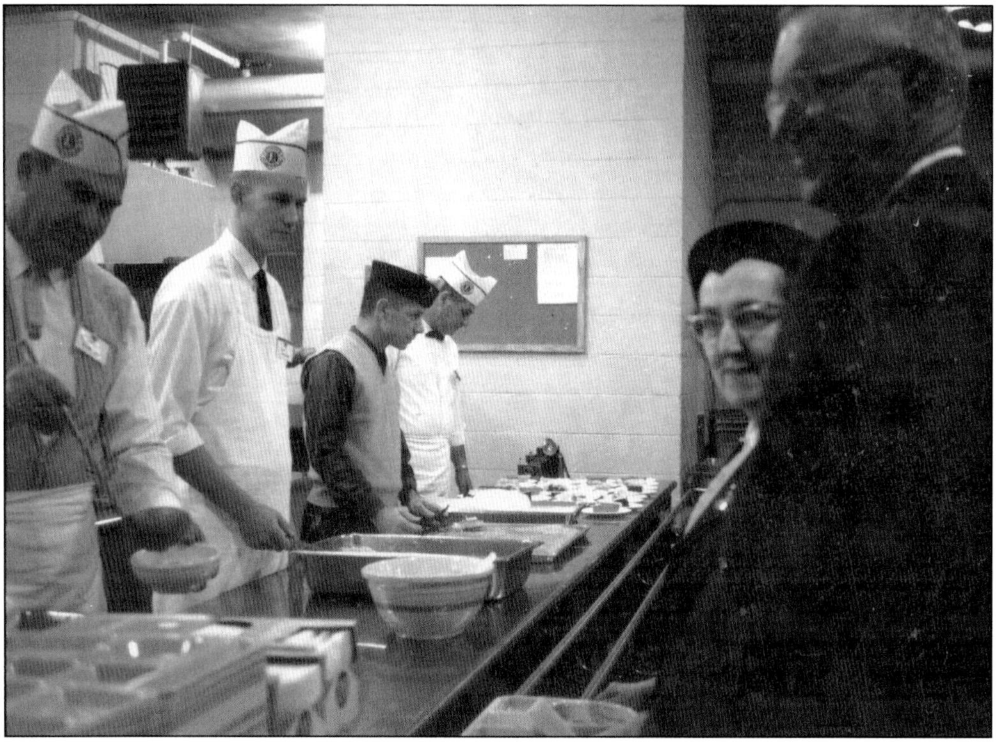

The Lions Club serves guests at a 1964 dinner at the College Avenue School cafeteria. The Brownsburg Lions Club was organized in 1929. The club, as a service-based organization, has spent the years since bettering the community through fundraising projects and service.

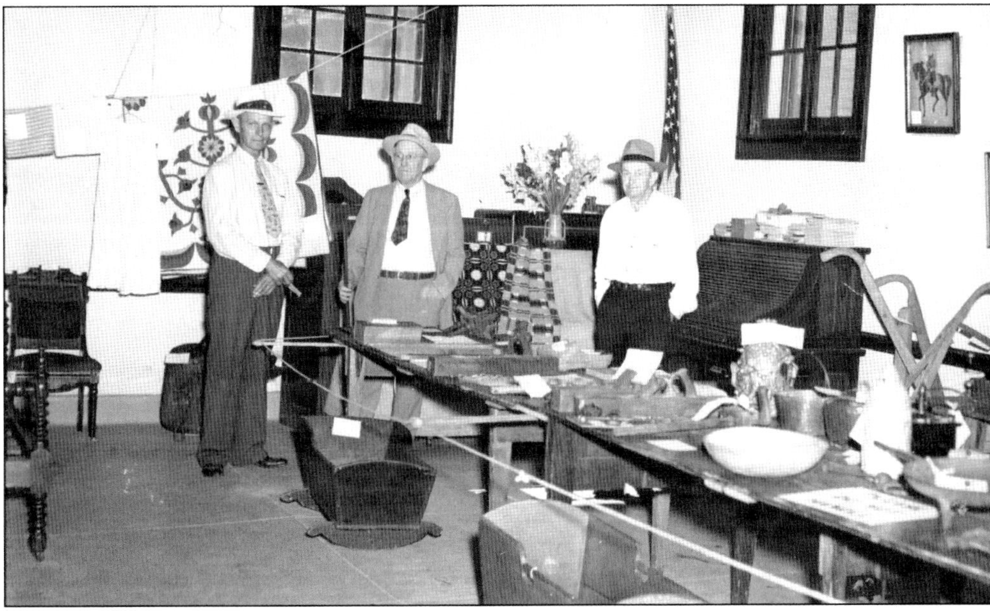

The room in this photograph may be recognizable to many people. These gentlemen are overseeing an antique show in the basement of the Carnegie Library building in 1948. The show was part of a display for the centennial celebration. There appears to be a large black "Town of Brownsburg" safe in the background. It would be incredible to see these items today.

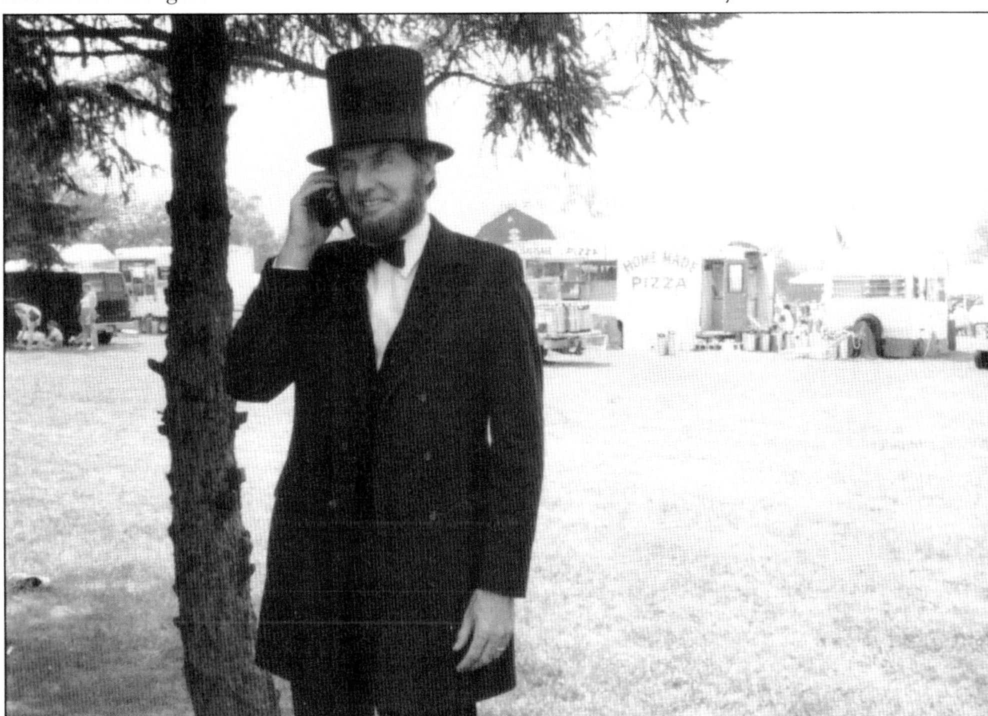

Abraham Lincoln, also known as Wilbur Tague, has lent his celebrity look alike skills to numerous events in the community throughout the years. Yet, Wilbur may be best known as the photographer of special events and class photographs to multiple generations of Brownsburg residents.

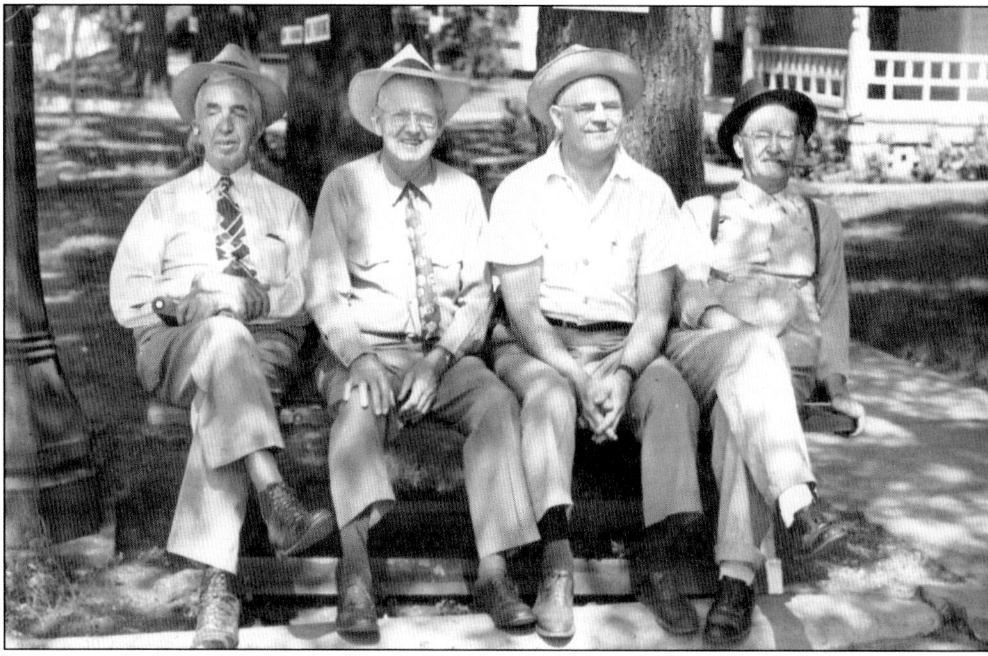

In a photograph labeled "The Liars Bench," these men are pictured relaxing on a bench in 1948. The men are, from left to right, George Reitzel, Russell Hughes, L.P. Anderson, and Harry Bell or Herman Canary (depending on the source). The phrase was a jab at men who liked to tell stories in their free time. All of the men here were gentlemen who contributed to their community.

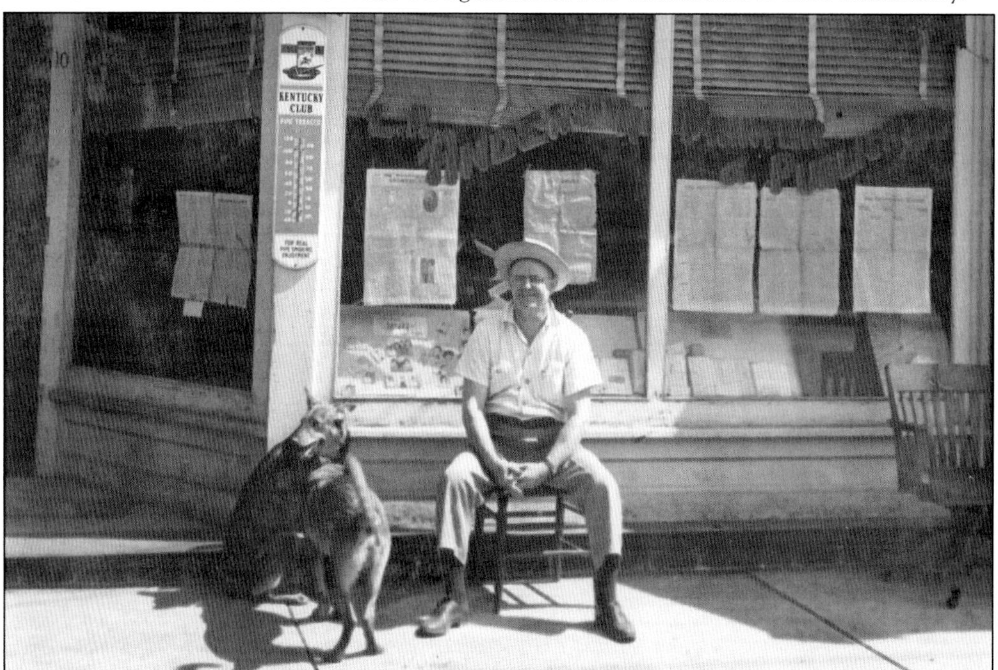

Levi P. Anderson, often referred to as L.P., sits outside of the *Brownsburg Record* office in 1948 with his dogs Karla and Prince. Anderson was the printer and publisher of the *Record*. He purchased the paper from the previous owner, George Guy Campbell.

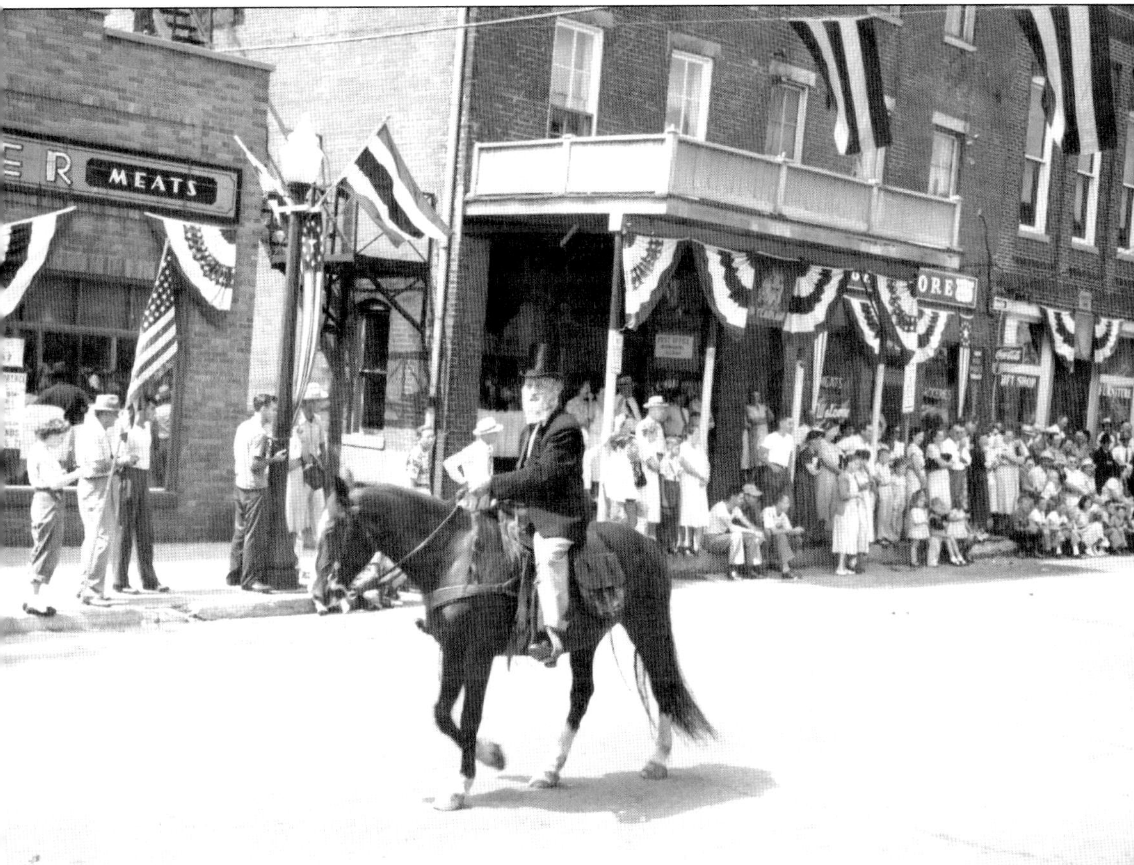

Dr. Arthur N. Scudder portrays the old country doctor in the 1948 centennial parade. Around this time, Scudder, had a medical office at 24 North Grant Street. Dr. Scudder began his practice in Brownsburg in 1933. The community regarded Dr. Scudder as a man of values who would not compromise them. In 1976, to honor Dr. Scudder, the town board declared April 10 as Dr. Scudder Day. Many people consider him a real country doctor in the way he served his community. Residents recalled the doctor making house calls with his black bag at anytime day or night. He cared for people even when they could not afford to pay him. On April 9, the public was invited to a program called *This Is Your Life, Dr. Scudder.* The program and reception were organized by well-wishers to express admiration for a man who cared for an entire community.

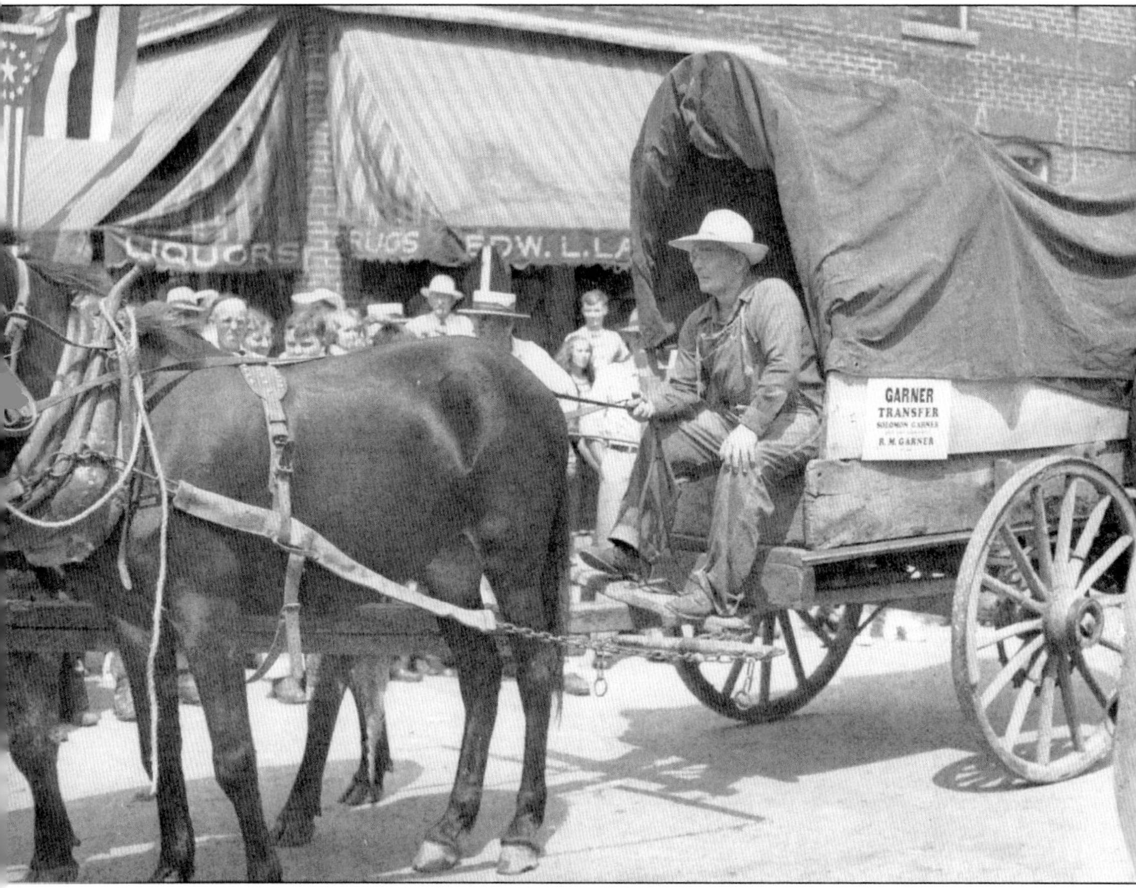

Russell M. Garner drives a wagon past the Lady Pharmacy on the northwest corner of Main and Green Streets in the 1948 centennial parade. Many people knew Russell better by the name "Bundy." Garner came to Brownsburg in 1922 and watched the town grow from small to large. He ran multiple businesses in town, including delivering ice, owning a restaurant, and operating the Garner Trucking Service. He operated the trucking service for 43 years while maintaining up to seven trucks. Even after his retirement, he cared for Eaton Hall and delivered packages from stores to local businesses and residents, among other things. He served on the Brownsburg town board and was president from 1950 to 1954. The Brownsburg Lions Club presented Russell with an award honoring his 43 years with the club as a charter member. He served as their president for a time as well.

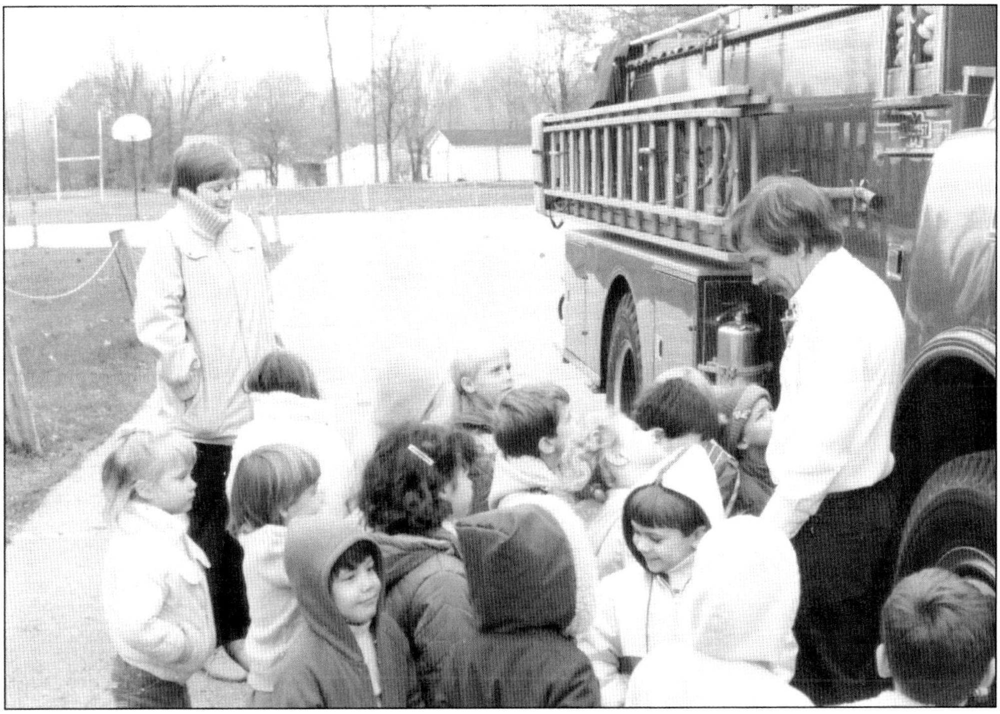

The Brownsburg Fire Territory headquarters can be found at 470 East Northfield Drive. Their mission is to protect citizens by safeguarding lives and property. Educating the public is part of the job as seen here in this 1985 photograph. Here, a group of students from St. Malachy School learn about fire safety in the parking lot.

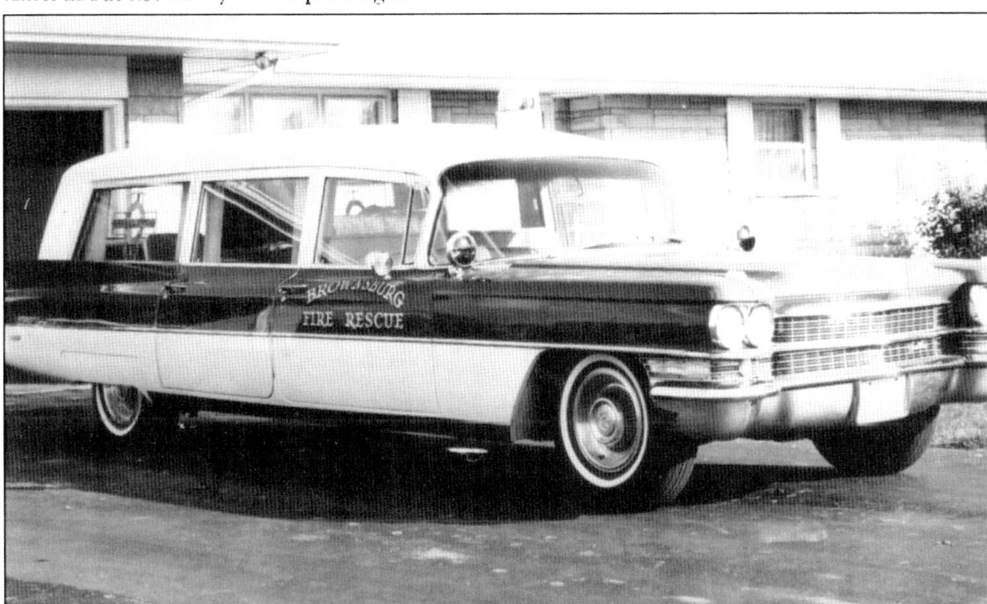

This shiny new ambulance sparkles in the sun in 1965. The Brownsburg Fire Department put its newest piece of equipment into service in November. The department felt that the new ambulance would provide faster service in the event of an emergency.

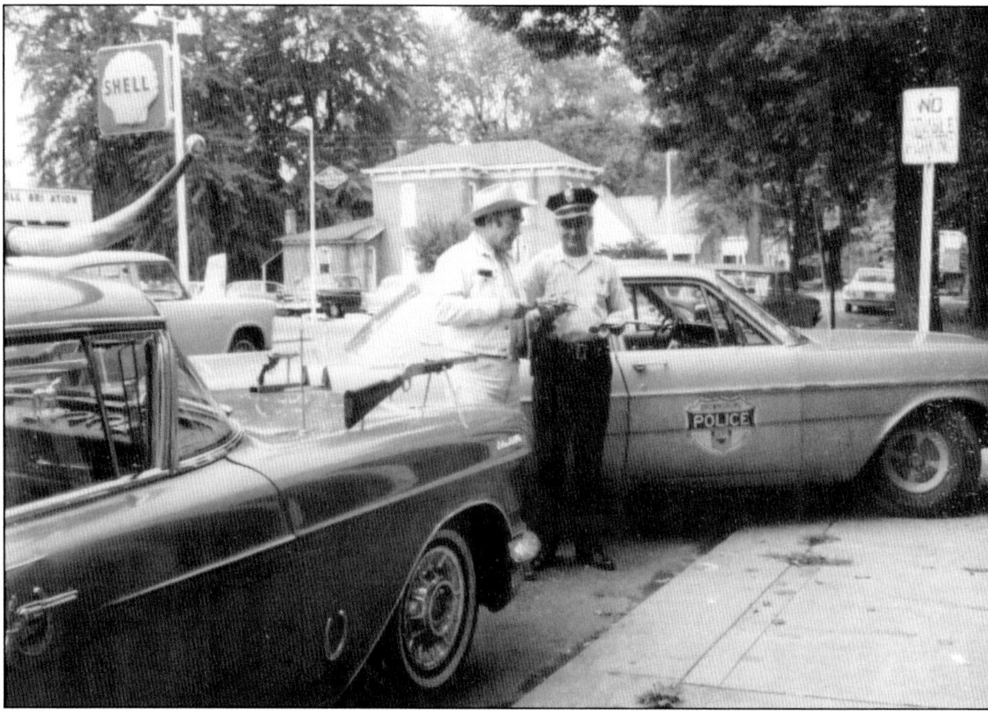

Parked under the "no double parking" sign, the Brownsburg Police officer appears to be examining a handgun belonging to a colorful individual. The gentleman, with steer horns and guns mounted to his car, and the officer are having their discussion on west Main Street in front of the Shell station. The Italianate home can be seen in the background.

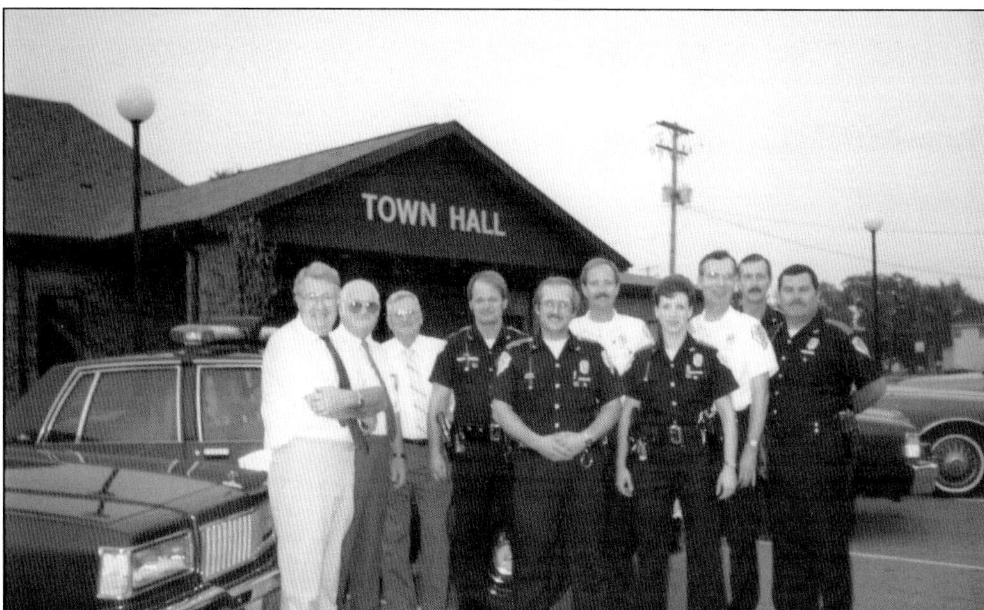

With the town hall in the background, Brownsburg Police officers, commissioners, and others gather for a photograph. The department was preparing to talk to residents for the National Night Out against crime. The department today is located at 31 north Green Street.

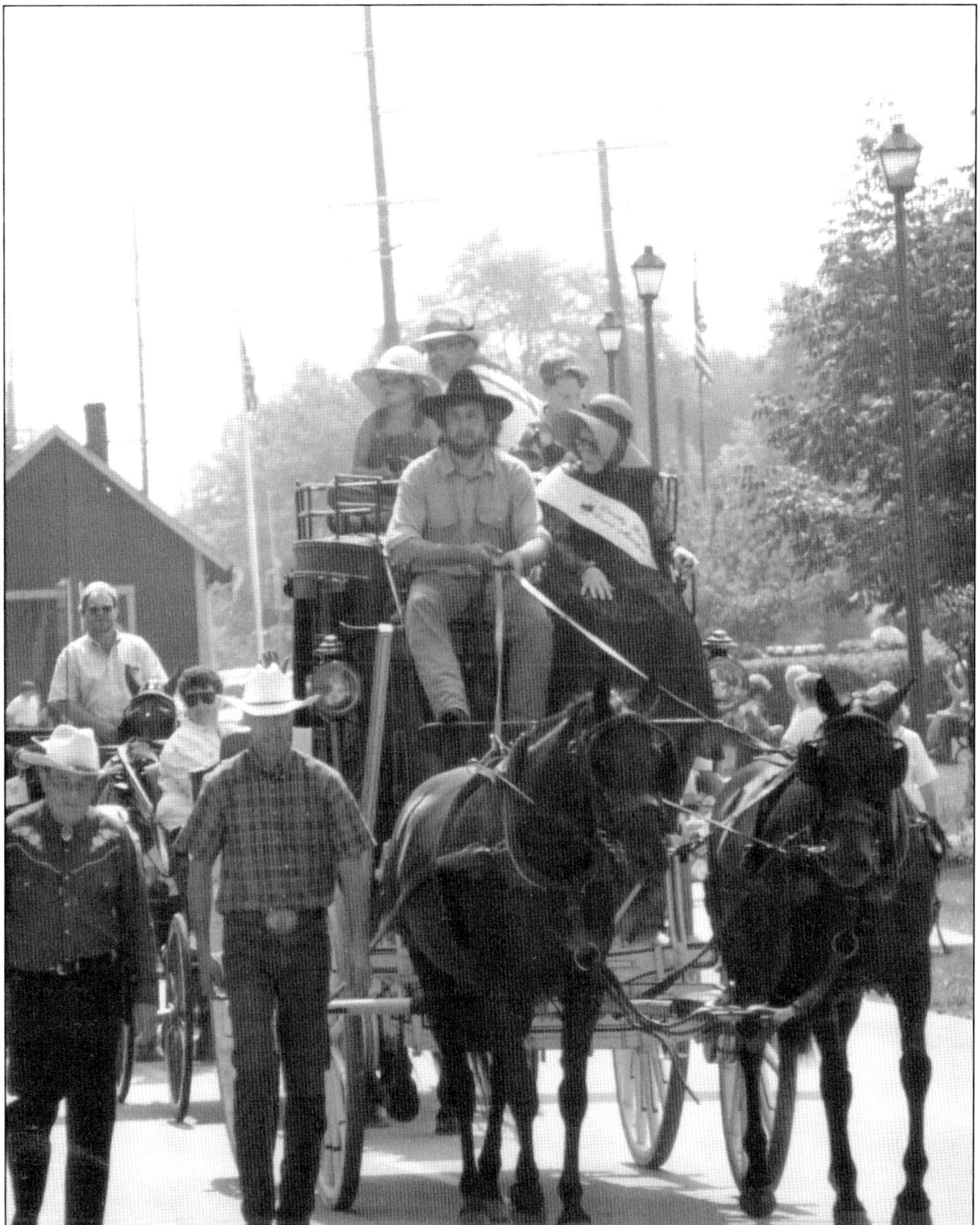

In August 1998, Brownsburg celebrated its sesquicentennial anniversary. In the photograph above, part of the parade makes its way into Arbuckle Acres Park from north Green Street. The wagon is escorting Dorothy Kelley, grand marshal, to the ceremonies and activities in the park. The old interurban depot can be seen in the back left of the photograph. Dorothy was selected as grand marshal due to her longtime residency and family history in Brownsburg. She was a descendant of the Prebster family who settled here for many generations. Dorothy and her husband Dwight and family lived off County Road 550 East, west of town. The road was also known by her family name, Prebster Road. Looking ahead to the future, grand marshal Kelley said she hoped that Brownsburg citizens would "remember their roots, and keep their beliefs and morals."

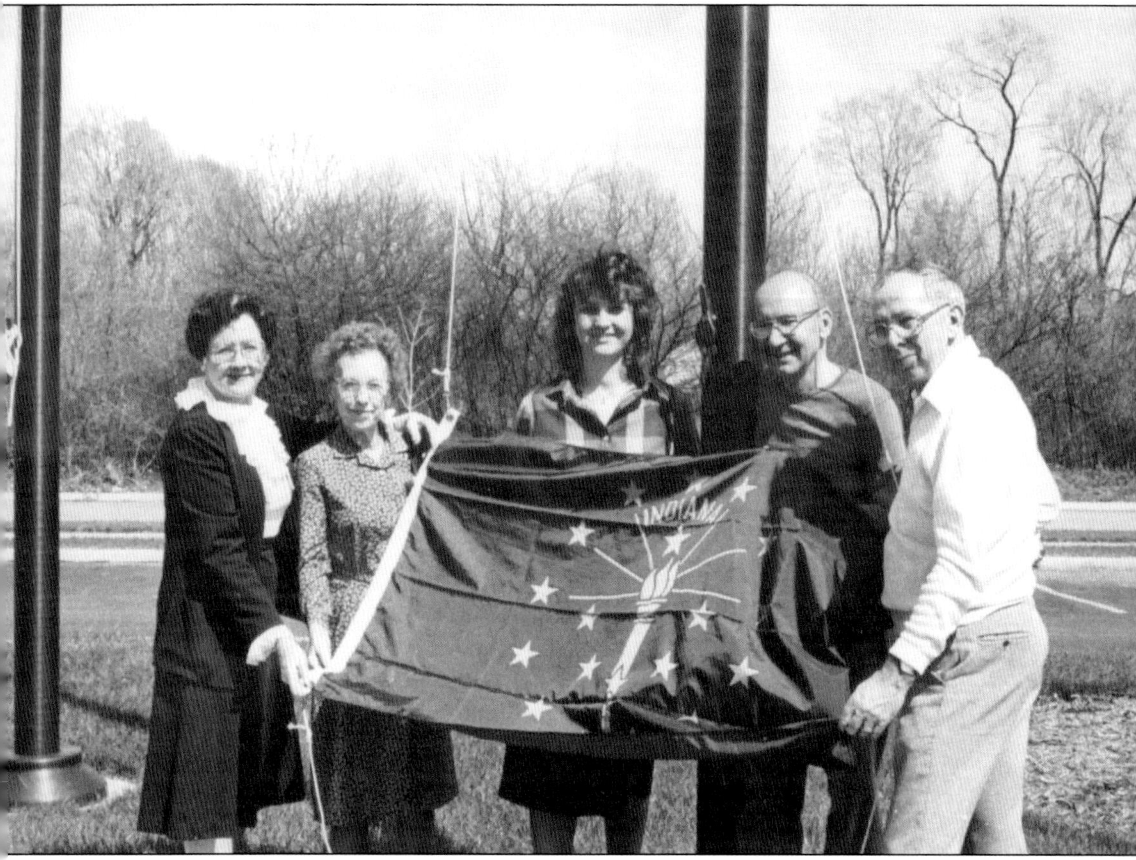

Brownsburg Public Library received a new flag in 1984 to replace the previous one that had been stolen. Fred Roark noticed the missing flag and donated an American flag, ropes, and hardware. Sen. Lillian Parent donated an Indiana state flag. Pictured here are, from left to right, Senator Parent, Jean Sharpe, Wanda Pearson, Henry Moore, and Cecil Sharpe. Locals will likely remember Jean Sharpe, who worked at the Brownsburg Public Library for 27 years before retiring in 1991. They will also undoubtedly remember Wanda Pearson, who served the Brownsburg Public Library for many years in different roles. She arrived at the library in 1981, and at the time of her retirement in 2014 she was serving as the director. Having seen the library through many years of changes and growth, Pearson was understandably chosen to be the 2014 Fourth of July parade grand marshal.

Seven

Other Fun Stuff

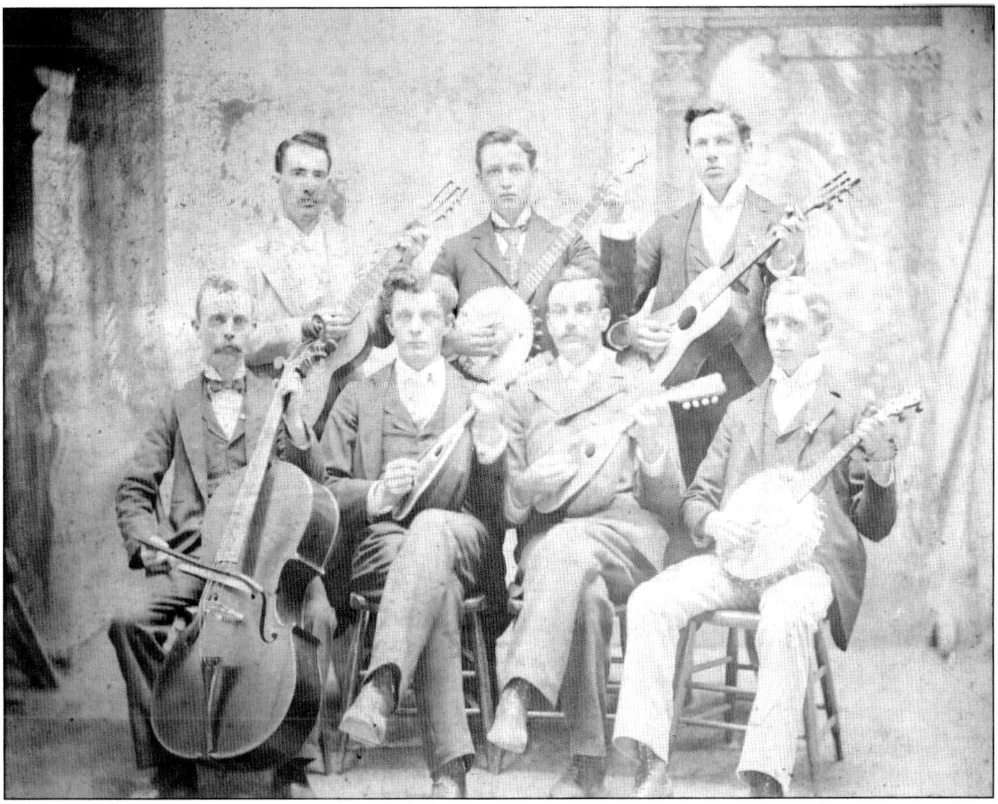

These dashing men form a string septet on their various string instruments. The men are, from left to right, (first row) George Andrew "Andy" Johnson, Claude Hollett, French Trucksess, and Ed Watts; (second row) unidentified, Hal Green, and Harley Ridgeway. The photograph is undated but was likely taken in the early 1900s.

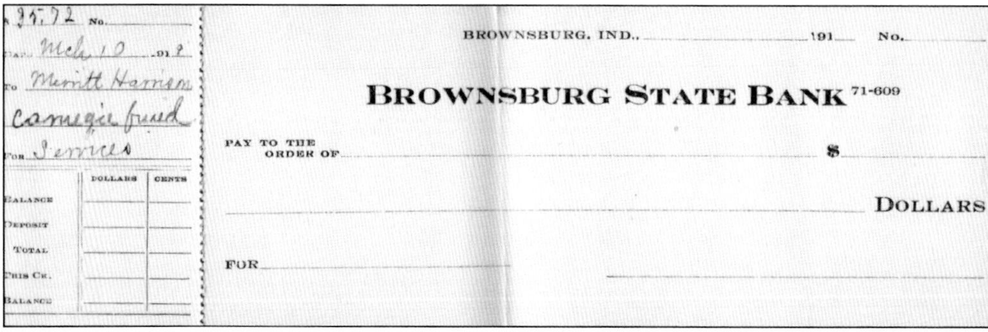

The old checkbook above may not look like much, but it says quite a bit about the past. The checks, drawn on the Brownsburg State Bank, were used by the Brownsburg Library Board to pay fees for the Carnegie Library building. The stub is made out to Merritt Harrison for $35.72 for services on March 10, 1919. The Carnegie Library building was initially contracted to and designed by the first architect on the project, Norman Haden Hill. Hill was reluctantly called away, and so, he very highly recommended Merritt Harrison to the board. Harrison, the architect who saw the Brownsburg Public Library to completion in 1918, is perhaps better known for his work in Indianapolis. He was the architect of the State Fair Coliseum, formerly Pepsi Coliseum, and now Indiana Farmer's Coliseum shown below.

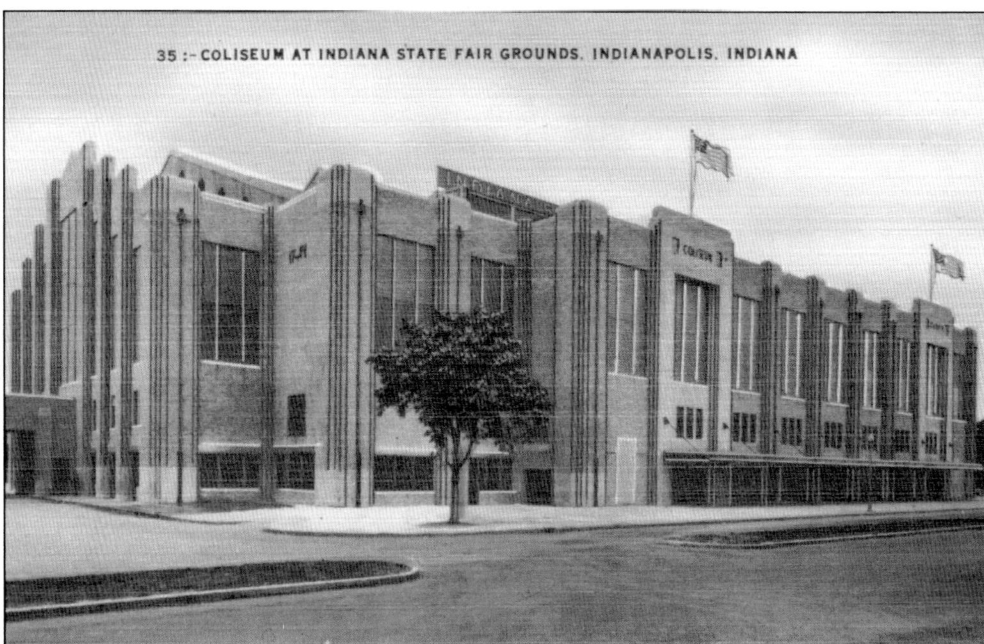

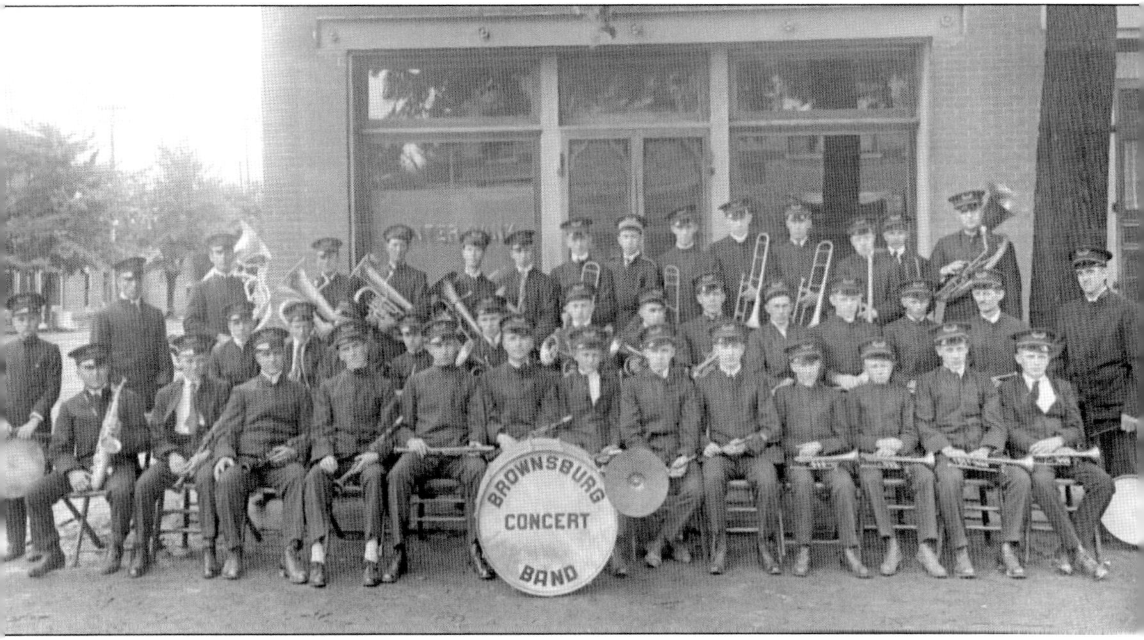

The Brownsburg Concert Band posed for a formal photograph in front of the old Hunter Bank building on the southwest corner of Main and Green Streets. The band is sitting on west Main Street, facing north. Green Street runs south behind them on the left of the picture. The band, manned by volunteers, held weekly practice sessions on the second floor of the Hunter Bank Building. Especially active in the 1920s, they performed around town and in Saturday night concerts sponsored by local store owners. In 1923, the boys played a concert of 10 songs under the directorship of C.L. Hunt. They would perform in the intersection of Green and Main Streets on a bandstand that had been stored until concert time. The street was lined with lights, and the locals enjoyed the evening. Eventually, the state highway department disapproved and the band faded out.

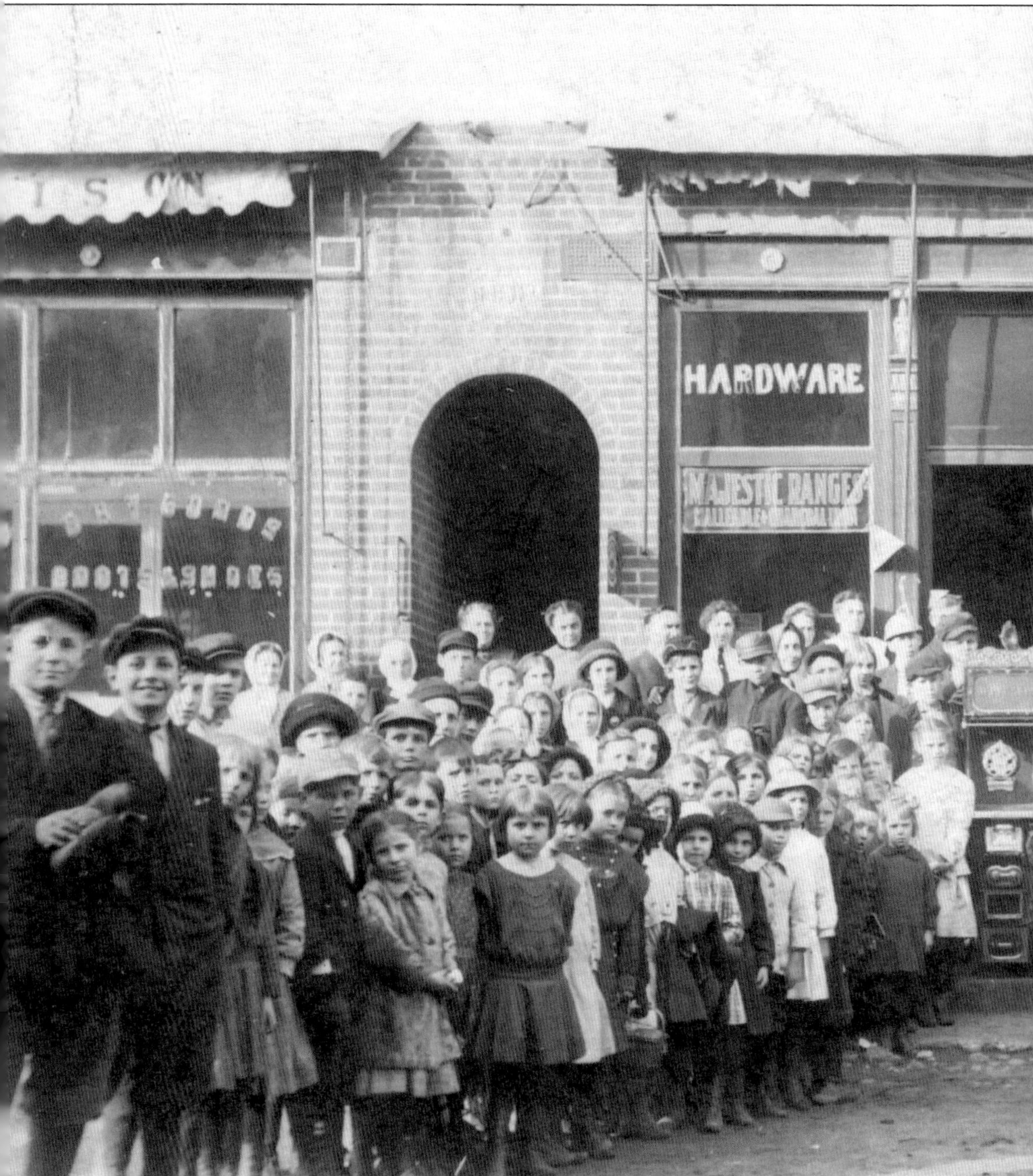

These children, also pictured on the book cover, are captured around 1908 in front of William F. Evans Furniture and Undertaking. As the name on the store implies, Evans was a jack-of-all-trades. He served at one time as the president of the Brownsburg State Bank, sold insurance, and hardware. Additionally, as part of his furniture business, it was Evans who supplied the furniture,

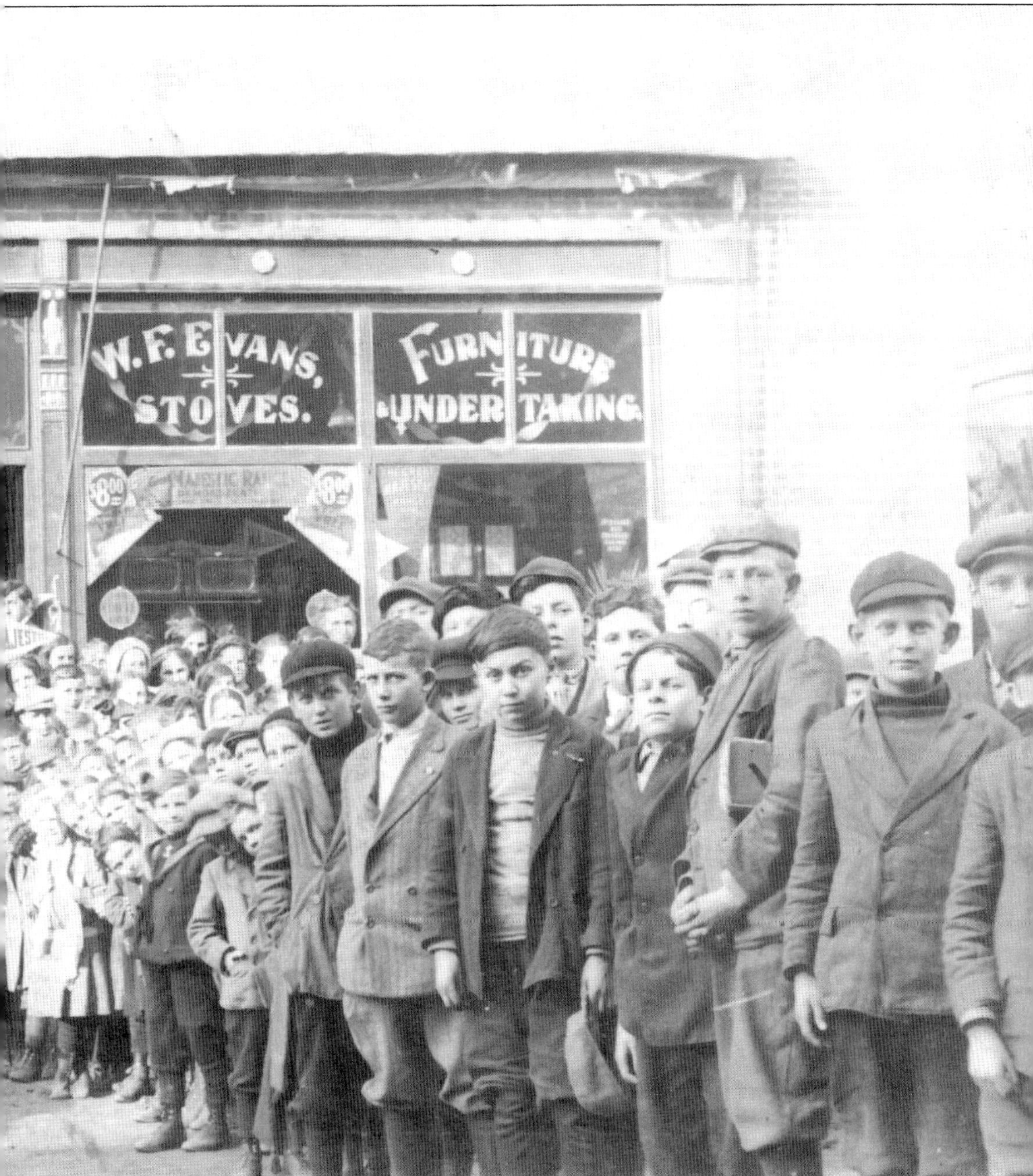

tables, chairs, and desks for the Brownsburg Carnegie Library's opening in 1918. As an undertaker, Evans studied at the Myers School of Embalming located in Indianapolis. Refer to page 2 for additional information about William F. Evans Furniture and Undertaking.

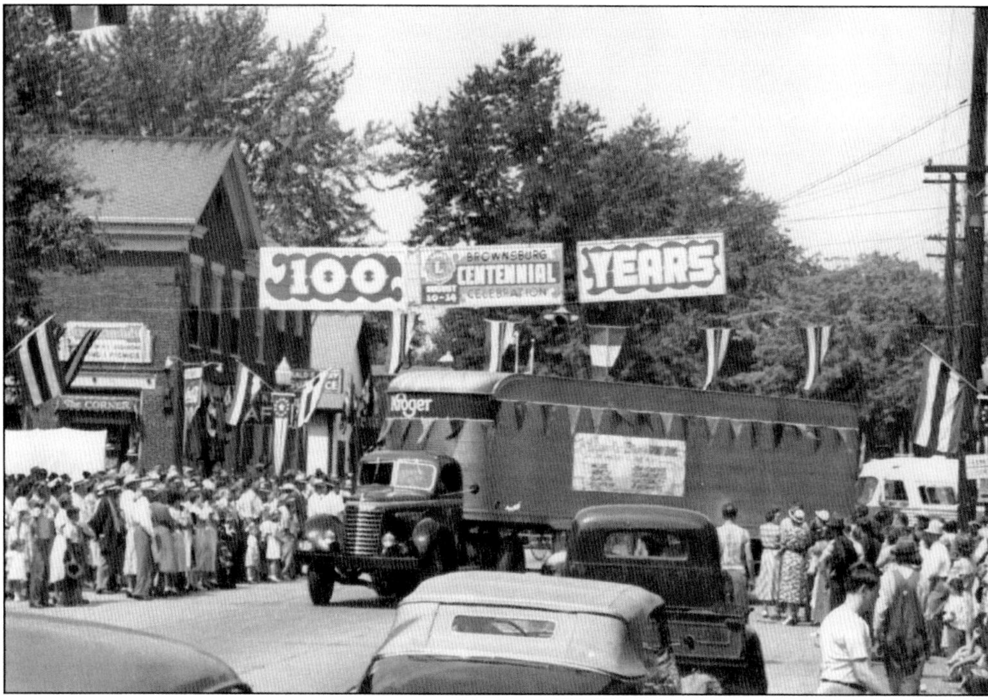

The beauty of the 1948 photograph above lies in the people of Brownsburg that line the streets. Most of the people in the crowd are dressed in their finest dresses and hats. The Hunter Bank building can be seen on the left of the photograph as the Kroger truck makes the turn onto east Main Street.

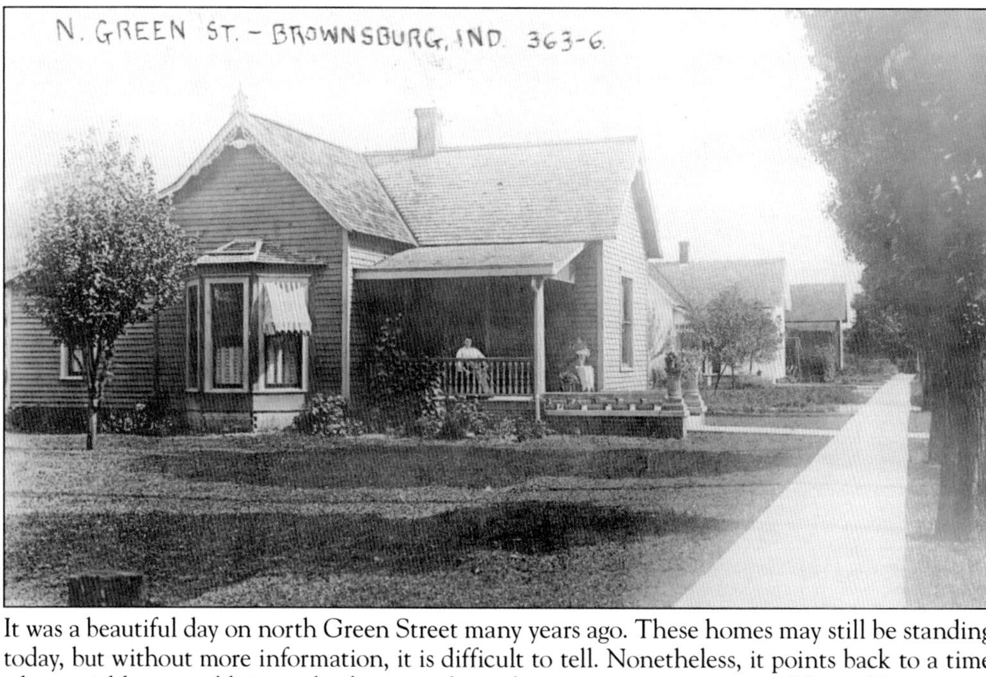

It was a beautiful day on north Green Street many years ago. These homes may still be standing today, but without more information, it is difficult to tell. Nonetheless, it points back to a time when neighbors would sit on the front porch, as this woman is, to greet neighbors. (Courtesy of Roger A. Zimmerman.)

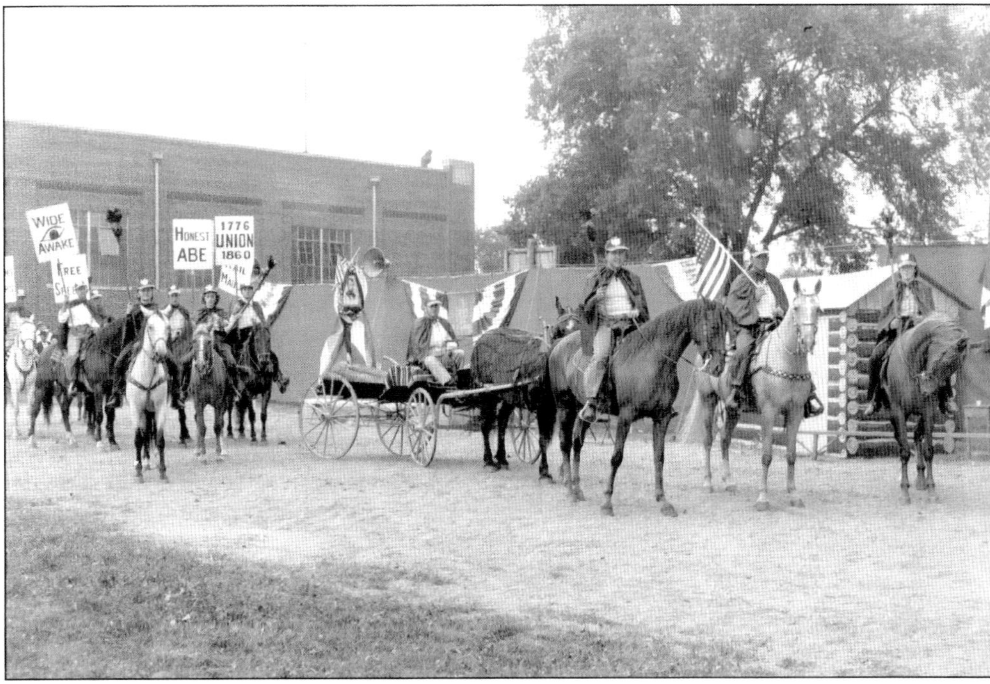

Part of the centennial celebration in 1948 included a pageant on the Brownsburg school grounds on College Avenue. The community building can be seen in the background of the above photograph. In the photograph above, the scene represents the Lincoln campaign of 1860. Various groups such as the Wide Awakes, Rail Maulers, and Lincoln's Rangers celebrated, shouted, and marched in support of his campaign. In the photograph below, the scene depicts the years between World War I and World War II. The years swung from "get rich" and community improvements to a period of economic depression.

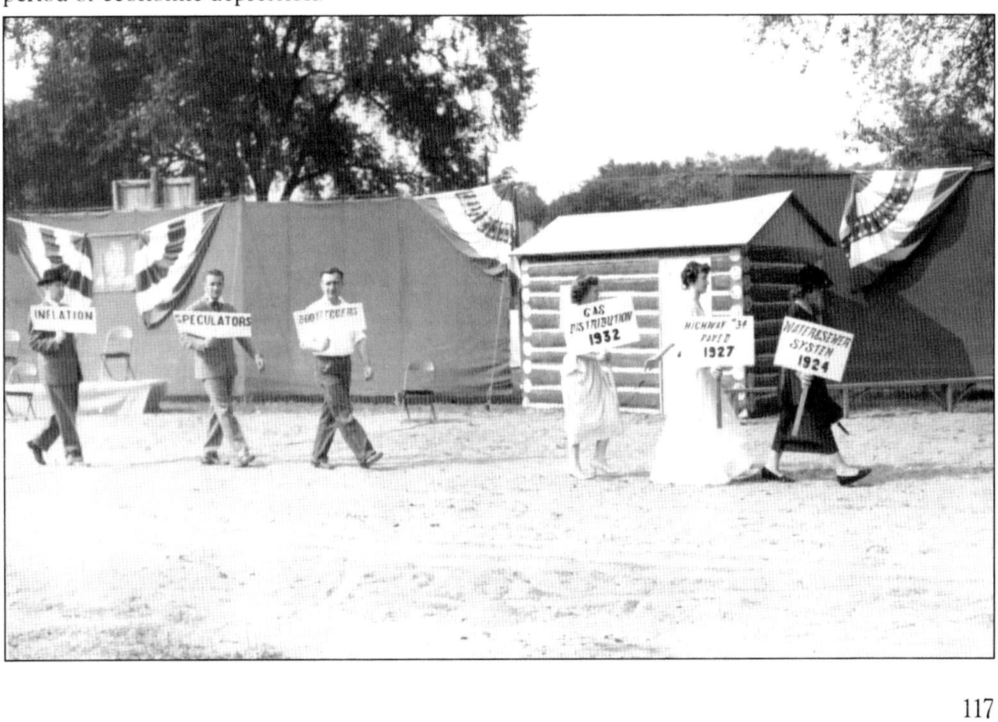

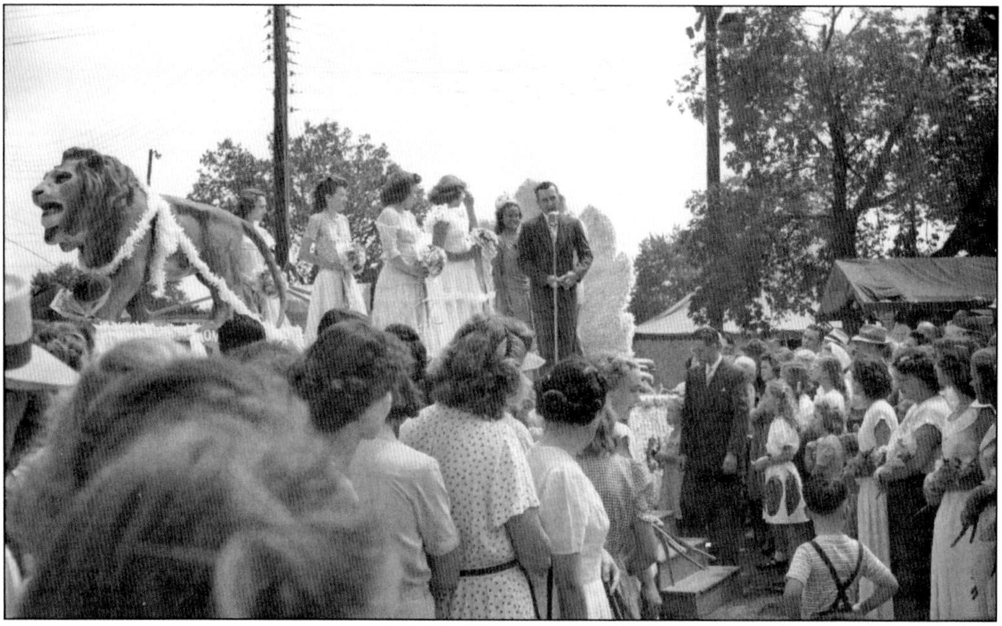

The crowning of the Brownsburg Centennial Pageant queen took place on August 14, 1948. In the photograph above, the ladies are standing on the float next to the decorated Lions Club lion. Standing partially obscured behind the lion are, from left to right, Jane Owens, Rosemary Wiley, Joan Pedigo, Barbara Elkins, Marjorie Cornett, and announcer Floyd Hufford. Adoring community members gather around the women while queen Marjorie Cornett (wearing the centennial crown) and her court enjoy the exciting atmosphere. The celebration of the event also included Coca-Cola, whose apt slogan at the time was "Where There's a Coke, There's Hospitality."

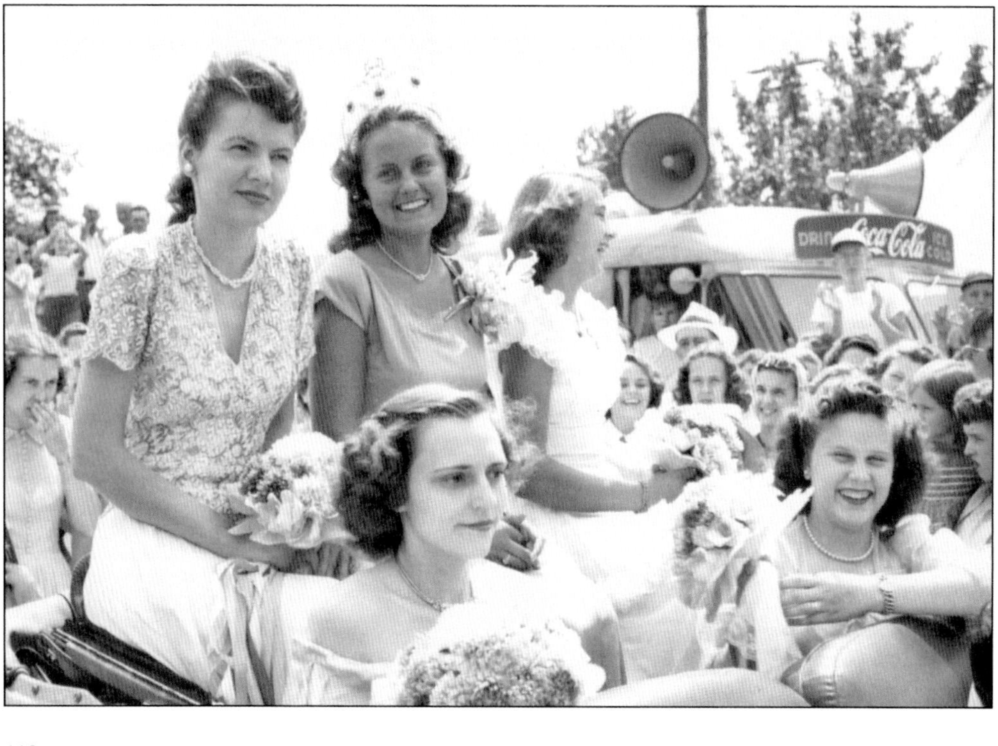

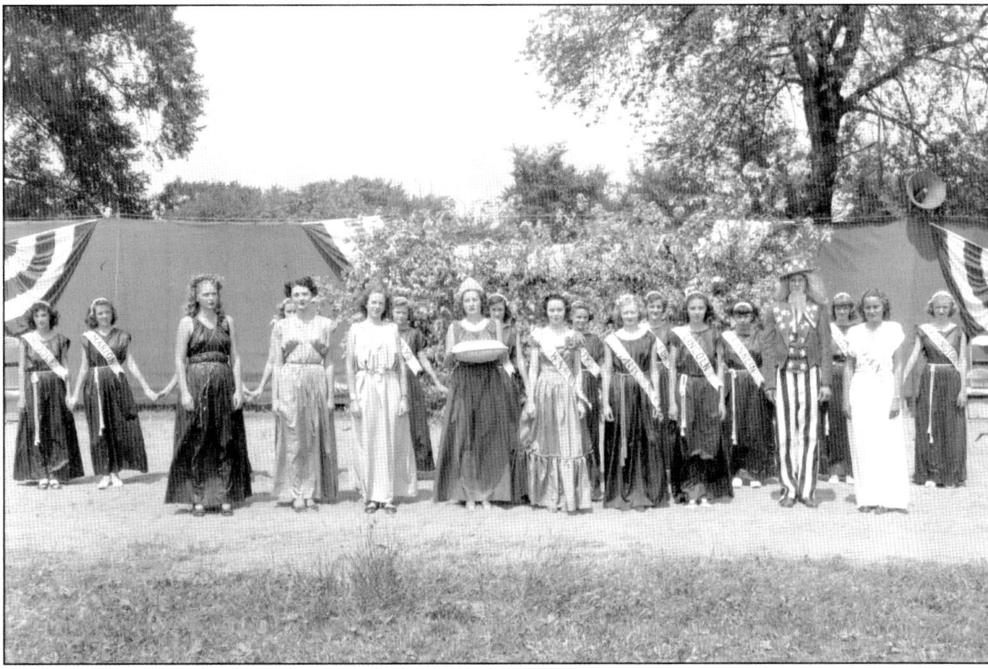

Representing the forward progress of the town, Uncle Sam stands next to Miss Indiana, Miss Hendricks County, Miss Brownsburg, and Miss Lincoln Township. With him and behind are the additional townships of the county. The scene was written for the centennial pageant in 1948.

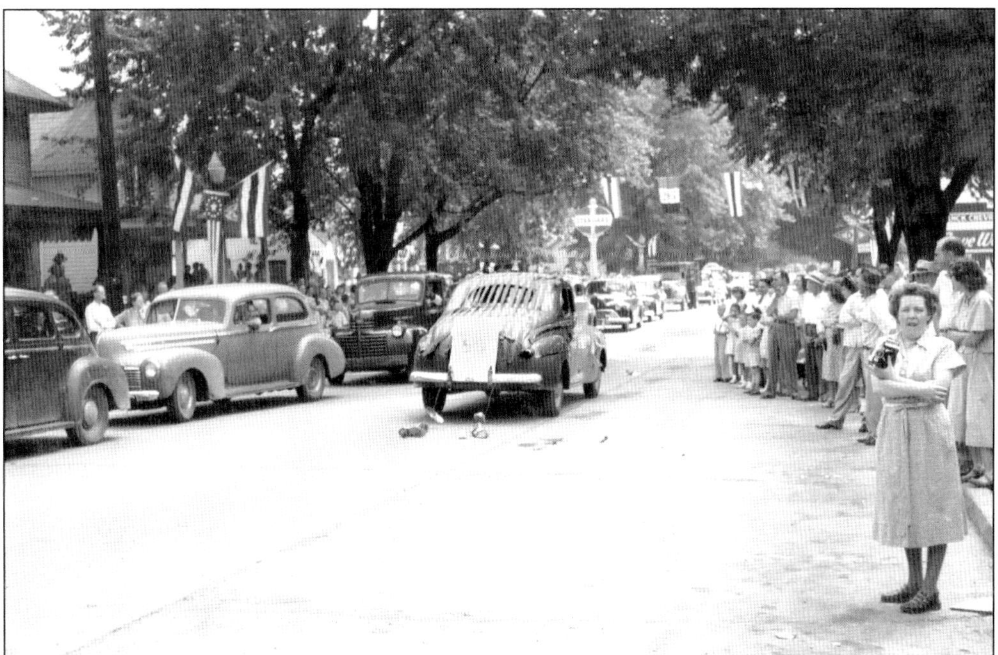

This 1948 view looking east captures a beautiful tree-lined street with Blanck Chevrolet sign on the right and Standard filling station on the left. Cars from the 1940s line the street along the town, and spectators watch the parade events. The car in the center of the photograph is dragging shoes and bears a sign that states, "Just Married 50 Years Ago Today."

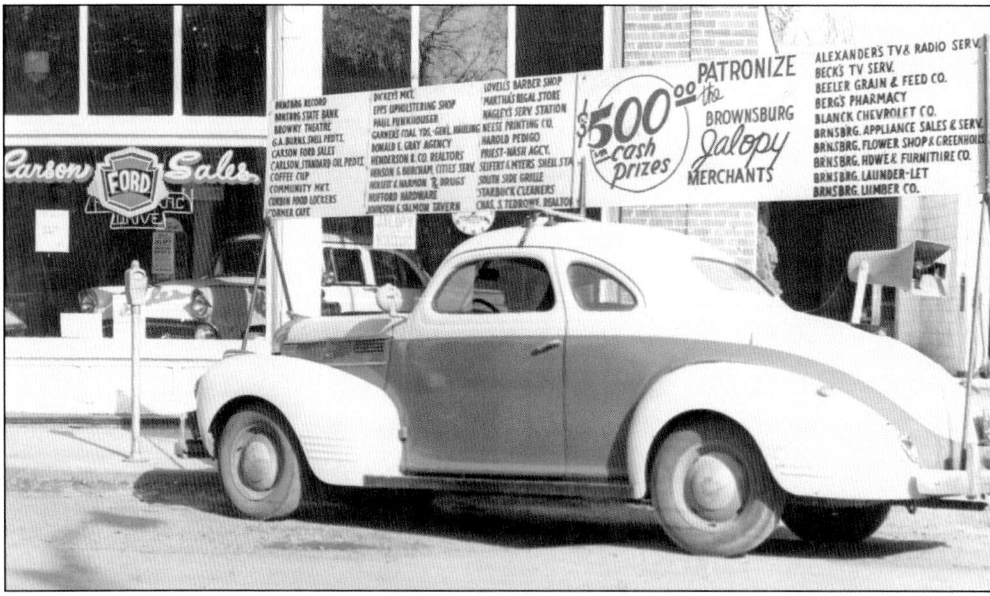

Carson Ford Sales advertises "Jalopy Days" in town. The promotion in 1955 was a joint effort of many Brownsburg town merchants. Patrons could win a jalopy and $500 in merchandise certificates by shopping with Brownsburg merchants who displayed the jalopy sign. A list of merchants at the time can be seen on the sign hanging behind the jalopy.

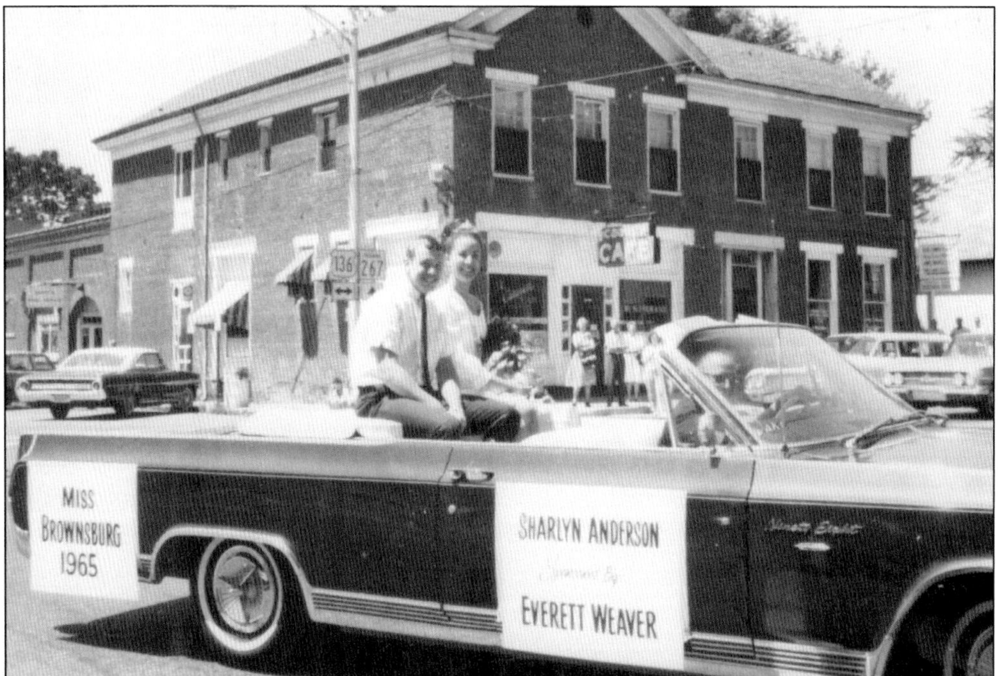

Miss Brownsburg 1965 makes her way around the corner from Main Street to north Green Street. The very recognizable Hunter building is in the background. The Corner Café was located in the corner of the building. On the far left of the photograph is a sign hanging from the Hunter building, for Scott's Shoe Repair, located on south Green Street, owned by Ivan Scott.

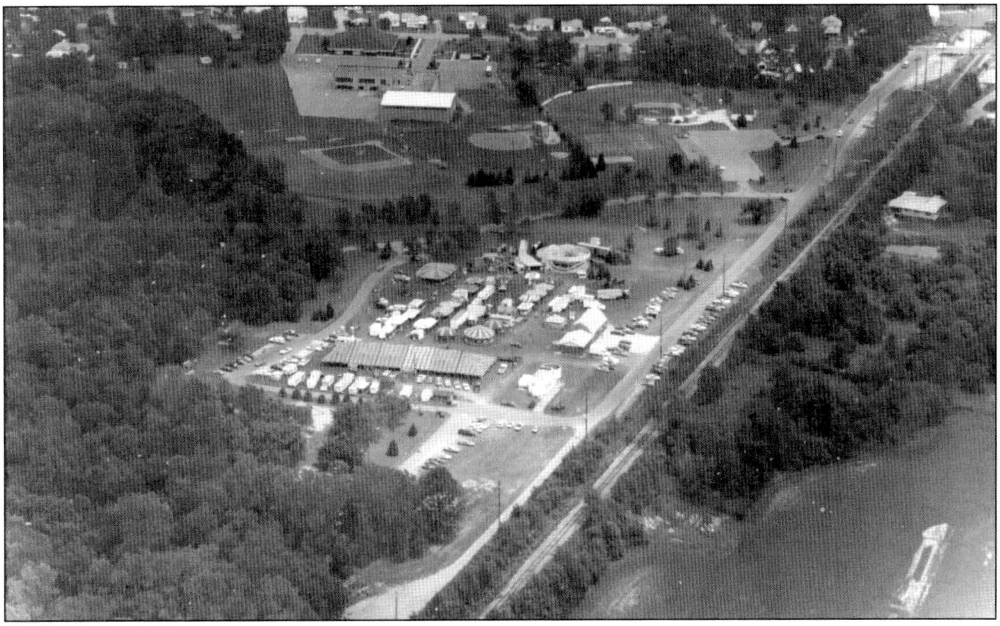

Nestled in a lush pocket in Arbuckle Acres Park is the Lions Club Extravaganza of 1985. The Brownsburg Lions Club, organized in 1929, provides many benefits to the community including eye care programs, youth programs, and scholarships, among contributions to community betterment projects. The Fourth of July Extravaganza is a favorite of the community. The Lions Club meets in the heart of Arbuckle Acres Park at Bundy Lodge.

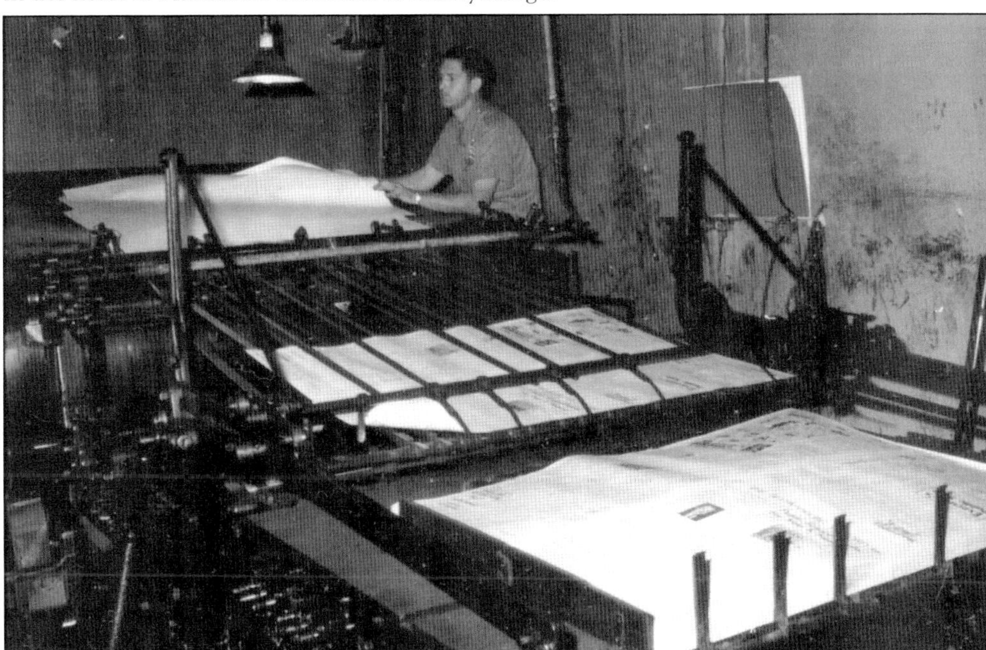

According to the photograph identification, this is the last issue of the *Brownsburg Record* being run on "old style." The name of the newspaper can be seen on the bottom-right corner. The *Brownsburg Record* was born from its predecessor the *Modern Era* in the 1880s.

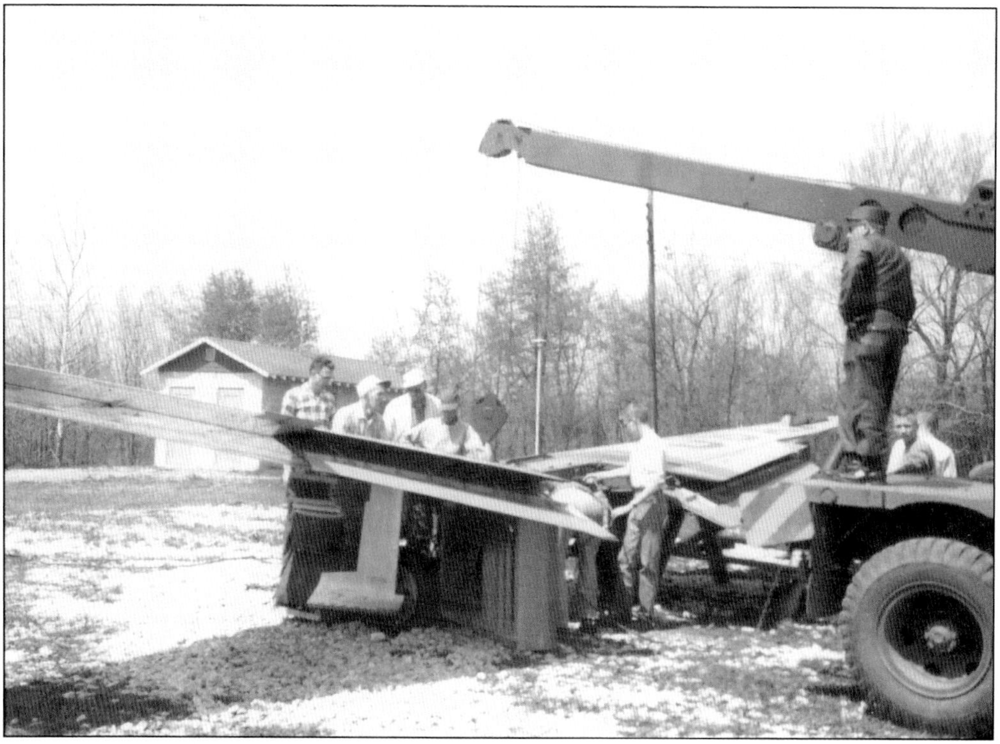

In 1963, some fun flew to Arbuckle Acres Park for local children. Many will remember the F94C jet plane that arrived in pieces in the park and was assembled for youth to play upon. In this photograph, the wing and tail are shown. The plane remained until parents became concerned about the safety, and in July 1975 the town board voted to destroy it.

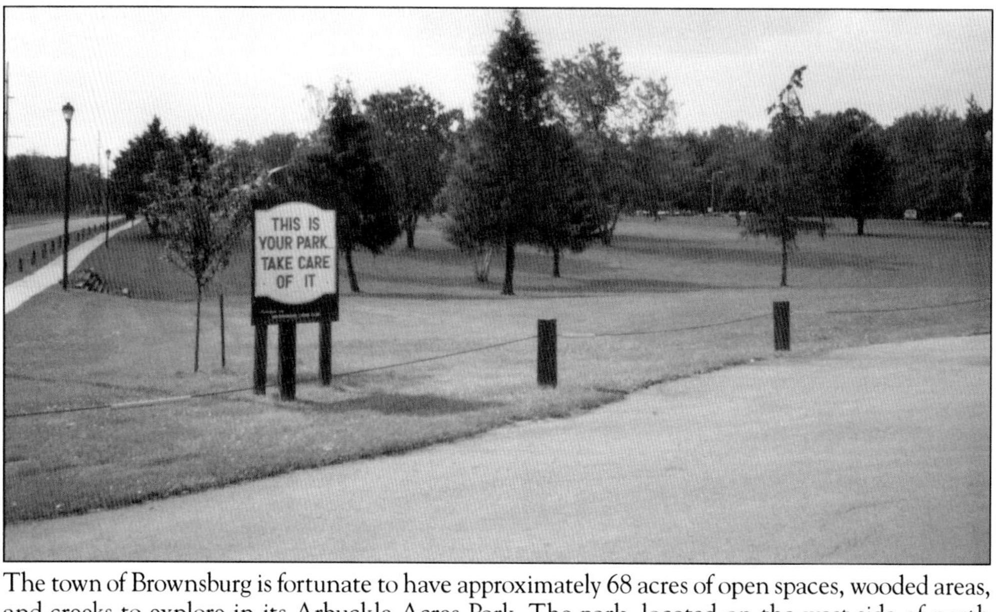

The town of Brownsburg is fortunate to have approximately 68 acres of open spaces, wooded areas, and creeks to explore in its Arbuckle Acres Park. The park, located on the west side of north Green Street, was originally a purchase of 38 acres in 1958, from a descendant of the Arbuckle family. The park was named in honor of the family.

This monument, located in the Brownsburg Cemetery, was built to recognize all of the men and women who served their country. In the distance looking west, the white cross of the St. Malachy Cemetery can be seen in the background.

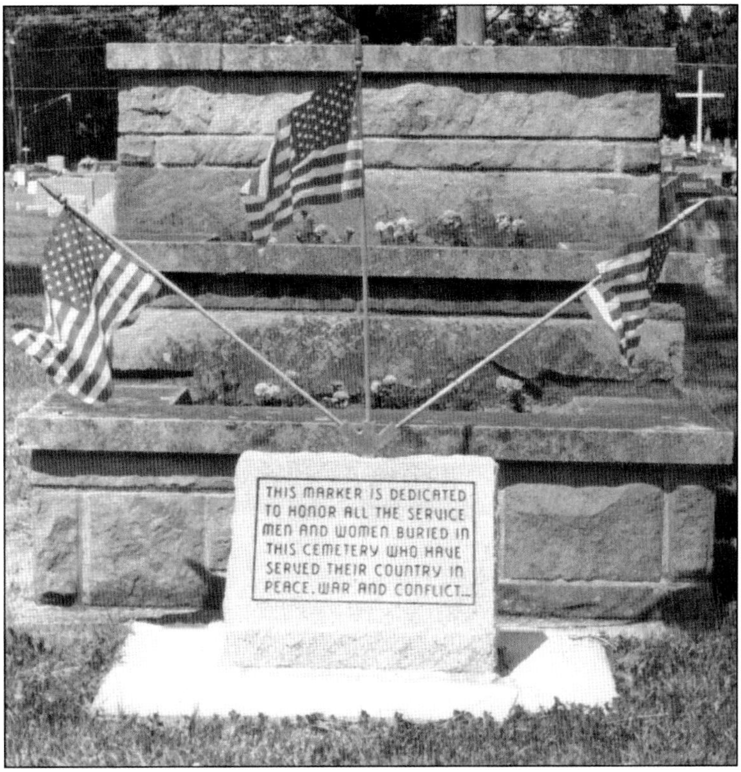

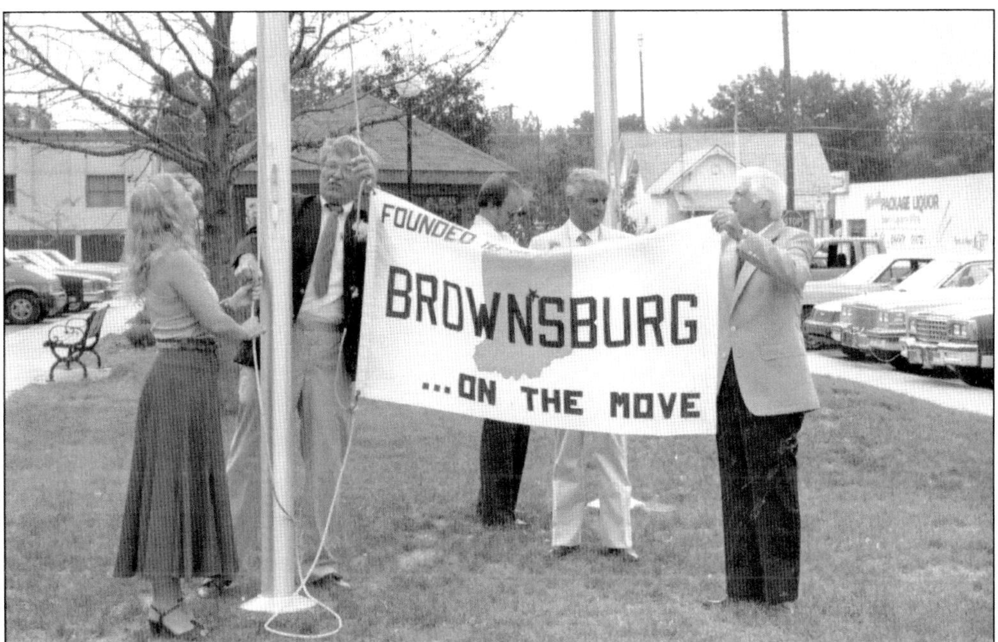

In 1988, the new Brownsburg Town flag was revealed. Identified on the photograph and raising the flag are, from left to right, S. Hall, flag designer; Paul Kilian; Ed Schrier; and Don Gray. Police officer George Ingle is in the background. The group is hoisting the flag on the pole behind the town gazebo on the north side of Main Street.

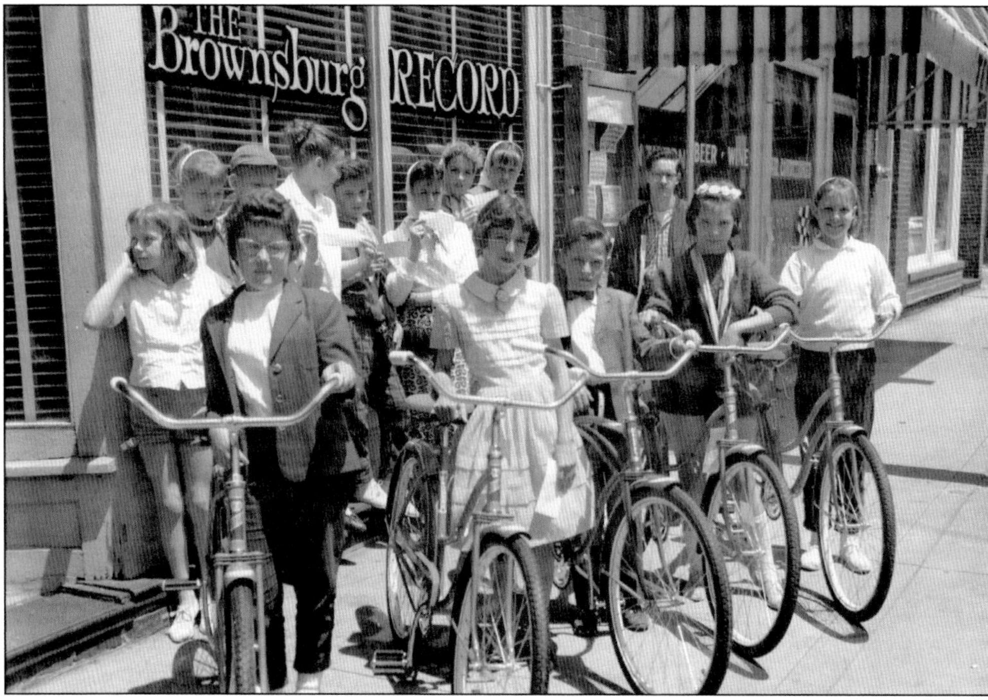

These industrious young people have good reason to celebrate. The children here participated in the *Brownsburg Record*'s subscription drive in 1961. Standing in front of the *Record* office, the top sellers received a bicycle for their sales efforts. The children are holding checks that they received for the $1 per subscription sold.

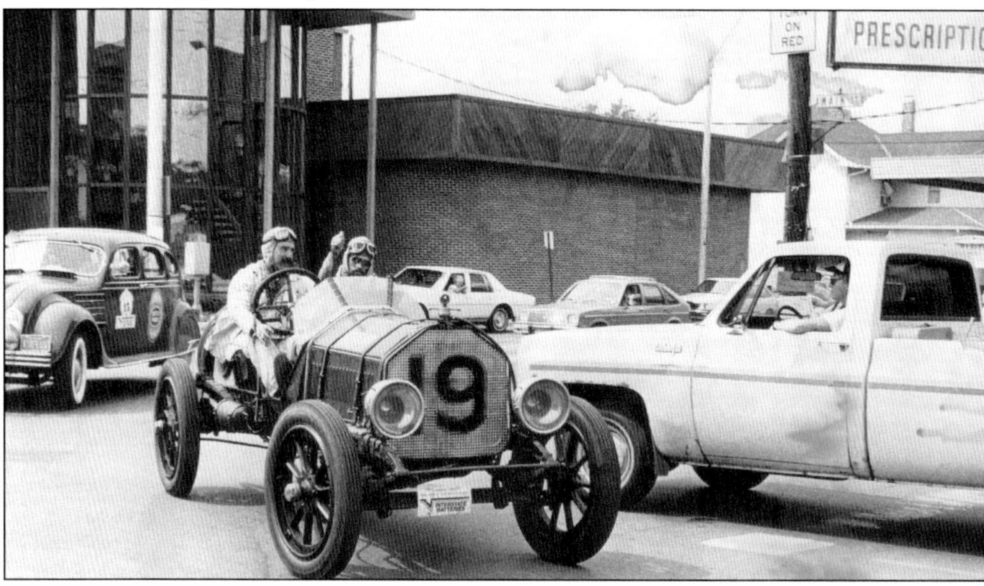

This vintage Indianapolis race car is rounding the corner from Green Street to head east on Main Street in 1984. The car is marked with Interstate Batteries, "The Great American Race," on the license plate. The race finished at Raceway Park after leaving California for the 3,000-mile trip. Harley's Restaurant, which had occupied the northwest corner of Main and Green Streets, can be seen in the background of the photograph.

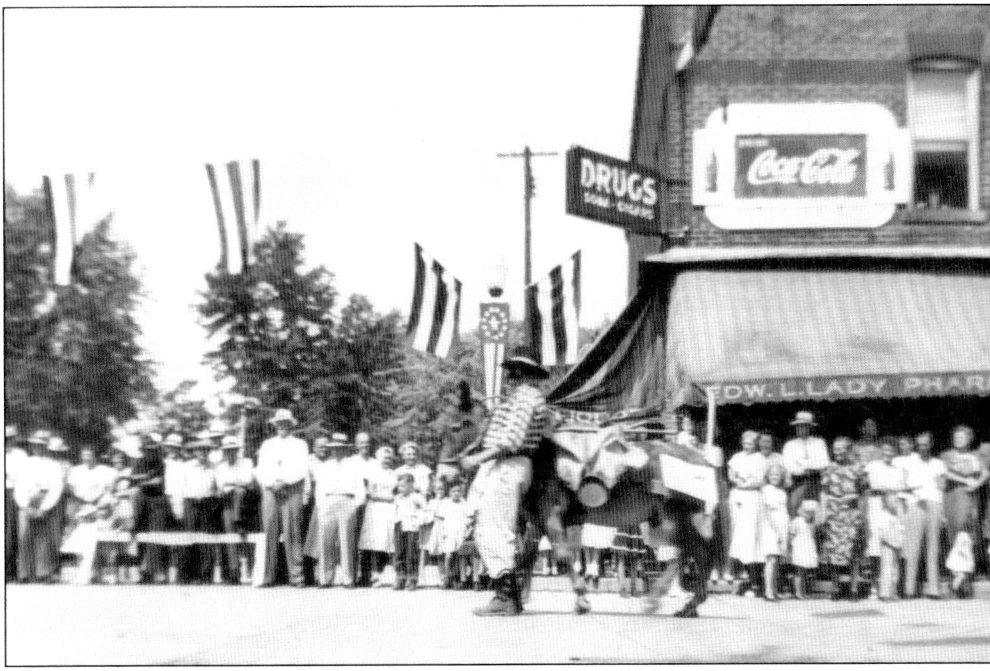

A prospector marches past the Edward L. Lady Pharmacy in 1948. The pharmacy was located in the building on the northwest corner of Main and Green Streets. Harley's Restaurant was another occupant later filling this same location. Lady was listed in the 1940 census as a pharmacist in Center Township, Indianapolis.

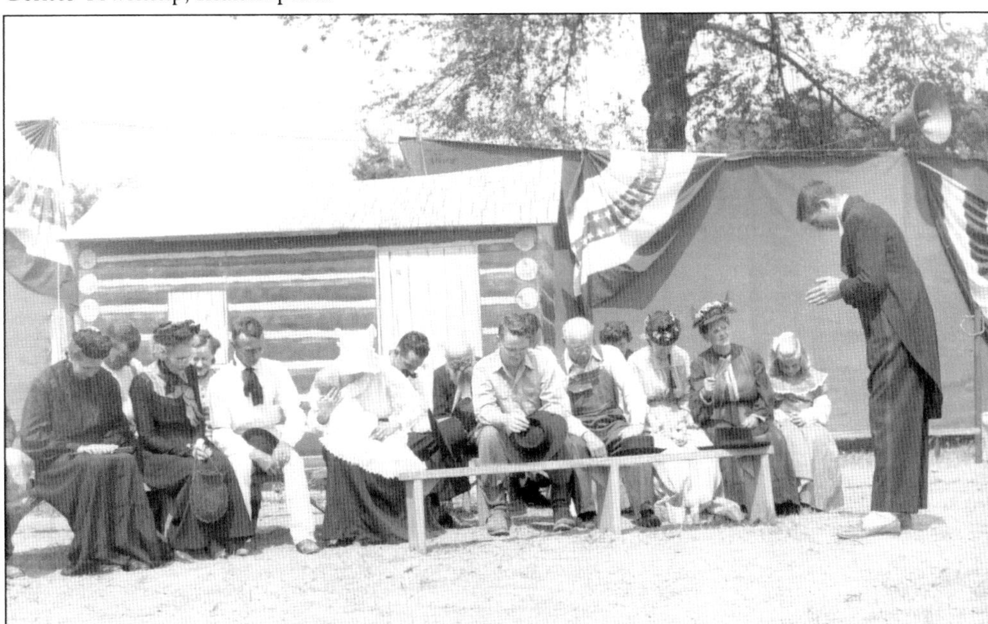

These 1948 actors are portraying the founding of the early churches in Brownsburg. Churches played a pivotal role in establishing places for families to interact and worship. Additionally, many of these early churches were formed in rudimentary log buildings that could double as schools for the children.

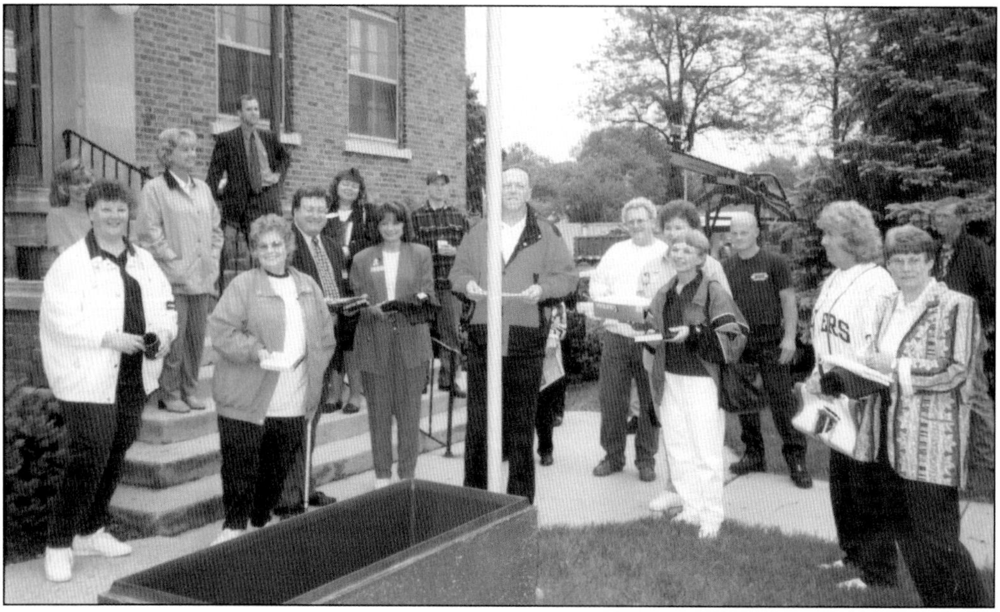

Perhaps it is fitting to end the pictorial journey of the community with these two photographs from the 1998 sesquicentennial celebration. The event, headed by chairman David R. Stumm and supported by many wonderful contributors, was designed to remind the community of its history and preserve it for the future. In the above photograph, community members gathered outside of the Carnegie Library building to deposit items into a time capsule. Inside the vault, below, Officer Stumm helps place items such as newspaper articles, photographs, and a copy of *The Village of Brownsburg*, among other things. The capsule, donated by Matthews Mortuary, was a vault designed to keep the contents sealed and safe in the old library lawn until Brownsburg's bicentennial in 2048.

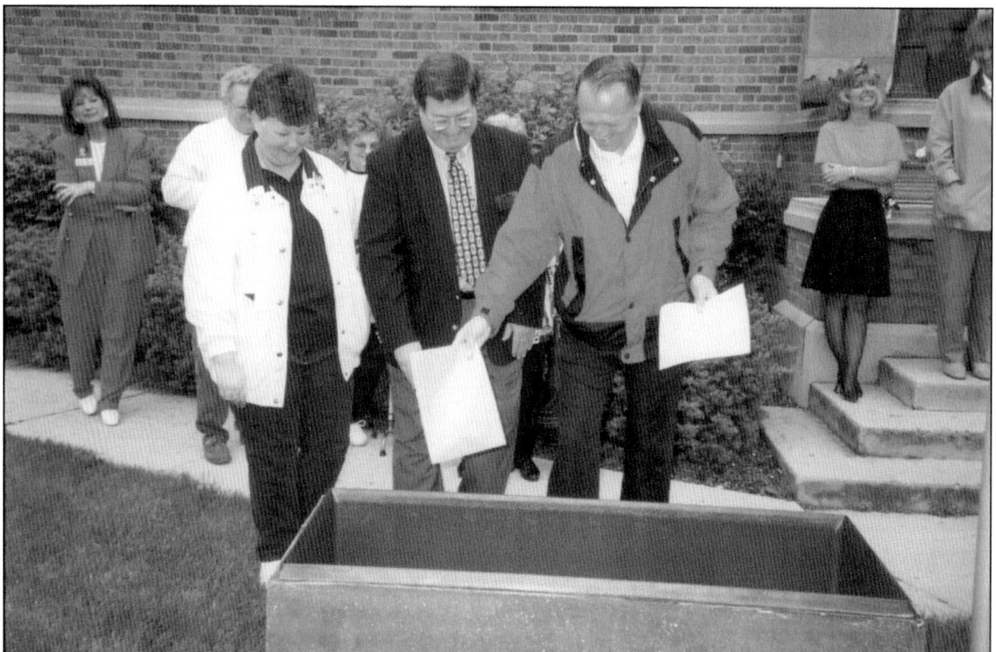

BIBLIOGRAPHY

Brownsburg Guide. Microfilm collection. Brownsburg, IN: 1963–1993.

Brownsburg Record. Microfilm collection. Brownsburg, IN: 1889–1966.

Hadley, J.V., ed. *History of Hendricks County Her People, Industries, and Institutions*. Indianapolis, IN: B.F. Bowen and Company, 1914.

Historical Vertical Files. Brownsburg, IN: Brownsburg Public Library.

History of Hendricks County, Indiana. Chicago, IL: Inter-State Publishing Company, 1885.

Industrial Souvenir of Hendricks County. Plainfield, IN: Friends Press, 1904.

Kolp, Mildred Leone Robinson. *One Century: Brownsburg, 1848–1948*. Brownsburg, IN: 1948.

McDowell, John R., ed. *The History of Hendricks County, 1914–1976*. Danville, IN: Hendricks County Historical Society, 1976.

Smith, Mildred B. *Our Yesterdays*. Brownsburg, IN: 1948.

Trucksess, Alice. *Brownsburg History*. Loose-leaf binder collection. Brownsburg, IN: 1935.

Tremaine, Guy Everton. *A Romance of Methodism*. Brownsburg, IN: Calvary Methodist Episcopal Church, 1928.

Willard Jackson Collection. Loose-leaf binder collection. Brownsburg, IN.

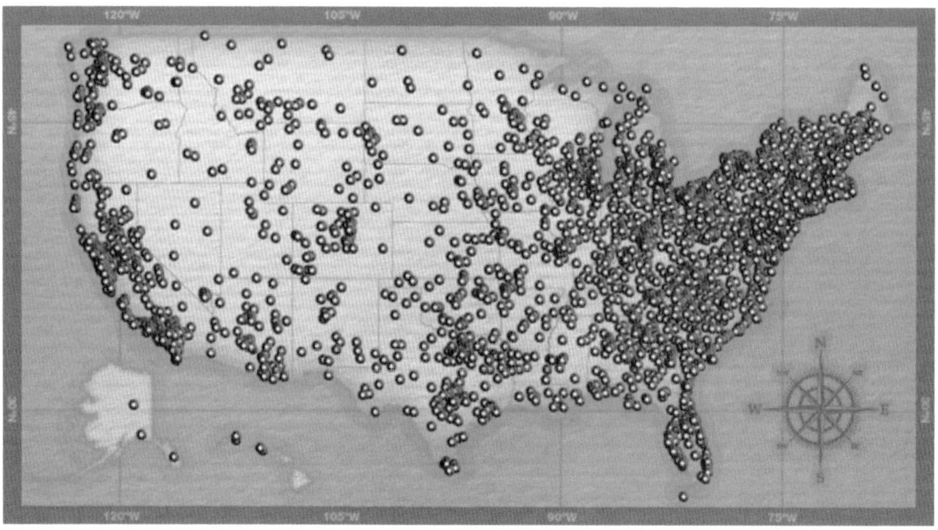

Consistent with our mission to preserve history on a local level, this book was printed in South Carolina on American-made paper and manufactured entirely in the United States. Products carrying the accredited Forest Stewardship Council (FSC) label are printed on 100 percent FSC-certified paper.

MADE IN THE USA